MANAGEMENT CONTROL OF DATA PROCESSING:
PREVENTING MANAGEMENT-BY-CRISIS

W. H. Inmon

Prentice-Hall, Inc. Englewood Cliffs, NJ 07632

Library of Congress Cataloging in Publication Data

INMON, WILLIAM H.
    Management control of data processing.

    Includes bibliographies and index.
    1. Electronic data processing—Management.   I. Title.
QA76.9.M3155 1982   658.4'0388   82-9112
ISBN 0-13-548123-6   AACR2

Prentice-Hall Series in Data Processing Management, Leonard Krauss, Advisor

Editorial/production supervision and interior design
    by *Aliza Greenblatt*

Cover design
    by *Edsal Enterprises*

Original cover art
    by *Duane Armstrong*

Manufacturing buyer
    Gordon Osbourne

Printed in the United States of America

10   9   8   7   6   5   4   3   2   1

ISBN 0-13-548123-6

PRENTICE-HALL INTERNATIONAL, INC., *London*
PRENTICE-HALL OF AUSTRALIA PTY. LIMITED, *Sydney*
PRENTICE-HALL CANADA INC., *Toronto*
PRENTICE-HALL OF INDIA PRIVATE LIMITED, *New Delhi*
PRENTICE-HALL OF JAPAN, INC., *Tokyo*
PRENTICE-HALL OF SOUTHEAST ASIA PTE. LTD., *Singapore*
WHITEHALL BOOKS LIMITED, *New Zealand*

ii

DEDICATION

This book is dedicated to Dr. Gene Amdahl, an inspiration to all who would run against the wind.

ACKNOWLEDGMENTS

Several people have been instrumental in the development of parts of this book. Jerry Corvino was a great help in the area of capacity planning. Independent reviews were done by Rose Scearcy and Jack Elza. Their input was quite useful.

A special thanks goes to Bill Lind, who indirectly added much to this work. And finally a very special thanks goes to Jeanne Friedman for editing, ideas, encouragement, and general contributions.

Thanks a million!

W. H. INMON

USE IN THE CLASSROOM OF THE QUESTIONS AT THE END OF EACH CHAPTER

The activities at the end of each chapter are to reinforce the concepts discussed in the chapter. There are three types of activities: (1) case studies—verbal descriptions of management problems with statements that will provoke comment; (2) a multiple-choice questionnaire; and (3) standard essay questions. Starred activities are more difficult than the others.

The case studies portray the problems that a manager faces daily. The problems presented represent one or more central points found in the chapter. By going through the 23 case studies the student will get a very representative cross section of what data processing management is like.

The second group of activities comprises nontraditional multiple-choice questions. Either all the choices are correct or all are incorrect. Each choice reflects a different perspective of the problem. The teacher can ask the student to make a decision between the choices. Another technique is to assign the student a choice, then ask the student to describe the issues. A third way the material can be used is to ask students to describe the differences between choices.

The final group in each chapter is composed of traditional exercises and essay questions about the material.

Contents

Preface *vii*

FUNDAMENTAL TOPICS

1   Management by Crisis   *3*

2   Evolution of Systems   *11*

3   System Life Cycle   *27*

4   Data and Data Integration   *38*

5   Availability   *61*

6   Standard Work Unit   *75*

7   Capacity Planning   *95*

8   Productivity   *105*

9   Security   *121*

SPECIFIC TOPICS

10   Selecting a DBMS   *133*

11   Selecting Projects for Data Base   *142*

12   The Transition from Batch to On-Line   *154*

13   Growing Out of a Machine   *178*

14   Management Perspectives on Data Dictionary   *192*

15   Software Architecture Limitations   *204*

16   Approaches to System Design *210*

17   User Requirements *224*

18   Design Review Methodology *235*

MANAGEMENT TOPICS

19   Discipline *247*

20   Managing Growth *260*

21   Management Styles *275*

22   Data Base Administration/Data Administration *286*

23   Organization of Data Administration *299*

IN SUMMARY

24   Controlling the Data Processing Organization *317*

Index *323*

PREFACE

□□

Management Control of Data Processing: Preventing Management by Crisis is divided into three major parts: "Fundamental Topics," "Specific Topics," and "Management Topics." The chapters in "Fundamental Topics" describe the fundamentals necessary to survive and succeed in managing in the present world of data processing. Each major area of concern is described. Emphasis is placed on the trade-offs involved in striking a balance among the many criteria of success, most of which work at cross purposes to each other.

The underlying theme of this book is: As a manager, how do I avoid painting myself into a corner that will be awkward to get out of later? In data processing there are *many* corners that can be devastating. Managers who are not aware of those corners are heading their organizations into troubled waters. The successful manager operates in a planned, action mode of leadership—not in a reaction mode, where external forces leave the manager no choices. "Fundamental Topics" prepares the manager for recognizing issues and controlling problems that relate to those issues.

The "Specific Topics" section addresses common problem areas faced by most data processing shops today. In this section the emphasis is on data base, because of its widespread acceptance and use. The discussions are not at a technical level, but at a higher conceptual level.

The section on "Management Topics" addresses the organization of data processing and the coordination of people and resources in the computer environment. Again, the emphasis is on broad issues that will be faced by management of both large and small data processing shops.

The major purpose of the book is to alert the manager of data processing to the most common dangers and pitfalls, and to help the manager survive and succeed in a world of growth, complexity, and constant change. Avoid crisis before it is unavoidable—that is the challenge facing today's data processing managers.

For the most part this book is not written at the technical level, even though technical concepts form a major part of some discussions. Only a few very important discussions go into any amount of detail, and even those discussions are first introduced conceptually so that the nontechnician is able to focus very clearly on what is being said. Because of this basic orientation, it can be stated that this book is written primarily for management, not for technicians. It is the author's opinion, however, that technicians will find the book enjoyable and useful, especially in the discussion of management, because technicians often have to live on a day-to-day basis with the types of management decisions discussed here, and the technician knows full well the importance of those decisions. The book should also prove useful to the technician going into management because of the breadth of issues discussed.

The primary audience to which this book is directed is: management, students of business and computer science, and technical personnel.

The reader may be interested in the background of the materials for this book. They have come from many sources. Where references in the literature exist, they are noted. In fact, this book should serve as a directory to other works because the book aims at covering the *breadth* of topics the manager needs to know. For the most part the chapters of this book can serve as introductions to entire subject areas. A major part of the background comes from surveys. Where feasible, these surveys are noted. Several private surveys contributed to this book which unfortunately could not be cited. For further details about them, contact the author. Other material has come from long association with data processing organizations and the author thanks the many companies that have contributed indirectly. The last source comprises from in-depth interviews with experienced consultants, managers, and designers.

Even though the worlds of data base and on-line systems form the nucleus of this book, the scope extends well beyond those realms. This book does not address data processing shops of a particular size; it addresses large and small shops, since discussions are at a conceptual level. Interestingly, the problems faced by data processing shops of different sizes tend to be the same; the only difference the size of the shop makes is in the scale of the problem.

It is the intent of the author to explain those management decisions and actions that often perplex outsiders and frustrate the people affected by the decisions. In short, this book prepares the reader to avoid crises in leading an organization. Even more important, after reading the book, the reader should understand *all* of the issues relevant to those decisions, as they are identified and discussed. If the reader is interested in the alternatives and trade-offs of good and bad management practices in the world of data processing, he or she should find a wealth of material in this book.

The reader will find a wide diversity of problems and topics addressed in the book. Some are technical, some are behavorial, some relate to the organization chart, some relate to budgets, and so forth. The diversity is planned and is representative of the issues facing a data processing manager on a day-to-day basis. One day a manager will face an on-line system going down. The next day the manager will face problems as to how departments can be organized. The next day the manager will sit back and philosophically reflect on the direction the organization is taking. The diversity of topics in this book are very much like the diversity of topics facing a data processing manager.

The questions found at the end of each chapter are meant to place the reader in the shoes of the manager. The problems presented are real (although the company names and scenarios that are presented are fictitious). The perspective of the problems is to put the reader into the role of manager as the manager walks into work each morning. From that point on, it is up to the reader to solve whatever problem has occurred.

W. H. Inmon

FUNDAMENTAL
TOPICS

□□□

1

Management by Crisis
□□□

1.1 LEVELS OF MANAGEMENT

There are at least two perspectives that managers of data processing can take in addressing the responsibilities and challenges facing them. They can address the problems at a superficial, daily level, that is, deal with problems in their most immediate manifestation. Or they can take the time to understand the real roots of problems and view them in a larger, more complete context.

When management views problems superficially, typical concerns are such things as: Did the report get out on time? Did all the network come up today? Why are terminals in a given location not getting adequate response time? Do we have software to manipulate data in such and such a fashion? And so forth. There is no doubt that *someone* must be concerned with the day-to-day details of running a data processing shop, but if that is *all* the manager is concerned with, it is simply a matter of time until one or more of the many major forces shaping the data processing environment gets out of control and causes the manager to face a crisis, perhaps one of monumental proportions.

1.2 FORCES INFLUENCING DATA PROCESSING

What are these forces in data processing that can overwhelm managers if they are not prepared?

The single largest force the data processing environment is driven by is the growth of demand for services—the need for more personnel, more hardware, more software, more applications, more of everything—and all at once. The data processing industry is, relatively speaking, in its infancy. Computers simply have not been in existence that long, especially computers with the capabilities of those being produced today.

The second major force that shapes the world of data processing managers is that of a changing and technological environment. Computerization requires a certain level of technical expertise and the type of expertise that is appropriate is always changing. Not only does the technological world open the door to many complexities not found in other environments, but those complexities are a moving target. This constant change means that managers can *never* rest on a firm knowledge of the technical world, because that knowledge is dated and in a finite amount of time will be obsolete.

The factors of complexity, growth, and change mean that managers have little latitude for error in their decisions (or indecisions). There are many ways in which problems occur that can lead to crises. The margin for error can be compared to the necessary degree of accuracy of a spaceship as it attempts to reenter the earth's atmosphere. If the ship comes in at too high an angle, it comes in too fast and burns up. If it comes in at too low an angle, it "bounces off" and goes into orbit. The difference between an angle for the spaceship that is too high or too low is a scant few degrees.

Data processing managers have precisely that same fine margin for error in coping with the major forces that *shape* them and their organizations if they wish to avoid crises. There is one outstanding difference between the captain of the spaceship and a data processing manager. When the spaceship is handled incorrectly, it means the demise of the ship and the crew, but when a data processing manager miscalculates, it ultimately costs *only* money. The errors in data processing are not usually fatal (think goodness!), but they are expensive—to employees, to the user, to upper management, and to the company.

Because the forces shaping data processing are so severe and powerful, in some cases managers may not really have a solution to their crisis, but a choice of what kind of crisis they would like to have when they have it, and how bad it will be. If a manager is facing Hobson's choice, it is even *more* important that the manager be aware of the shaping forces.

1.3 CRISES ARE A FACT OF LIFE

Given that some crises are unavoidable even in the best data processing organizations and are commonplace in most organizations (they are a fact of life), are crises a totally negative experience? Not at all. Crises are the most powerful and meaningful way in which people (and in a collective sense, organizations) learn. In that sense, then, crises represent a great opportunity for the organization, because the pain of a crisis causes people to avoid having the same crisis again. Unfortunately, in data processing it is usually not the person who caused the crisis who gets to learn from it. For one reason or other, the feedback loop in data processing is often inadequate, so that poor decision makers rarely have the opportunity to suffer the pain caused by their bad decisions. This book explores and demonstrates this theme in several places.

Since crises are unavoidable (and indirectly have an educational benefit to the company), the point of interest is really their frequency of occurrence and their size. A crisis is a situation that *demands* top-priority attention and/or resources for resolution. A data processing shop is run well when there are few crises. It is poorly run when there are many. What "few" and "many" are is necessarily subjective.

Crises that are typical of the data processing environment include:

1. *Program bug in the middle of the nightly production run.* A programmer gets out of bed, examines the problem, changes some edit criteria or logic in the program, reruns the offending program, and goes back to sleep.

2. *Staff turnover.* In two months' time five out of eight experienced programmers and designers leave for greener pastures.

3. *Maintenance strangulation.* Three years ago 35% of programmer time was dedicated to maintenance. Then five programmers were added to the staff. Two years ago 48% of programmer time was dedicated to maintenance and 10 programmers were added to the staff. Last year 65% of programmer time was dedicated to maintenance and 12 programmers were added to the staff. This year 78% of programmer time is spent on maintenance.

4. *On-line performance.* A year ago 25,000 on-line transactions ran at 1.2 seconds' average response time. This year 50,000 transactions run at 6.8 seconds' response time on a faster machine.

And so forth. Data processing is fraught with examples of crises.

1.4 NATURE OF CRISES

Some crises can be solved by a mere "change in a line of code," such as a debugging problem. Most data processing crises cannot be solved nearly so simply. It is those major crises that cannot be solved simply that plague the organization. A data processing shop is like an ocean liner under full steam. The next tens of feet of the liner's direction are set regardless of *any* action that anyone might take. If there are rocks in the water, the liner is going to have to strike them. To avoid the rocks, the ship should have turned long ago.

Those deep-seated, long-term problems that require much planning to avoid are the ones the really competent data processing manager must face and cope with. Many data processing managers (those that manage superficially) are not inclined to roll up their sleeves and get their hands dirty. They attempt to manage only the manifestation of the problem, addressing only the day-to-day concerns. It is *they* who are heading their organizations toward unwarranted crises.

That is why this book does not address the day-to-day problems of data processing (even though those problems are important and someone must come to grips with them). Instead, emphasis is on the areas that are relevant to the long-term problems of the data processing organization, such as system design, capacity planning, or organizational considerations, where much of the foundation of future events is laid.

1.5 FREQUENCY OF CRISES—THE TREADMILL

It has been suggested that crises happen over time in all organizations. The point of interest is how often they occur and how bad they are. Since crises *demand* attention and resources, there is nothing that can be done but address the crisis when it arrives. The thing that management should avoid is a treadmill of crises, where management decisions are *normally* in reaction to crises, and work is *usually* done in a crisis mode. Once an organization is on this reaction-mode treadmill, it is very difficult to get off. Management that is in control of the organization is in an action mode, not a reaction mode. Conversely, management that is not in control is in a reaction mode.

1.6 RELEVANCE OF TOPICS FOR DISCUSSION

Since a number of factors shape the data processing environment and the environment is a changing and complex one, it is not surprising that the manager coming to grips with the roots of crises faces many, often very different, subjects. Indeed, the chapters of this book often serve only as an overview of the topics relevant to coping with data processing crises. However, *each* topic is relevant to the understanding and prevention of management by crisis, however different that topic might be from other topics.

For the skeptic, remove any single topic presented in this book and there will be a significant risk of failure. For example, remove capacity planning and an organization will eventually face a problem in the orderly acquisition of equipment, thus causing a crisis when the demand for hardware outstrips supply. Remove availability and the organization will face a crisis when it is discovered that the on-line system stays down too long when it goes down. And so forth. Each topic has its own relevance to the success of managers who would prevent long-term crisis. Managers who choose *not* to come to grips with these topics lead their organizations into very dangerous waters.

Some of the topics and their relevance to crisis avoidance are:
• *Evolution of systems.* Recognition of the major movements in data processing and anticipation of forces that shape that evolution.
• *System life cycles.* Post-implementation development and why it has been instituted.

- *Data and data integration.* Minimization of the maintenance effort; expandability of systems.
- *Standard work unit.* On-line performance built at the point of design, not after the fact.
- *Capacity planning.* Planning acquisition rather than experiencing the "threshold of pain."
- *Security.* Learning about security before circumstances do the teaching.
- *Batch to on-line transition.* The single most difficult problem of most shops today—upgrading personnel, changing attitudes, changing procedures.
- *Design review.* Quality control of application design at *the* place it will do the most good.
- *Discipline.* The benefits of discipline; the cost of not having discipline.
- *Organizing data processing functions.* Territorial claims; avoiding unnecessary conflict; placing control at the right place in the organization.

These topics and the other ones presented in this book are at the heart of the success of data processing managers who want to control their environment, not be controlled by it.

CASE STUDY

The San Francisco Cable Car Company operates a whole set of subsidiaries, such as pizza parlors, retail outlets, bookstores, a recording company, and a loan company. The company, which is based in San Francisco, depends heavily on automation to control this collection of very diverse businesses. The company's computer system has been in existence quite a while. Because management is very profit oriented, the emphasis is constantly on fast results.

In January, one of the inventory systems is running and a problem is experienced. Mysteriously, the on-line program quits running. The operator has never seen this kind of problem before and notifies the data base administrator (DBA) because the DBA oversees the on-line system. In the meantime the on-line system comes down and all users complain to management. The DBA spends all night attempting to rectify the problem, but to no avail. The next day the small programming staff sets about looking for program bugs, the DBA continues to search for clues as to what is wrong, and the software vendor comes in and begins to analyze the situation.

In the meantime users become more and more frustrated and higher management becomes involved. After about 36 hours, a programmer notes that a program was put into the on-line environment incorrectly and in a way that had never been done before. The result produced the mysterious problem and corrections are soon made.

Two weeks later a top management meeting is held. It is disclosed that a new acquisition is to be made—a chain of service stations. Management is very excited about this acquisition because the short-term profitability looks very good. The only problem is that service stations have to comply with several sets of regulations—by the state, by the county, and by the city. This means that new accounting procedures must be adapted to the existing accounting system for Cable Car Company. The changes must be made in one month's time because the regulatory reporting is done on a monthly basis. The entire programming staff (including two nighttime operators) are told to drop their current activities and dig in on the accounting changes. The staff is told to work Saturdays and overtime—to do whatever it takes to get the job done.

In February, systems are running smoothly when the on-line system suddenly experiences a very unusual degradation of response time. The normal 8- to 10-second response time goes to 30 seconds! The users of the on-line system are very upset and call data processing management. The DBA is assigned the task of investigating the problem and told that it is a top-priority project. The DBA monitors the on-line system and determines that several transactions are misbehaving, that is, operating in a different fashion than they ever have before. He asks the user if there is any difference in the way the transaction is being used.

The user states that the transaction (which is used for forecasting) has heretofore been used for forecasting to a six-month horizon. Last week the user discovered that he could forecast up to 10 years! The user is very excited about this new capability. The DBA tells him that he cannot use this facility because of the impact on the on-line system and the user immediately escalates his complaint up the management chain. Data processing management is told to "fix" the programs so that the user can have what he wants.

The DBA investigates alternatives and discovers that there is a way to give the user some of the function he desires and still not affect performance too much. Unfortunately, it will require major changes to two data bases, which will cause about 40 programs to be changed. Data processing management tells the development staff to drop everything and make the changes as quickly as possible.   ■

Comment on the Following

1. Data processing is operating in a mode that is controlled by crisis.
2. The two months depicted here just happen to be unlucky months. Things will smooth out eventually.
3. What is the basis of each of the problems? What is the basis of all the problems?
4. The user *must* be pleased, which means that the user can expect any service that will make his life easier.

5. More capacity (faster machines, more disks, a bigger network, etc.) would greatly relieve the problems here.

6. If data processing management had a more competent staff, these problems would not happen.

7. The top management of the Cable Car Company needs to reassess its view of the role of data processing.

8. A larger staff would solve many of the problems.

9. Personnel with more technical competence would greatly alleviate management problems.

MULTIPLE-CHOICE QUESTIONS

1. A system designer made a serious error in judgment in miscalculating the way certain on-line transactions are to be used. The user operates the transactions in a different fashion than was intended and this has a great effect on the performance of the on-line system.
   A. The designer should be demoted.
   B. The designer will learn from her mistakes by seeing the results of her poor decision.
   C. The user should have warned the designer that there was a problem with the way in which the designer perceived the transaction.
   D. The transaction can be "tuned" so that it will not affect the on-line system.
   E. The user cannot change his mind about how a transaction will be used.

2. A government regulation has just been enacted that greatly affects the cash flow of the Anteater Company. It is imperative that the data systems reflect the new regulations as soon as possible. An analysis is made of just how many programs must be changed. One hundred fifteen programs are affected. Management allocates 20 programmers to the project. It is estimated that they can get the changes done in eight weeks. Management calls the local contract programming office and hires 15 more programmers so that the eight-week lead time can be shortened to four weeks or so.
   A. The changes may take *longer* to make with more programmers, not shorter.
   B. Communications between programmers is often a major factor in productivity.
   C. Some programs are written so that work on program A should be completed before work on program B begins.
   D. Reducing the number of programmers to work on the changes

from 20 to 2 will probably lengthen the amount of time it takes
to change the programs.

E. If the programs have been designed and written so that they are
easily changeable, the lead time will be greatly reduced over what
would otherwise be the case.

EXERCISES AND ESSAYS

1. How can management lead an organization out of a crisis mode once it
gets into that mode?

2. Are crises inevitable in data processing? Are they a totally negative
experience? How can the positive aspects of a crisis be emphasized?

3. What happens when an organization has no control over an environment for which it is responsible? Is this a tenable situation? In the
short run? In the long run?

4. What can be done about management that does not recognize the real
cause of crises, just the symptoms?

5. Can accountability be used as a tool for getting out of the crisis mode?
If so, how? At what levels?

6. What is the cost in terms of dollars of operating in the crisis mode? In
terms of morale? In terms of user satisfaction?

//

Evolution of Systems

□□

There is a rather predictable evolution of systems in most commercial data processing shops. Awareness of this perspective can be important to a manager for at least two reasons:

- It is comforting to know that other shops are going through the same process.
- Understanding the various phases and why there is a next phase can be useful as a planning tool.

If it is appropriate and inevitable that a shop evolve to its next stage and for one reason or the other the evolution is greatly resisted, many problems will arise as a result. It is the purpose of this chapter to describe the evolutionary process and to present descriptions of why the evolution occurred, then to draw some conclusions from the process.

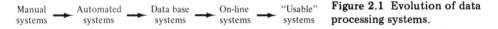

| Manual systems | → | Automated systems | → | Data base systems | → | On-line systems | → | "Usable" systems |

Figure 2.1 Evolution of data processing systems.

2.1 VARIOUS STAGES OF EVOLUTION

The evolution of systems can be depicted as shown in Figure 2.1. The five stages of evolution of data processing systems are: manual systems, automated sequential systems, data base systems, on-line systems, and "usable"* systems. The last stage, usable systems, does not imply that previous systems were not usable; instead, the emphasis is on a much higher degree of usability, much more so than at any other stage. Thus the term "usable systems" applies.

*The term "usable" is nonstandard data processing terminology. Unfortunately, no other currently accepted term fits. The term "usable" implies a versatile, "user-friendly," flexible, highly available, and prompt system, which has usually proliferated into a number of places and uses within the company. These systems are usually for planning, trend analysis, etc. rather than operational processing.

2.2 MANUAL SYSTEMS

As an example of the size and scope of a manual system, consider Figure 2.2.

Figure 2.2 Manual systems.

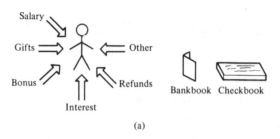

(a)

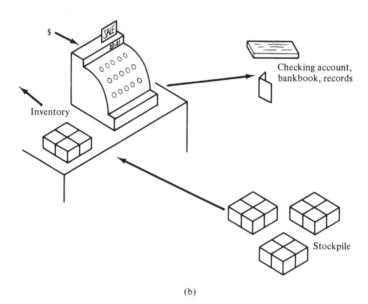

(b)

A man who manages his own business sets up a system for his income. He tracks such things as salary, gifts, and bonus. All he needs is his bankbook and checkbook. He spends an hour or two a month balancing the figures, making sure that things are in order. Keep this simple example in mind as we describe manual systems.

Manual systems are those that are operated partially or entirely by human activity. Occasional use of a calculator (or "adding machine") or typewriter does not change the basic orientation of the system, which is work being done by human beings. These systems are obviously very labor intensive and, compared to larger, automated systems, very slow. Some of the trappings of manual systems are files, memos, reports, balances, and cross balances. In short, there was (and is, for there are plenty of manual systems in existence) a lot of "paper shuffling."

The *information cycle* (Figure 2.2a), which is the time from when an enterprise first gains information to the time when that information is accessible and usable to all appropriate individuals in the enterprise, is very long when more than one individual is involved. The issues the designer faces in building manual systems are: How have we done this type of system before? What do we need to satisfy our business needs? What expenses are involved in building the system?

These issues have to be defined within the context and limitation of the tools with which the designer has to work. Again, in relation to the tools the designer has in an automated environment, the designer of a manual system has some severe limitations, such as how large a volume of work can be handled, how much data can be physically stored in a location (not to mention how the data can be meaningfully indexed for later retrieval), and how the data can be reported or made available to all the different parts of the enterprise that have a need to see the data.

The criteria for success for workers operating manual systems are: how *efficiently* the work gets done, how *much* work gets done, how *accurately* work gets done, and how *regularly* work is done. Interestingly, the same criteria appear in other forms in automated systems. The amazing thing about the criteria for success for using manual systems is that the work being performed is so repetitive, thus minimizing the satisfaction or interest of those doing the work. Maintaining a proper attitude for success in the face of a high degree of repetition is very difficult. No wonder the computer can be called the modern "beast of burden."

As the size of systems grows, the desire arises to automate wherever possible. The sheer volume of work, the limitations of manual systems, the continuously increasing cost of labor, storage, and materials, coupled with the decreasing costs of automation—all pave the way for the age of computerization. In those cases where an organization is slow to change from manual systems to automation but in fact *should* be changing, the problems manifest themselves sharply by driving up a company's operating expense (in relation to similar companies that are automated), and by giving the companies with automation more capabilities, which ultimately leads to a competitive edge for the automated companies.

2.3 AUTOMATED SYSTEMS

Using the example of the system for manually tracking the income of an individual, the individual now unites with several other people to form a small business. There is still a need to track the income of the business, and the basic sources of income have not drastically changed—but now there is a different set of needs. There is more income to be tracked, it needs to be tracked in a more formal fashion, and the timeliness of the information is more important. Also, communication concerning income must be made available to the individuals in the small business.

Figure 2.3 reflects an automated system built to serve the needs of a small business. The automated system presented here is simple. It is really nothing more than transferring data from manual form to automated form—a listing and perhaps subtotaling of the information captured. This simple system may help the reader to envision a small automated system.

Figure 2.3 Automated systems.

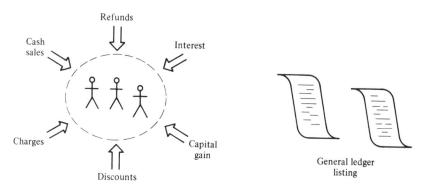

The first step away from manual systems is automated systems. The computers used in this environment are a definite step toward a fully automated system, yet compared to the very large, fast computers that are available, are very primitive in terms of function, speed, and size. The move toward automation has many substeps. One of those steps is learning *how* to automate. Once a shop learns the mechanics of automation, it can concern itself with *how to automate well*, which is a somewhat different matter. Some of the paraphernalia of sequential systems are punched cards, paper tapes, tapes, disks, and limited amounts of memory in which to store programs. The output of all this processing generally is reports—long sequential reports, produced from massive merges of master files of data, sorts, and batched updates. In general, the information cycle is shortened from the manual system mode. This type of processing is referred to as "batch" because activity is collected or "batched" and then processed together, when the files of the system become available for processing. Because of automation, it becomes possible to construct entirely new types of systems that are not feasible in a manual environment. Even though the information cycle is shortened, the cycle could still be counted in numbers of days because of the batching, keying of data, editing of data, and so on, that is endemic to the nature of the sequential cycle.

The criteria for workers to succeed in a sequential environment were (and *are* for existing sequential shops): getting jobs automated as quickly as possible, getting reports out, creating and updating master files, writing programs quickly and accurately, and changing existing systems as rapidly as possible when maintenance must be done. As more and more sequential systems are built, maintenance (the changing and caring for existing programs and data) becomes a problem.

One of the fundamental limitations of the sequential environment is that several programs cannot access data concurrently. This means that each system and subsystem in effect must "own" its data to ensure that necessary processing can occur. In the long run this "ownership" of data leads to a proliferation of systems which are very similar in content and processing, but which are supported by entirely separate programs and definitions of data. One of the criteria for success in the sequential world, then, is managing change in light of many separate yet interrelated subsystems. Over time, sequential systems tend to become complex, cumbersome, and contain a considerable amount of duplication.

The issues central to sequential systems come in essentially two forms. The first issue is: How does automation occur? How can data be mechanized? The next (and ultimately larger) question is: Once automated, how do sequential systems handle growth—both growth in the volume of system activity and growth in the way the system can be shaped? Because of the limitations of the media on which sequential systems exist (cards, tape, etc.), changing the basic definition of data on which sequential systems run is a complicated affair. The complications arise not in the act of actually changing the form of the data and in converting from the old form to the new form, but in changing all the programs in which the data is used. In a really large sequential environment (where there is much processing and much diversity of processing), program change is both cumbersome (in the total amount of work that must be done) and very complex (in that program and program logic must be modified and there is a *very* low tolerance for error).

The transition from sequential systems to data base systems is caused primarily by the growth in the amount of processing to be done and the way that processing needs to grow. There are some very real and definite limitations to sequential processing (such as the inability to access part of a sequential file without accessing the entire file) that are not too obvious in the initial stages of growth but become more and more obvious as systems grow and age. In general, sequential systems do not age well. Some of the reasons a shop in the sequential processing mode will want to evolve to a data base is because of the potential for storing data in ways more suited to the application, the benefits of data integration (i.e., unifying systems with common data), and the ability to make the most of direct-access processing.

In the cases where management insists on hanging on to the sequential world when it should not, there may not be a problem as long as either the data processing needs or the company's growth do not expand beyond a moderate growth rate. Old sequential systems, in the face of a large growth curve, can cause *much* unneeded dissension and result in precious manpower dollars being spent unproductively. Sequential systems are not responsive to the needs of decision makers in general.

2.4 DATA BASE SYSTEMS

Using the example of the system that tracks income, this simple system is now applied to data base systems. The small business is now transformed into a medium-size company with an entirely new scope of information needs. The basic sources of the income have not really changed, but the scope of the system has, and in a dramatic way. The total amount of data to be tracked has grown greatly, the procedures for handling the income are much more formalized, and there is a greater need for using the information in various ways. New information needs might be: Where are sales going up? Going down? Who produced the most revenue? The least? What is the ratio of expense to revenue for each operating unit? And so forth. Because of large amounts of data and the diverse requirements for the use of data, data base is implemented.

Figure 2.4 Data base systems.

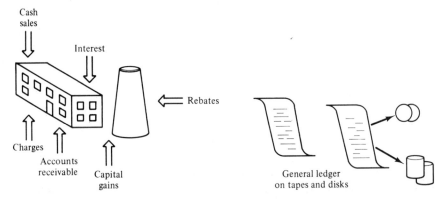

Figure 2.4 shows that in essence the general ledger information is merely put onto a disk device. Going to direct-access storage (disk) and data base implies that (1) more data can be handled; (2) it can be handled in more than a sequential mode; (3) the data can be viewed in a number of ways; and (4) it can be accessed concurrently.

The primary advantage which data base offers over sequential systems is that data can be accessed concurrently and directly. No longer does a programmer have to spin a tape accessing 100% of the data to get at a desired

5% of the data. No longer does a program have to wait to report from a data base because another program is writing a different report. Because the same data can be accessed by more than one program, it makes sense that the data should be capable of being viewed in more than one way. Through the facilities of a DBMS (data base management system), one programmer can view the same data as another programmer in an essentially different manner. The processing is still done in the batch* mode. The output of the data base environment (e.g., reports) does not change much from the output of sequential systems. Reports, temporary files, batch updates, and so on, remain. But the information cycle is shortened again, primarily because of the capability of concurrent access of data.

The criteria for success in the data base environment include the ability to write programs quickly and accurately, to run reports quickly, to use existing data bases to get reports out, and to master the technical aspects of the tools that are available. Because of the direct accessibility of data, new types of systems can be written that were not available in sequential systems.

One of the dangers of "going data base" is that data base is not used as anything more than a sophisticated way of organizing data, rather than as a tool to unify the way data is viewed and used. When this is the case, a company shortchanges itself by not realizing all the possible benefits of data base. Hand in hand with the issue of using data base as a sophisticated way of organizing data is the issue of the needed organizational control that goes with using data base. If data can be stored and used on a community basis, numerous organizations within the company should have a say in the design of the common data base. But sequential systems are normally built around a very local concept of data in which the design of systems and data is very private.

This subtle (but very real) shift in attitudes is the cause of a great deal of conflict with the advent of data base systems. Many organizations side-step this conflict by ignoring it and allowing a number of copies of identical data to exist, thus mollifying users who do not want to share their data and are resistant to change. This mollification ultimately cost the company a *great* deal of unnecessary processing, development, and maintenance. Managers who do not recognize the ultimate long term cost of political expediency in this instance cost their companies *very* significant amounts of money that need not have been spent.

The transition to on-line systems comes about when a company recognizes that on-line data base systems can greatly reduce the information cycle from that of sequential systems. By reducing the information cycle to the shortest amount of time possible, a company can make the best use of the time of the system's users. Excellent examples of minimal information

---

*"Batch" refers the practice of collecting activity, batching it together, and processing all at once. Batch systems can be sequential or data based in their orientation. The opposite of batch is online.

cycles are those of the airline and banking industries, whose operations are intimately tied to their on-line systems.

In the worst case, if a company decides to delay going to on-line systems when it is appropriate that it should, the batch data base systems grow and the information cycle of a company reaches a constant or slightly increasing value which represents a limitation on how short the information cycle can ever be. This means that the responsiveness of a company to information is less than optimal.

2.5 ON-LINE SYSTEMS

Using the simple example of the income system, when the data a company has grows large and important enough, it may be cost-effective to make the information available to users in the most rapid fashion. This means putting the data "on-line." Note that the original source and nature of the data—income to the business—have not changed. In fact, the fundamental nature of the data has not really changed. The only changes that have occurred are in the timeliness of the data, the amount of data, and the use of the data.

Figure 2.5 shows data that is available on-line. This implies that a user in the company can directly access the data (usually through a cathode ray tube, CRT) in a timely fashion (i.e., a few seconds). The nature of the data has not really changed. It is still a ledger on a disk, but now it is readily available. In addition to accessing data concurrently, the on-line environment allows the user to update data concurrently.

Figure 2.5 On-line data base systems.

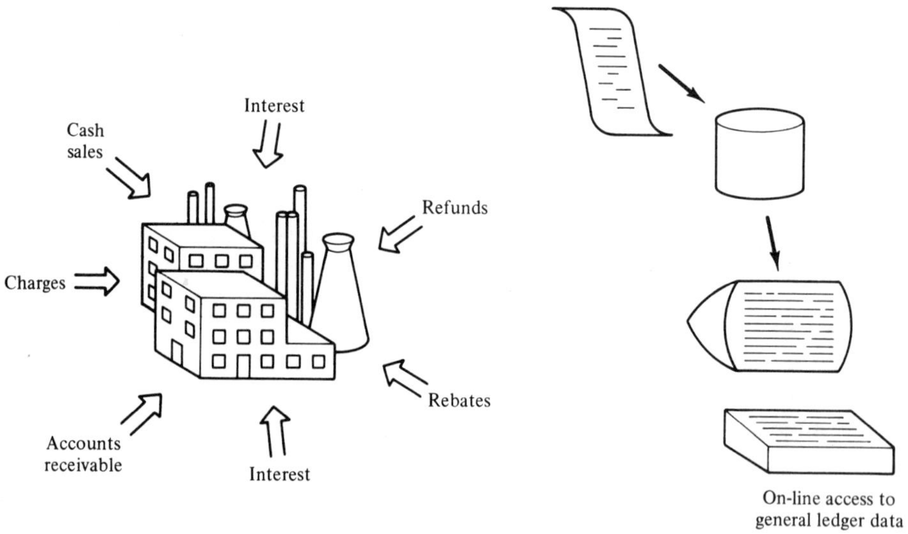

Cash sales
Interest
Refunds
Charges
Rebates
Accounts receivable
Interest

On-line access to general ledger data

The move to on-line systems comes in phases, as did the move to other modes of operation. The primary phase involves building and mastering the mechanics of on-line systems. This phase is concerned simply with the act of getting through the technical barriers in order to construct a system. Once a shop develops the expertise to construct on-line systems, it must go through another phase, which is concerned with how well on-line systems are constructed—an entirely different matter. In fact, the question of the quality of on-line systems is one of the major issues that a manager will face.

System quality refers to the responsiveness of an on-line system, the total amount of time that the online system is up and available, the ability of the system to undergo change gracefully, and the cost effectiveness of construction and operation of the system. When on-line systems do not have the proper degree of quality built in, they waste a *great* deal of money because they are not cheap to construct or to change once constructed.

One major difference of this environment is that on-line systems ultimately share common resources with other on-line systems, much more than in any other environment. This leads to the need for a higher degree of organizational control and discipline than has been required or enforced previously. Since it is the nature of on-line systems to share common resources, one of the fundamentals of on-line system design is that a given application system under the online controller must be careful how it uses its resources because poor utilization of resources will affect *other systems* also under the online controller, as well as the offending system. This consideration is new to the organization that has just arrived in the on-line environment and requires a new level of discipline. For whatever reasons, organizations traditionally fiercely resist new levels of discipline. Furthermore, the visibility of problems in the on-line environment is such that an organization *cannot* sweep the issue of discipline under the rug (as they usually do in data base and batch systems).

When an on-line system does not function properly, it is obvious to the entire world. In batch systems there is a wide tolerance for problems because problems may never be noticed by the user. There is a much greater margin for error in the design of batch and sequential systems. In on-line systems, a minimum of problems will have the user busily harassing data processing management for better service, whereas with batch systems problems of much greater significance are tolerated by the user. Service is measured by response time in on-line systems and response time is measured in seconds. As systems grow, simultaneous users can queue and compete for resources, while the seconds tick away.

Furthermore, the parameters for success for developing on-line systems are different from the parameters for success in the batch environment. Certainly, programmers who code speedily and well are at a premium. But there is a whole new and additional set of parameters for success in design and development. Designers must also build in performance (i.e., response time) and availability (i.e., the total time the system is up) of on-line systems, or the user will complain, regardless of how well or quickly the system is programmed otherwise. One of the *major* problems of the on-line environment is that management rewards development personnel for building on-line systems based on the success criteria of batch systems. This is one of the subtle causes of the dissension associated with the construction of on-line systems.

By far the main issue of on-line systems is that of system performance (i.e., response time). This means that the information cycle is cut to the shortest time possible and that there are completely new ways of using the computer that are not possible otherwise. A secondary issue but a very important one is system availability (i.e., system uptime). Availability refers to the time the on-line system is up and usable. The maximum range of availability is 24 hours a day, 7 days a week, 365 days a year. Most shops do somewhat less than that. There is no question that on-line systems create an environment of information responsiveness for the entire company.

The transition to "usable" systems (refer to the earlier explanation of "usable") is brought about by the explosion of demand for computer services. It has been said that once on-line systems capture data, the challenge is then to use the data. There is an increasing demand for data and processing. A major part of that demand is to be able to change data and to view existing data in new, undefined ways. Thus the trend to highly usable systems is born.

Managers who are naive about the pitfalls and pleasures of the on-line data base environment will undoubtedly cost their companies money because the pitfalls here are complex, many, subtle, and so easy to fall into that many shops accept them as normal.

2.6 "USABLE" SYSTEMS

The next progression from on-line data base systems is to usable systems. (*Note:* The term "usable" has special nonstandard connotations as discussed in this book.) Once an organization has grown considerably, its needs expand with its size. There is a great need to see the data, or subsets of the data, in many forms, so much so that a single data base cannot adequately meet the many needs of the users. So usable systems are created.

Figure 2.6 shows that the basic sources of the data have not changed and the basic format of the data has not changed. What has changed is the amount of data, the different needs for the data, and the way the data is stored and accessed.

The information cycle is not necessarily shortened by the advent of usable systems, at least as the definition of the information cycle applies to the other stages of system evolution. Instead, the very nature of the information cycle changes and needs to be viewed from a different perspective. Heretofore, the information cycle referred to the time when data became known to a company to the time it became generally available to the company. That definition usually applied to the data becoming available to a

Figure 2.6 Usable systems.

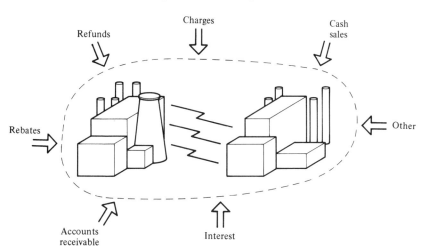

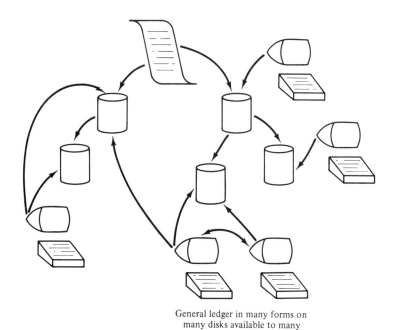

General ledger in many forms on
many disks available to many
users on-line

given system, usually the system associated primarily with the creation, update, and retrieval of the data.

What was not implied was that the data was made generally available *outside* its primary system. If a broader perspective of the information cycle is considered and it is taken to mean the time from when data is known until it is available *throughout* a company's information systems (not just to the primary system), then usable systems certainly do address a shortening of the information cycle. This means that, once the information is captured and made available outside its primary system, the user has *direct* accessibility to the data.

Some of the signs of usable systems are subsystems (such as FOCUS, RAMIS, QBE, or software packages that usually run in support of larger systems) that run in, primarily, a retrieval mode. Extracts and conversions of data from the primary system are typical of usable systems. Ad hoc requests written by the user (not data processing) and ad hoc programs that are run only once are other trademarks. Much of the technology of usable systems is yet to appear, although some very elegant and powerful tools exist today.

The issues of usable systems are an ability to change the semantic form of data easily and to be selective in the type and format of requests that are to be run. The requests for data throughout the company at this point are normally much more elementary than in other environments. A rigid system—one that cannot easily undergo change— has a short life span in a high "usability" environment. The amount of time from a user's desire to get at data (especially existing data) to the point where that request is fulfilled is also a major issue.

The manager who should be building usable systems (but is not) finds that the backlog of new processing requests grows much faster than the data processing organization can respond.

2.7 SYNTHESIS OF EVOLUTION

Some interesting points should be made about the evolution of systems:

1. Each stage involves a transition brought about by a changing environment in response to problems. At the very heart of *all* those problems was growth of one sort or another. Without growth, it is possible that manual systems would be the *only* type of system known today.
2. Each stage solved some problems, but opened the door to a whole new set of problems. In its time and place, each stage has been heralded as a panacea, and again, in its time and place, each stage has proven not to be a panacea, just another stage of a large progression.
3. Each stage reduced personnel requirements and increased machine

requirements. Furthermore, the sophistication and capacity of the machines have grown with each stage, and the cost of units of processing has gone down.

4. Each stage shortened (and/or broadened) the information cycle.
5. Each stage opened up possibilities and opportunities not feasible previously.

2.8 SUMMARY

An evolution of systems has occurred and is occurring. Understanding what the stages of the evolution are and why the next stage evolved can be very useful to a manager. The usefulness is that a manager can recognize what stage a shop is in and thus anticipate problems before they become acute.

When a manager is facing a new stage of evolution and resists, the problems that cause a shop to evolve naturally from one stage to the next grow much larger (and ultimately much more expensive) than they need to be. Also, the capabilities of a company are impaired when evolution should occur but does not.

CASE STUDY

Aspen Aspirations is a women's clothing manufacturer, distributor, and styling company. Aspen has worldwide distribution. In the United States, there is a distribution center in most major cities and in fashion resorts such as Palm Springs, Aspen, and Monterey/Carmel.

Aspen currently runs a large on-line system that controls accounts, manufacturing deliveries, scheduled deliveries, distribution deadlines, and so on. In the on line system, the status of any account can be found. It can be said that this system is the backbone of Aspen Aspirations.

For quite a while, management has recognized a need for a different kind of computer system. Not coincidentally, the system needed will heavily use the data found in the on-line distribution system. The system that is needed is for planning and trend analysis. It is one thing to keep track of the orders and deliveries to all of Aspen's accounts, but it is another thing to step back and analyze buying trends on a six-month or yearly basis. For the purpose of trend analysis, the status of an individual account is not particularly important, nor does it need to be accurate up to the second. Much data needs to be scanned and compared, at a summary level, against summary data taken from a previous time.

Aspen has tried to use software packages against the on-line distribution system, but there have been many problems. The software packages often have a negative effect on the on-line system. The on-line system is geared for rapid limited access of data, whereas the software packages attempt to do data base scans and analysis, which causes a conflict in the on-line system. Doing data base scans against on-line systems uses many resources, because the on-line system is not optimized for that type of processing. Furthermore, in doing planning and trend analysis, the user needs to change frequently the type of data viewed and the way the data is viewed. Those changes are very slow and difficult to bring about in the on-line environment.

There are other problems and contradictions. The user is interested in the status and summaries of data, not in the ability to update or change the data, but the on-line environment gives the user the capability to update make changes (on an individual account basis). A further contradiction is that the user could care less about the integrity features of the data base management system. Because of the slow speed of servicing the user requests for trend analysis and planning, the backlog of requests is growing much faster than data processing can service the requests.

After much soul searching, data processing management abandons the effort to use software packages on the data that exist on the on-line system. The local software vendor introduces data processing management to an entirely new approach to solving the problems of planning and trend analysis systems. The new approach involves software that processes on-line data out of the on-line environment. The data is stripped off the on-line system and put in front of the user. The user cannot do updates at the account level, but that is no loss. Also, the user does not have to involve data processing development and maintenance in the use of the data once the data is stripped. Further loss of capability is that the user has only a "snapshot" of the data (i.e., the information is current only up to the moment it was stripped). For trend analysis and planning, this is no problem.

The great advantage is that the user is free to alter data, sort it, summarize it as the user wishes, and do many other things independent of data processing because the software the user is running is optimized for user convenience and is not run in the on-line environment.

After a few months, the data processing manager makes some observations. Machine utilization is higher than ever before, and the number of user requests in the backlog of activities is beginning to fall.   ∎

Comment on the Following

1. Management is embarking on the era of usable systems.
2. Just as some problems will be solved and other problems will be created as a shop goes from one stage of evolution to the next, what problems have been solved and what problems will be created by going to usable systems?

3. What will happen should the user want update capabilities for planning and trend analysis systems?

4. What is the cost of allowing the user to reformat data? Is that an un-reasonable thing to do? Why is reformatting of data so painful in an on-line system?

5. Is there a danger in allowing the user great freedom to do data processing functions in the absence of data processing personnel?

MULTIPLE-CHOICE QUESTIONS

1. A shop has been running sequential systems (non-data base) for the past six years. New systems were produced frequently in the first few years. Lately, systems have become more and more complex because the interfaces between systems are increasingly complex. Maintenance is becoming a bigger problem. As systems grow older and more maintenance is required, the maintenance programmer's job has become increasingly difficult. In an effort to reduce data processing expenses, management firmly refuses to consider a change of scenarios that would take the shop toward data base or on-line systems.

   A. The costs management saves in hardware will probably be lost elsewhere.

   B. The maintenance problem is not going to get any better.

   C. The complexities of interfacing systems will probably not im-prove.

   D. Synchronization of data values is a real problem in this environ-ment.

   E. Since data is redundant among systems, more programs must be written to support the data than would be necessary if the data was integrated.

2. Management opts to go to the data base environment. In the data base environment, data can be integrated, systems will be easier to write, data will be easy to control, data can easily be accessed directly, and synchronization of data is not a problem.

   A. Using data base ensures that data and systems will be integrated.

   B. Data values are synchronized in a data base environment.

   C. There is a minimum of redundancy in the data base environment.

   D. Systems can be produced much faster in the data base environ-ment.

   E. Maintenance is not a big problem in the data base environment.

EXERCISES AND ESSAYS

1. Outline the reasons why shops evolve from one stage to the next. Determine what those stages are. What happens when a shop resists the evolution? What are the new sets of problems encountered in the stage being evolved to?

2. What are the roots of growth? Where is the end of growth? What parameters control growth?

3. Trace the length and breadth of the information cycle throughout the stages of evolution.

4. What is the next stage of evolution after usable systems?

5. Are there any valid reasons why a shop should resist evolution? If so, what are they?

III

System Life Cycle

☐☐☐

To understand many of the problems of data processing today, the manager must have a firm grip on the process by which systems are built, are run, and are finally aged and discarded. Central to the understanding of this process is the life cycle of systems, which is fairly uniform from shop to shop. Systems usually begin with a feasibility study, progress to a deeper analysis, go to design, then programming, testing, implementation, and maintenance. This progression and the relative amount of work spent in each phase are shown by Figure 3.1.

Feasibility → analysis → design → programming → testing → implementation → maintenance

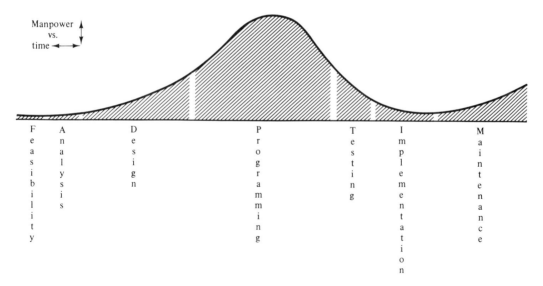

Figure 3.1 System life cycle.

The traditional phases of the system life cycle are fairly universal and are accepted by management and the data processing community in general. There is another phase that exists in many shops that is not formally discussed, because it is the result of factors that management would rather ignore. Often, it is swept under the rug in the guise of maintenance. It is the *post-implementation design and development stage*, which is really a *re*design and *re*development stage. Management does not like to call attention to this phase because it is a sign that (1) deadlines have been set that were unrealistic, (2) there has been a flaw in the design (which management feels might reflect on its competence), (3) users have not established firmly their expectations, or (4) miscellaneous other reasons.

This stage is often a ploy added by anxious designers to help them meet schedules or to redo work that was not done properly the first time. In this phase, user requirements are satisfied on schedule in that deadlines are met and a program (in some form or the other) exists to satisfy user requirements. (*Note:* The program only *exists*; it does not actually perform as it should.) Once the heat of the deadline is past, the program is reworked or even rewritten from scratch after it has been determined that it is inadequate in one or more ways during implementation or in the production environment.

This approach is especially useful in the environment of on-line systems, where (1) almost any program will satisfy the initial user specifications (because the user specifications have not been properly prepared) and (2) the length of time from the first pass at implementation until the true operational characteristics of the system are known can be in the neighborhood of *years*. There is no doubt that artificial satisfaction of deadlines is a primary cause of post-implementation design. A secondary cause is that users do not perceive the processing possibilities until they actually experience their on-line system. At that point whole new vistas open up to them, but their system design is based on an architecture that cannot support their imagination. A third cause is that system designers have not prioritized exactly what is most important in the system. For example, during development, system development time is optimized, but during the first phases of operation the designer decides that the system should be optimized for performance. It is too late at that point to retrofit a reordering of system priorities. Post-implementation design is very expensive and unnecessary. When it occurs, competent managers should be aware of it and do all they can to ensure that it will not happen again.

Often, users will be ambiguous and/or incomplete when it comes to specifying requirements. Their attitude can be described as saying: "Give me what I say I want, then I will tell you what I really want." This attitude can lead to a vicious iterative cycle in which it may be very expensive to determine what is required. There are several *major* pitfalls to this attitude. The first is that satisfaction of a set of requirements is a major undertaking and usually cannot be changed fundamentally with ease, so satisfying "iterated" requirements is very expensive. The second major problem with this attitude is that if users are allowed to reiterate their requirements, how many times can they reiterate them? Once? Twice? Ten times? *Each* iteration is expensive and leads to the phenomenon of post-implementation design.

Another very similar (yet fundamentally different) reason for user requirements causing post-implementation design is the case where the user's environment undergoes a large, profound change from the time of specification of requirements until implementation. In this case, the result will be post-implementation development and design, but the difference is that it will not be reiterated. In the eventuality that the user's environment *is* undergoing rapid change, the designer should construct the system with as much elasticity as possible and/or construct only a minimal subset of the system until such time as the user's environment stabilizes.

Another cause of post-implementation design is due to a poor design, a poor implementation of the design, or both. The most common cause is poor design but on occasion, poor implementation of a good design is found. Usually, this phenomenon is found as a shop progresses to a new mode of building systems, such as going from sequential systems to data base, or more frequently, from data base to on-line systems. On occasion, a shop will be well versed in the proper design techniques of a mode of design, but the individuals constructing the systems will not be qualified, and the resultant design is poor. Unfortunately, in the on-line environment it often happens that a shop will not learn of its design errors until late in the system life cycle, owing to the *delayed development feedback phenomenon* (Chapter 20).

Whatever the cause of post-implementation development and design, the cost is very high, in light of the fact that (1) the effort itself typically costs as much as the original project development cycle, and (2) the resultant system is a conglomeration of data and programs that were originally architected with other purposes in mind (thus making the system difficult to maintain from the outset).

The remainder of this chapter describes the traditional phases of project development. It is written as an overview and is for the reader new to data processing. Major issues are identified without an in-depth discussion. Further references are included for the reader interested in a deeper study of these phases.

3.1 FEASIBILITY

The traditional system life cycle begins with a feasibility study. Some of the typical concerns at this point in the system's life are:

• What, in very general terms, is the system to do?

- *Can* the system be implemented?
- *Should* the system be implemented?
- At a gross level, what resources will be required to build the system? To operate the system?

It is worth noting that a system that *can* be built perhaps *should not* be built, for a variety of reasons. Both questions are equally germane to the feasibility study.

The criteria for justifications that should occur at this point are:

- *Financial.* Is the system going to make money for the company? Save the company money? Is the marginal amount saved over the life of the system worth the cost of development and implementation?
- *Technological.* Will the technology work? Will it be outdated? Is there a better technology? What are the risks?
- *Political.* What impact will construction and operation of the system have on the organization? Do adequate resources exist? If they do exist, can they be allocated? Are there long-term considerations in regard to the organizational structure?

In large shops these considerations are normally formalized. In smaller shops they are usually done informally. There are advantages and disadvantages to both the informal and formal approaches. When done formally the specifications of feasibility serve as a base document for user requirements. Inherent limitations and intentions will be clearly delineated so that future misunderstandings are minimized. When done informally, specifications are not subject to long delays due to rewriting a specification or modifying complex parts of it when changes need to be made.

The major drawback of not formalizing specifications is that the specifications are open to interpretation. This may be the cause of misunderstanding in that a user may have certain expectations, the designer thinks that he or she has fulfilled those expectations, and there is a wide discrepancy between the two.

3.2 ANALYSIS

The next traditional phase of system development is analysis. From the feasibility study comes user requirements (in one form or the other). The first step in analysis is to refine these requirements into a form that has meaning in the data processing environment. Data modeling usually follows (either formally or informally). In the formal case this often includes *data normalization* and the construction of *canonical data structures* (see Chapters 13 to 15 in James Martin's *Computer Data Base Organization*). As data modeling is being done, the definition of the processing needs is begun. A very rough idea of the shape of the system is then formed from the data model and processes.

Some of the pitfalls of analysis occur when decisions are made that do not mesh with the user's perception of the system and when analysts add unnecessary and unwanted refinements to the system. The analyst may add one or more features thinking that those features will enhance the system, when in fact they do not—unfortunately, the user was not informed of the additional features.

3.3 DESIGN

The design phase of a project occurs when the conceptual understanding of the system becomes shaped into a physical form (i.e., in the form of data layouts, program specifications, etc.). While in the conceptual form, a system is very easy to change. The further the system goes from conceptualization to actualization, the more difficult changes become. This is so because changes cause more and more work to be undone the further the system progresses. The data is translated from the data model to a "storage" (or physical) model. At this point the data is defined in a tangible form that a programmer can work with, (that is, into a form recognizable to software and hardware). Once the data has been defined in a stable form, program specifications can be finalized.

One of the pitfalls of design is an emphasis on the workability of the system, rather than on system quality. Given the tools that exist today, it is no great feat to come up with a workable design; instead, it is a worthy feat to come up with the *best* design that is workable. Even the word "best" has some strange connotations, because what is best to any two people is probably different.

For instance, the developer may view the best design as the one that can be done the fastest. The user views the best design as the one that has the most user function. The operator views the best design as the one that is simplest and easiest to operate. And so forth. Thus the first task of the designer is to determine the system parameters of success that will determine what "best" really is, then how to fulfill these parameters. When a designer settles on the first scheme that occurs to him or her (i.e., the first "workable" design), the resultant system design usually satisfies very few of the real "best" parameters of success.

3.4 PROGRAMMING

The programming phase of a system starts when program specifications have been solidified and the programmer has a "road map" by which to begin to construct programs. The programmer is normally judged by the speed at which he or she turns out code and how well the code satisfies specifications. In a complex environment such as the on-line environment, there are additional parameters of programming success, such as speed of execution, uniformity of resource consumption, and other factors.

Some pitfalls of programming include not fulfilling specifications, incorporating more function than was specified, and incorrectly interpreting specifications. In some cases a programmer will hyperoptimize a program for efficiency of execution, so much so that future changes to the code are very difficult, because of the way in which the code is written. In addition to hyperefficient code that is difficult to read and change, coding styles and practices have a major bearing on the maintainability of code. The ideal is to meet design specifications while maximizing code understanding and flexibility.

3.5 TESTING

The next traditional phase of system development is that of testing. Code that is generated must be tested in a stand-alone mode, where the code is tested in the absence of other, related code (i.e., other code that passes or receives data from the code being tested), and in an integrated environment (where code is tested in conjunction with other related code). These types of tests are commonly referred to as unit tests and system tests. Both valid data and invalid data should be run through the program. Valid data should exercise all of the logic paths of the program and invalid data should be entered to determine how the program responds. The presence of invalid input data should not bring a system to a halt; the data should be gracefully rejected by the program. As an example, a key entry operator enters "C" for a person's sex when only "M" or "F" qualify. The program should make note of it and reject the entry rather than allowing data to enter a file or data base or causing the program to terminate abnormally.

There are other levels of test. In an on-line environment it may be desirable to run a stress test—a test not of correctness of code but of efficiency of execution—which is not concerned with the accuracy of the program, but with the volume of programs that can be run in a live, production environment. Another type of test is a security test, where existing levels of security are verified and attempts are made to circumvent them.

3.6 IMPLEMENTATION

The next traditional phase of a project is implementation. At this point the program tests have been completed and errors that have been discovered are corrected. Upon correction, the tested programs are made available in a production mode (i.e., for use by the user on live data and run in concert with other production programs). Certain test data may be converted to a production form. Other massive data conversions may be done to generate the first set of production data. As the code is readied for production, it may be passed through an automatic optimizer (a piece of software that does not change the accuracy of execution but concerns itself with the speed of execution) to improve operational efficiency. Usually, a certain amount of preparation is necessary for the operating system when an application goes into production. This may be as simple as ensuring that enough space exists on which to store production programs to as complex an operation as defining a new application to the software that operates an on-line system.

Some of the pitfalls of implementation occur when the implementation effort is not coordinated and needs to be, when programs are put into production when they are not ready, when adequate resources do not exist that are needed for the production effort, and when the implementation effort involves new technology not previously handled by the organization. When an abortive implementation is forced by management or the user, it is a *big* mistake and will lead to many problems in the future.

3.7 MAINTENANCE

Every user's environment changes over time. The only difference from user to user is the rate of change. As change occurs, so do user requirements, and with the change in user requirements comes maintenance of existing systems. Maintenance can usually be categorized into three categories: "fixit" maintenance (problem resolution), change maintenance (modify existing code), or add-on (extend existing code). Another form of maintenance, which relates indirectly to the forms noted above, is that of system rewrites.

Over time, code can be changed so often that it becomes mangled and is difficult, if not impossible, to understand or follow. Also, program style, standards, and specifications have a great deal to do with how flexible programs can be. Another major factor relating to maintenance is that of changes to the data on which programs operate. All of these factors relate to how easy or difficult the job of the maintenance programmer will be.

Considering the large and increasing amount of staff time being spent on maintenance, it is surprising that there are not more automated aids available to assist the programmer.

3.8 SUMMARY

Management should be aware of the problems that arise during the development life cycle of the system. The post-implementation design and development effort can, in itself, cause crises of monumental proportion and can greatly exaggerate related problem areas, such as morale, productivity, and user satisfaction. This phenomenon is very costly—in terms of money, personnel, and morale. The manager should do several things to minimize the problems of post-implementation design: make sure that deadlines are set in concurrence with the people responsible for meeting these deadlines, make sure that user requirements are firmly established in a clear and quantifiable way before deadlines are set, and make sure that technical problems that will occur will not greatly affect (negatively) the project. In general, management must be aware of the realities of producing the project.

Also, management should make sure that the user is "kept in the loop" throughout the development cycle. In cases where the user is aloof from the project, there is a good chance that a great deal of effort will be wasted because the end result does not perform a useful function, however well built it is.

REFERENCE

Martin, James, *Computer Data Base Organization*, 2nd ed., Prentice-Hall, Inc., Englewood Cliffs, N.J., 1977.

CASE STUDY

The Northern California Wine and Grape Co-op operates winery, marketing, publicity, and distribution facilities. For the past six years, American wine consumption has gone up an amazing 22% per year. What once was a small business is now large and is handling several times as much money as was ever imagined.

Wine and Grape has had batch systems before, but now, with their size and profitability, the company believes that it is ready for the on-line environment. Their first system in the on-line environment will be one that will connect their distributors across the United States. It will control not only orders, but the servicing of orders.

Management is concerned with the rising costs of computerization and mandates that the top priority is programmer "productivity." They base their wisdom on the fact that labor costs are rising faster than computer costs. The best designer of past batch systems is selected to lead the project. He sets out quickly to design the system. In a very short time the system is designed and is into programming. About this time, a member of the data base administration staff and a vendor enter into discussions about the design of the system. They comment to management that the system design has "problems." Management confronts the designer, the designer asserts that the design will work, and management admonishes the DBA and vendor not to interfere.

In a short time—eight months—the first part of the system is through testing and implementation, much to the pride of the designer and management. The development effort has taken 120 person months of effort. The remainder of the system goes into production and with the exception of one or two minor problems, the system "settles" nicely.

The system begins to be used locally before the nationwide distributors are turned on-line. For the first few months, the system uses 10% of machine capacity. During the fourth month, one of the data bases has a problem and comes down. Because of the system design, this data base brings the entire system to a halt. It takes 22 hours to recover the system, during which time orders for wine and the distribution of wine come to a halt. Needless to say, upper management is *quite* concerned.

Once the crisis is over, an analysis of the problem is made. It is pointed out that as more data is put into the system, the recovery time will lengthen. The designer determines that operations could have handled the recovery process more efficiently, perhaps in 14 to 16 hours. Management is concerned because even 14 hours of downtime is really distressing. The DBA points out that a redesign of two data bases and a reprogramming of 25 programs could greatly reduce the downtime—to as little as half an hour. Management allocates personnel for this "maintenance" effort.

In the meantime, the response time of the system, which was 3 to 5 seconds, has gone to 9 to 10 seconds (occasionally up to 30 seconds) as more distributors are cut over to the system. A tuner is brought in and reduces response time to 7 to 8 seconds. This requires a two-week effort and the tuning expert charges $800 per day.

For the next few months, things are calm, except that as the system is being used more often, response time climbs. New users are discouraged to find that the average response time is 15 seconds, with waits up to 1½ minutes. The users become very upset with the system and put pressure on data processing management.

Another ("more competent") tuning expert is brought in and works six weeks to get response time down to 10 to 12 seconds. This expert charges $1000 per day.

Finally, a whole new set of distributors east of the Mississippi is added and response time goes to 2 to 3 minutes. Upper management calls the expert tuner in for a session. She says that tuning will never solve some of the fundamental problems of the system. What can be done is to:

1. Recode small parts of the system that are obviously inefficient.
2. Redesign the system and rewrite it.

She makes the point that the current architecture of the system will probably *never* be efficient, and urges management to have the system rewritten.

Management feels that a system rewrite would be an admission of incompetence and, besides, they have promised the users the system. So a piecemeal rewrite is opted for. The basic problems of the system are not attacked.

After three years, the results are:

1. The system provides a 25- to 45-second response time, with occasional waits of up to 4 minutes.
2. A total of 920 person-months have been spent in tuning, rewrites, and so on.
3. If response time is ever to be satisfactory, a basic system rewrite must be undertaken.

Comment on the Following

1. Management is—politically—in a very tenuous position when it opts to ignore long-term considerations.
2. Optimizing for development time can be an extremely expensive thing to do.
3. Tuning can only do so much for a system once it is built.
4. Desirable attributes of a system—such as performance, availability, and flexibility—are put into a system at the moment of design. Retrofitting them is either impossible or impractical.
5. A certain reasonable amount of post-implementation design is normal.
6. Post-implementation design problems are much more common in large, complex, on-line systems.
7. The problems faced by management are *never* going to get any better unless the system is rewritten.

MULTIPLE-CHOICE QUESTIONS

1. A user wants to optimize development time while development is under way. Once the system is up and running, he will want to optimize performance. When the system goes down, he will want availability to be optimized. When the system needs to be changed, the user will want to optimize flexibility.

   A. By optimizing development time, the user may be preempting his chance at having other adequate systems features.

    B. Just because development time takes a long time, it does not necessarily mean that the resulting design will be adequate.

    C. Trade-offs must be made somewhere, because a design optimized for performance will not be optimized for flexibility.

    D. Machine speed should *not* be relied on as the only consideration of performance.

    E. Large data bases are contrary to the optimization of availability, performance, *and* flexibility.

2. A project is started. Ten months later it is completed. By the time it goes into production, the user's environment has undergone several changes that need to be implemented into the system.

    A. This is one of the roots of post-implementation development.

    B. Every user's environment changes. The only difference from user to user is the rate of change.

    C. This may be a symptom of the "give me what I say I want, then I will tell you what I really want" syndrome.

    D. If the design has been done with a high degree of flexibility, the change will have minimal impact.

    E. If the design has been based strictly on user requirements rather than on a "natural" structuring of the data, the changes are likely to be difficult to make.

EXERCISES AND ESSAYS

1. Describe the various phases of design. Outline milestones and deliverables of each phase. Project the personnel requirements for each phase. How difficult are design changes to make at each phase?

2. How can a manager distinguish between a user's environment that really does undergo a high degree of change and the "give me what I say I want, then I will tell you what I really want" syndrome?

3. When is it best to formalize system requirements? To keep them informal?

4. What exactly is the cost of post-implementation design? In its worst case?

5. Why is the on-line environment so prone to post-implementation design?

6. On the one hand, speeding through development can be costly. How about the reverse? Is going through design slowly insurance that system quality will be built in? How can a manager ensure that system quality can be built in?

IV

Data and Data Integration

□□

Data is the foundation on which commercial data processing systems run. Data reflects what exists in the user's environment. The points of interest are how the data is shaped, how much data there is, what data there isn't, and the media on which the data resides. Each of these considerations has a profound effect on how the data can be used. Coming to grips with the issues of data and data integration can save a great deal of money because the savings are realized globally and on a large scale. Conversely, not coming to grips with these issues wastes money.

4.1 HIERARCHY OF STORAGE

Data can exist on several media, and those media have their own hierarchy. In general, the rawer the data and the greater the bulk (i.e., the less refined and the closer the data is to its source), the more difficult the data is to use and the cheaper the storage media on which it is stored. The rawer the data, the closer it is to the user or to the source that caused the creation of the data. Data normally exists in two forms: machine readable and non-machine readable. Examples of data in non-machine-readable form are business letters, conversations, newspapers, invoices, orders, and memos. Machine-readable data typically exists on punched cards, paper or magnetic tape, disks, drums, or data cells, or in the main storage of a computer. Figure 4.1 shows the relative economies of the various media.

One of the main concerns of data processing management is to see that the correct data is residing on the right media. It does not make sense to put bulk data—data in raw, unrefined, unedited form—in main storage, because main storage is expensive and the probability of access of any piece of bulk data is low. By the same token, it does not make sense to put frequently accessed data on punched cards, because the time and effort consumed in retrieving and modifying the data would be prohibitive. It is thus up to the designer or system architect to balance the costs of storage and retrieval of data against the likelihood of the access of the data. An imbalance here

38

results in a waste of storage (which is expensive) or a waste of processing time (which is also expensive).

Figure 4.1 Relative costs of various media.

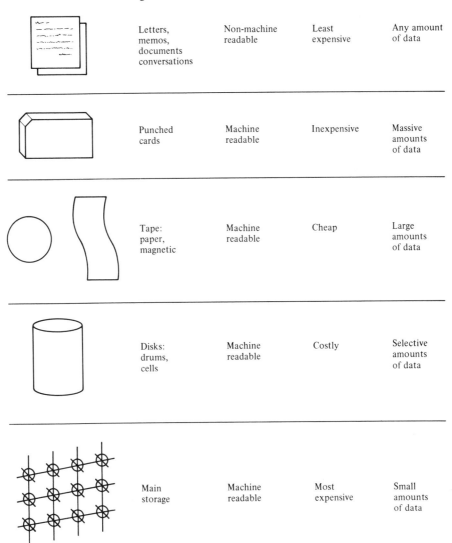

	Letters, memos, documents conversations	Non-machine readable	Least expensive	Any amount of data
	Punched cards	Machine readable	Inexpensive	Massive amounts of data
	Tape: paper, magnetic	Machine readable	Cheap	Large amounts of data
	Disks: drums, cells	Machine readable	Costly	Selective amounts of data
	Main storage	Machine readable	Most expensive	Small amounts of data

4.2 CAPTURE OF DATA

How does data cross the boundary from non-machine-readable form to machine-readable form? The traditional way (in batch) is through some form of data entry, such as card punching or keying onto disk (entering data directly onto a direct-access storage device). There are other technologies that will allow data to be captured automatically, such as character recognition, magnetic encoding, and other forms. Another way that data enters a system (but is not necessarily captured) is through programming interfaces, such as merges of large files or extracts of data from one or more files.

In some cases data values can be calculated or extrapolated at the point of interface (the contact with other systems). In an on-line environment data can be entered directly into the system by the user as the system is being operated. Figure 4.2 illustrates various ways in which data can get into a system.

Figure 4.2 Ways in which data can enter system.

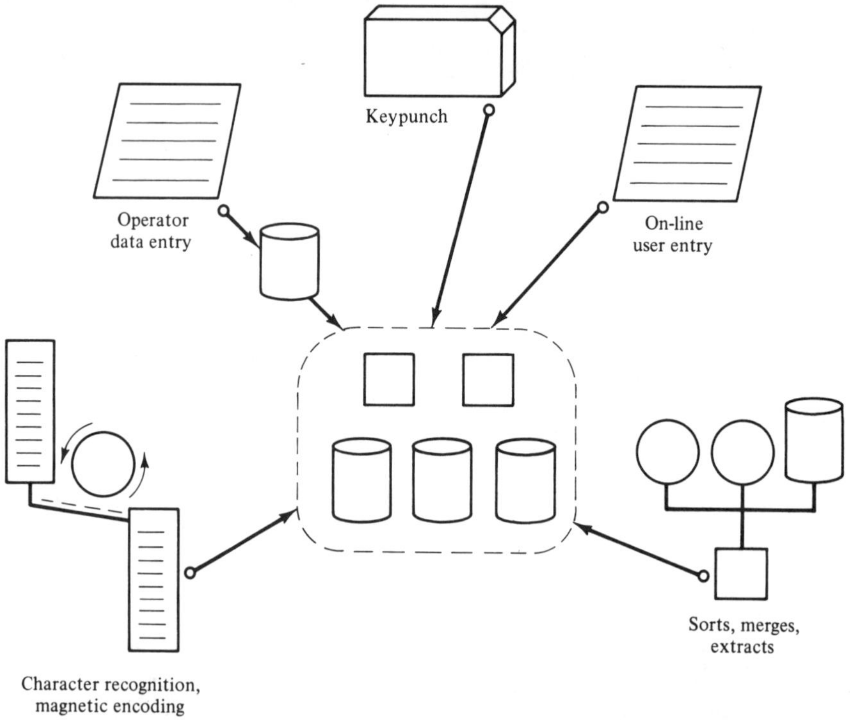

Keypunch

Operator
data entry

On-line
user entry

Character recognition,
magnetic encoding

Sorts, merges,
extracts

4.3 ARCHIVING OF DATA

Just as data enters the system, at some point it leaves the system as well. In some cases it is merely deleted from the system and lost. This may be an expensive practice if the data is ever likely to be needed again, because the cost of recapturing or recalculating the data can be very expensive. In some cases all the resources in the world will not help to restore data because when data is lost, it is lost forever and cannot be reconstructed. So it usually makes sense to archive data once it has been captured and is about to be deleted. This means the data that is to be deleted is written off to a less expensive medium, perhaps even to a non-machine-readable medium such as microfiche—a high-density microscopic medium for the long-term storage of massive amounts of data. At the very least, a company will have *some* record of the data in the eventuality that the data is needed later. One reason for archiving might be extensive government requirements or a historical basis for future planning.

One of the problems with archiving is that, with time, the definition of data structures change and this means that the person attempting to view that data over archival volumes must be aware of the changes in the definition. This changing of data definitions plays a big role in data processing and is referred to as "semantic" changes. As an example, suppose that the programmer refers to the zip code as being five positions in length. The government changes its mind about the zip code and now the programmer must think of it as occupying nine positions, except that all the programs the programmer has written still consider zip to require five positions.

This is a simple example of a "semantic" change of data. The program that views the data and its structure in a particular way today probably will not be able to operate on yesterday's data because of the change in the shape of the data.* Another problem of archiving is that the *content* of the data changes over time as well as the form, and this change, too, should be noted if the person attempting to use archival data is to have success. The point is that merely storing data is not enough. The meaning of the content and exact shape of the structure of the data must be stored as well.

The full life cycle of data is illustrated in Figure 4.3.

Figure 4.3 Data life cycle.

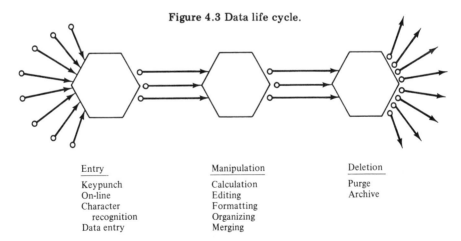

Entry	Manipulation	Deletion
Keypunch	Calculation	Purge
On-line	Editing	Archive
Character	Formatting	
recognition	Organizing	
Data entry	Merging	

*When a program operates on data, it normally views the data as having a single physical shape. When that shape changes, the program must be changed to expect the data in the new form.

4.4 USE OF DATA

Once data has entered a system, it is stored in a form that is useful for auto-mated processing. Data is operated on directly by programs, and those pro-grams are directed (one way or the other) by people (i.e., by the efforts of the programmer and the operators of the system). The result seen by a person who has caused a program to run may be a report, a reply on a screen, or perhaps no direct acknowledgment at all to the person entering the data. This indirect mode of using data (through a program) is both a blessing and a curse. It is a blessing in that the program gives the user much function—formatting, selectivity, and so on. It is a curse in that data has no great meaning *without* programs (i.e., programs must be used to convert data into information). Programs are expensive to write and even more expensive to change. As data changes (and *all* data changes over time), pro-grams must change.

The way data is used changes in two ways: semantically and by con-tent. A semantic change of data refers to a change in the form of the data (e.g., size of data elements, grouping of data elements, physical organization of groups of data elements, etc.). A semantic change implies that all pro-grams that view that data must also change, and those changes can be (and normally are) costly. One of the major problems facing the data processing industry is the closeness of the relationship between data and programs (called "data dependence"). There are many proposed techniques and products (such as data base, data dictionaries, etc.) that address data de-pendence, but to some degree (usually a large one), data dependence remains a problem.

The other way the use of data changes is in content. The form of the data remains the same, but the content of the data values changes. The main problem posed by a change of data contents is in the storage requirements and in the internal "cleanliness" of the data (over time, data has a tendency to become internally disorganized in a highly volatile environment). The two ways in which data changes are shown by Figure 4.4.

```
Name   — B Biddle              Name    — B Biddle
Age    — 38                    Age     — 38
Sex    — Male                  Sex     — Male
Job    — Bouncer               Job     — Bouncer
                               Salary  — 600/mo
                               Eyes    — Blue
                               Hair    — Blonde
```

(a)

```
Name   — D Shackleford         Name    — D Shackleford
Age    — 35                    Age     — 36
Sex    — Female                Sex     — Female
Job    — Chorus Line           Job     — Bartender
```

(b)

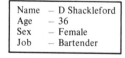

Figure 4.4 Two types of change of data: (a) semantic change of data; (b) change of data content.

4.5 COSTS OF DATA

The costs related to data stem from its storage, use, and the changes that occur in the data. Storage costs refer primarily to the cost of the media on which the data is stored. Figure 4.1 gives the relative costs of the various media. It is of interest to note that the cost of the most expensive storage has dropped over time; for example, main memory is much less expensive today than it was 10 years ago.

The second set of costs associated with data are associated with how the data can be used. These costs relate to the programs that use the data— the costs of creating the program initially, of running the program, and of changing the program when the data undergoes semantic changes. Other miscellaneous costs relate to the storage of the programs, their documentation, supporting utilities, and so on. For a single program these costs are not especially awesome, but when data is defined redundantly, it is seen that *each* of the separate definitions of data requires its own unique set of programs or code, so that redundancy of data definition is costly.

The third cost associated with data relates to actual changes in the data. When data undergoes semantic changes, there are two types of costs: the mapping of the data from the old format into the new one, and the cost of redefining the data to all the programs that are affected by the change. The latter costs are by far the greater. On a corporate-wide basis, when a commonly used data element must be redefined and redundancy exists, the costs of change are magnified by the redundancy.

4.6 ISSUES OF DATA

There are four major issues (and some minor ones) of which managers should be aware when managing data. The first issue is that of data availability— where data exists within a system but cannot be accessed for one reason or other. Some reasons why data may exist but not be available are:

- An updating program is running and has exclusive control of the data; no other program may access the data until this program is finished.
- A recovery (i.e., a restoration of data to an acceptable state after an error has occurred) is running and has exclusive control of the data.
- A reorganization (i.e., an internal restructuring of data) is running and has exclusive control of the data.
- The on-line system is down and the programs that access the data can only be run on-line.

From the reasons listed above for unavailability of data it is seen that there are two major problems: exclusive control of data or limited accessibility. Exclusive control of data is indirectly and yet intimately related with size of data. Simply stated, the more data that is controlled exclusively, the longer it will be necessary to control the data (i.e., any exclusive process will take longer to run the more data there is to be processed, thus locking out other processes from the data). This leads to the conclusion that smallness of data sizes is good insofar as the issue of availability is concerned.

The other issue—that of limited accessibility—is a calculated risk taken by all who choose to automate systems. Limited accessibility of data is the limitation imposed by the very media on which systems are run, such as a computer or an operating system. Whenever the computer is not available, it follows that the application is not available as well. System-wide availability is addressed by hardware and software technicians, whereas application-wide availability is addressed at the local design level. In a nutshell, smallness of units of data and disjunctiveness of data and programs lead to systems that are loosely bound together and can "fail soft."

When data is divided into small independent units, and one of those units is not available, only a small amount of data is affected. When programs are not tightly related or dependent on other programs, and one program fails, the entire system does not fail. This means that when a single part of the system—data or programs—fails, the entire system does not come to a halt. Thus smallness and disjunction are desirable in light of the issue of limited access to data. Chapter 5 gives a detailed explanation of the issues of availability.

The next major issue related to the usage of data is that of performance. In the batch environment, performance is equivalent to system throughput. System throughput is greatly enhanced by adding more machine power. Performance in the on-line environment (usually thought of as response time) is nothing more than the amount of time from the entry of a transaction by the user until the user sees the reply to the transaction. Performance in the on-line environment is *much* more complex and difficult to achieve than in the batch environment. One of the fundamentals to performance in the on-line environment is the standard work unit concept (Chapter 6), but there is more to performance than just the standard work unit. For a discussion of the many variables of performance, refer to Chapters 6, 7, and 8 of *Design Review Methodology for a Data Base Environment*, by W. H. Inmon and L. J. Friedman.

The third issue relating to the use of data that the manager must be aware of is that of flexibility. Flexibility is the ability to change the physical implementation of data as the data logically change in the user's environment with minimal impact on application programs. The real impact is not on the changing of the form of the data but on the programs that access that data, as has been discussed. The issue of data flexibility is discussed thoroughly in Chapters 5 and 6 of *Effective Data Base Design*, by W. H. Inmon.

The fourth major issue relating to the use of data that the manager must be aware of is that of data integration, which is discussed in depth in the following section. Other issues pertinent to the use of data are security, multiple uses of data, and operational considerations.

4.7 DATA INTEGRATION

Much has been written about data integration and it is generally agreed that it is a good idea, but very little has been done beyond theory. It is the purpose of the remainder of this chapter to explore data integration from a pragmatic standpoint, examining the promises of integration, the problems, and what exists today in the world of data processing.

The appropriate starting point of the discussion of data integration begins with its definition—not a definition based on theory but a definition based on the world in which data integration must either succeed or fail. A good working definition of integration is as follows:

Data (and data elements) are integrated when they are:

1. *Defined* at the lowest fundamental level, that is, as it exists in the logical data model based on the user's environment.
2. *Accessed* by a single definition, which includes:
   a. The physical shape of the data element
   b. The unique and uniform relation of the data relative to other data elements sharing the same boundary of physical storage and transportation

At first glance, parts of this definition may appear to be ambiguous or unclear, so amplification is worthwhile. The first and most immediate result of the definition of data integration is that the status of data *must* be removed from the semantic definition and relegated to a data field. This means that data exists in its most fundamentally primitive form regardless of its status, and that status should be represented by a change in data content. This subtle and *very important* distinction will be illustrated by an example.

Consider the data designer who must represent men and women in several forms: married, single, divorced, alive, and deceased. A very simplistic (and somewhat intuitively appealing) approach is to design a data base for each state of existence a person may be in. This is shown by Figure 4.5. It

Figure 4.5 Data defined differently into separate data bases.

Married man
Age –
Salary –
Name –
Single man
Salary –
Age –
Name –
Dead man
Date of death –
Age at death –
Name –
Divorced man
Name –
Age –
Salary –
Single woman
Age –
Salary –
Name –
Dead woman
Date of death –
Name –
Age at death –
Divorced woman
Salary –
Age –
Name –
Married woman
Name –
Age –
Salary –

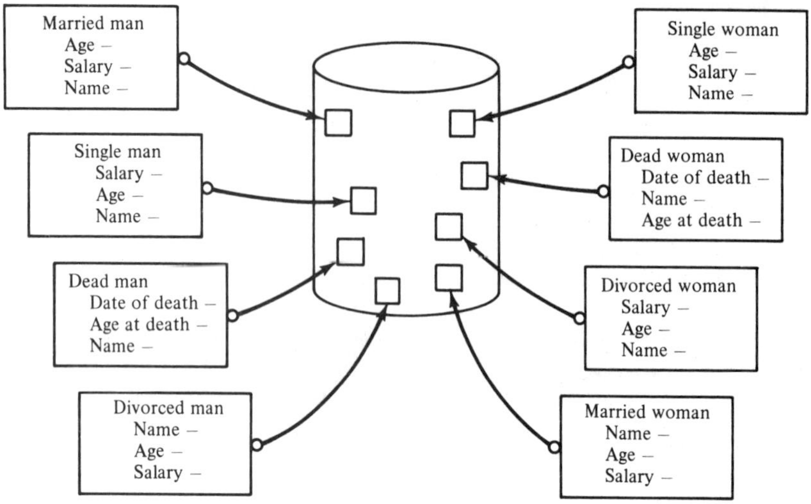

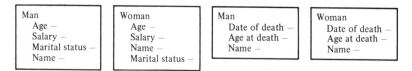

is clear from the figure that people can be described in one state or the other. However, those descriptions are very unintegrated (however closely they are related) because they are supported by *separate* data definitions which require *separate* programs to be written. Furthermore, when a man dies, he may be removed from the appropriate single, divorced, or married data base and *never* be put onto the dead data base. Or, worse yet, he may be put onto the dead data base and not be removed from the married, single, or divorced data base. Thus, reconciling the data among the data bases is seen to be as large an issue as writing the programs that support the data bases.

At a very basic level, what can be done? The data can be integrated! The first step to integration, as seen by the working definition, is to understand the data in terms of a data model. Among other things this means removing status as a consideration for key values, and this results in changes in the structuring of the data. In Figure 4.6 it is seen that marital status has

Figure 4.6 Replacement of status by data content.

Man
Age –
Salary –
Marital status –
Name –
Woman
Age –
Salary –
Name –
Marital status –
Man
Date of death –
Age at death –
Name –
Woman
Date of death –
Age at death –
Name –

been removed *structurally* and has been replaced by *data content.* This means that marital status changes without a need for deletion and creation of a new record, and without need for programs that support those activities. Thus the *total* number of programs needed is lessened considerably. There are some other refinements that should be made. Can men and women be reduced to a more fundamental form—that of the human form? The answer is yes. Other than the obvious sexual differences, men and women fundamentally are types of the same form, the human form. It behooves the information analyst to remove the "status" of sex and represent the forms more basically.

This next progression toward integrated data is shown by Figure 4.7. In this figure data is reduced to a very fundamental form by representing the status of sex by data content. At this point data is represented very fundamentally and is capable of withstanding change gracefully—or as gracefully as possible. Were data to be physically implemented in this form, one implementation would be "relational"—in "tuples"—the unit of storage for relational modeling of data.

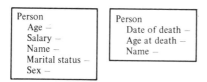

Figure 4.7 Reducing data to a very fundamental form.

Other physical implementations are also possible, such as that of the hierarchical definition of the data, shown in Figure 4.8. In this case it is seen that the person is viewed as an entity that can both be married or single at one point, and dead at another. Such universal data as name and sex (which normally do not change) remain with other universal identifying data. Other data, relating to marital status and general life characteristics, are grouped together; and other facts about the demise of the individual are further assimilated and organized. This model is feasible in a hierarchical model but *may* or *may not* be desirable because connecting mutually exclusive data in the same data base may not be a good idea.

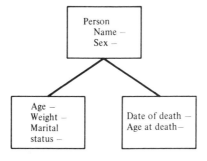

Figure 4.8 Hierarchical definition of data.

For instance, salary, age, height, or weight are no longer relevant as collectible data once a person has died. By the same token, date of death is not relevant as long as a person is living. Thus it may or may not make sense to have these data elements in the same data base. If the data base is used for all employees of a company's payroll, it probably will not make sense to combine such diversely related information. On the other hand, if the data is used for the life insurance policies of a company, it may make sense to combine mutually exclusive data. The deciding factor is the nature of the processing of the data itself.

There is another possible implementation: in *either* a relational or a hierarchical form, as shown in Figure 4.9. In this figure it is seen that data

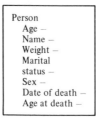

Figure 4.9 Implementation in either relational or hierarchical form.

relating to marital status, general living conditions, and death are combined. It makes *no sense whatsoever* to combine these data elements from an integration standpoint. The problem is in the programs that must support the data. Unfortunately, a program referencing the data must account for the physical structure of the data. Thus it does not matter whether a program accesses the data for sex, marital status, date of death, or whatever— whenever any of the data changes, the program must change. So when the coroner's office rules that it must add data concerning the attending physician, programs that update the weight of a newborn infant will be affected by this restructuring of data. This is absurd, of course, and is at the heart of data inelasticity and unintegrated data. It does not matter then *what* physical implementation the structuring of data takes, because the result would be an inelastic structure.

4.8 ANALYSIS OF THE POSSIBILITIES

The two extremes presented will be called unintegrated data structures and integrated data structures. Unintegrated data structures will refer to data viewed as shown in Figure 4.5, where like data was defined in many ways. Integrated data is described in Figures 4.7 and 4.8, in either a relational form or a hierarchical form. The point of interest is how these structures of data will react to some very real day-to-day pressures. The following questions will be considered:

- Where does the programmer go to make changes?
- What is the effect of change?
- How many programs must be written to support the basic structuring of data?
- When data changes in the user's environment, how many definitions of the data must change?
- If data must be cross-referenced or balanced, where can differences be resolved?

Figure 4.10 addresses those questions.

Figure 4.10 Comparison of unintegrated and integrated data structures.

	Unintegrated	Integrated
Where do programmers go to make changes?	Many places	Minimum number of places
What is the impact of change?	Huge	Least
How many programs must be written to support the basic data structure?	One for every separate data structure: many	One for every separate data structure: minimum number
When data changes in the user environment, how many definitions of data in programs must be changed?	Every and many	Every and minimum number
If data must be cross-referenced or balanced, where can the differences be resolved?	At many points; nowhere	At a single point; at a controlled point

4.9 POINT OF DEFINITION OF DATA

One subtle and yet very important point that may have escaped the reader in the working definition of data integration is that the critical point of physical data definition is *not* where the data is actually physically defined but *where the data is defined to the program.* This distinction may sound trivial but it is actually *very* important, because it allows for physical implementations of very large data bases that would otherwise be in violation of the concept of data integration, among other things.

For example, consider the following data base design. An account data base is designed so that it is implemented into three physically separate data bases split along key values, as shown in Figure 4.11. In the figure much data is semantically redundant in that name, address, and so on, are physically

Figure 4.11 Account data base implemented into three physically separate data bases split along key values.

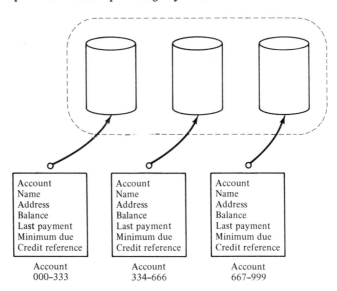

Account Name Address Balance Last payment Minimum due Credit reference	Account Name Address Balance Last payment Minimum due Credit reference	Account Name Address Balance Last payment Minimum due Credit reference
Account 000–333	Account 334–666	Account 667–999

defined in a number of places, and this would seem to nullify the precepts of data integration. But is the data really unintegrated? No, because it can be accessed by a *single* program definition, even though that definition is physically applicable over a number of layouts. The definition of data is uniform—which satisfies the second condition of data integration.

To understand the difference between data definition at the physical level and data definition at the program level, and the impact on the issue of integration, consider the example of Figure 4.12. In this case it is seen that

Part Description Location Shipper Address Contact phone Date received Amount received Expediter Voucher number Data of voucher	Shipping agent Address Phone Last activity date Delivery rating Balance owed Bulk discount Part supplied (1) Part supplied (2) Part supplied (3) Part supplied (4) Part supplied (5)	Account payable Auditor Last activity date Activity amount Shipping company Address Phone Voucher reference Bulk discount Date overdue Penalty

Figure 4.12 Classically unintegrated data.

data is physically defined in a number of places in several data bases, but there is an important and fundamental difference. The data that is redundantly defined is *not* uniformly defined in the places where it appears, and programs updating the data do not necessarily have to maintain the integrity of the content of the data. For example, (1) when a change occurs in the shipper's environment, the change proliferates through many programs in many ways; and (2) when the data relating to parts shipped or amount owed are not in synchronization from one data base to the next, it is not clear where to turn to rectify the discrepancy. Thus the data is classically unintegrated.

The reader may be curious as to how this data might be better structured so that it is integrated. A better structuring is shown in Figure 4.13.

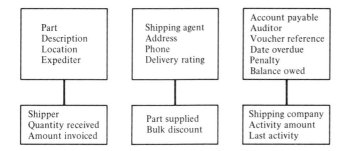

Figure 4.13 Integrated data.

In this example, integrated data is not entirely implementation dependent. Such internal data base management system considerations as pointers or concatenated keys are a consideration for performance and logical integrity. Comparing this example to the previous unintegrated form, it is seen that much redundancy has been removed. Removing the redundancy does not mean that there is a loss of user function; it simply means that the user function will be accomplished in other ways. It also means that the programs that support this structuring of data will be easier to maintain.

Thus the data is nonredundant for the most part, with the previously redundant data elements residing with the most functionally related elements. In the transition from Figure 4.12 to Figure 4.13, two very real and somewhat sophisticated points are noticeable. The first is that there are degrees of integration. This means that the reasons for data integration will be served in degrees, not entirely or not at all. The second important point is that considerations of data integration must be weighed against other considerations, such as performance. This is identical to the trade-offs between performance and flexibility, as discussed in Chapter 5 of the author's *Effective Data Base Design*.

Rarely, if ever, is data integration absolute or perfect (as is the design of data bases in light of other issues ever absolute or perfect). Another point worth noting is that considerations of integration *cannot* be divorced from the considerations of implementation, although quite a few of the considerations can be handled at an abstract level. Data integration done entirely on a theoretical basis will probably fail or be ineffective when reaching the point of implementation. On the other hand, data integration done without a sound theoretical basis will be in jeopardy because of the danger of not properly understanding the basic nature of the data. For data integration to be successful, there must be a balance between theory and practice.

4.10 ADVANTAGES OF DATA INTEGRATION

The advantages of data integration are so numerous and so great that they are almost obvious. It is interesting to note that most shops do not reap many of the benefits of data integration because those shops deem other, more obvious benefits to be more worthwhile or easier to achieve (such as on-line performance). Because data integration is really an almost passive activity and one that must be accomplished over long periods of time, management often overlooks its real importance. Data integration is one of the most significant factors in programmer productivity, yet it is so indirect (or passive) that management fails to perceive its importance.

How is data integration relevant to productivity (which at first glance appears to be a non sequitur)? When data is highly integrated there are fewer programs to be written, thus reducing the total amount of work to be done by the programmer. But the real aid to productivity comes at the time of maintenance. Since fewer programs were written originally, there are fewer programs to maintain. And even more important, since the data is centralized, it is easy for the programmer to locate where and how changes should be made. In this sense, then, data integration addresses productivity at a "macro" level, and even though it is an indirect factor, it is as important (or more important) than any other factor. The increased level of control that exists in an integrated environment (again, at a very high level) increases the effectiveness of management. Management is much less at the mercy of the world that it is supposed to be controlling. Management that does not understand or support data integration is laying a time bomb that will cost the organization very significant amounts of money in the long run.

Another obvious advantage of data integration is the ability of the organization to change as the world and the user's environment change. The less integrated (and less elastic) an organization's systems are, the more important this facility becomes. Ironically, this facility is not appreciated unless an organization is *not* in a position to change. Another more mundane advantage of data integration is that computer operations are greatly simplified and streamlined by the reduction of the *total* number of things to be done. After all these advantages (and they are very real), since data integration is passively achieved, it is of interest to note that the advantages are seldom reaped.

4.11 TRACK RECORD OF INTEGRATION

Historically, data has not been integrated. In a few shops in a few cases, integration has occurred, but on an industry-wide basis, data processing is guilty of producing terribly unintegrated systems. One of the great selling points of going data base was that systems could now be integrated. This was due to the fact that a number of application programs could access the same data base concurrently, thus freeing the designer of one of the major evils of the sequential media.

This difference is illustrated in Figure 4.14. In a sequential mode, data is accessible at a single moment by only one program. Other programs needing to access the data must wait. In a data base environment, a number of programs can access data simultaneously, thus allowing data to be integrated. Without this facility for concurrent access of data, it is *contrary* to an organization's best interest to integrate data, because data centrally stored that is serially accessible will create unreasonable processing queues.

Figure 4.14 (a) Sequential mode versus (b) a data base environment.

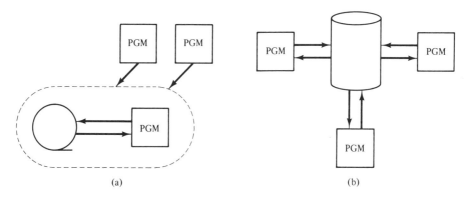

(a)   (b)

However, in most cases going to a data base from a sequential mode did little to enhance the posture of data integration. In most cases data base management systems were used as nothing more than a sophisticated access method (although they were often used *quite well* that way). The potential of data integration was much greater than that achieved because in many cases sequential files were merely converted using the same application architecture but with the data base access method.

Part of the problem of integrating data lies in the way in which the organization attempted to implement and control the data base. The major emphasis and effort was on the wrong areas. For example, management's attitude was that the use and existence of a data dictionary would automatically achieve integration of data. Over and over this approach has been a failure. The failure ultimately was the result of attempting to use technology to solve organizational problems, which has continually proven to be disastrous.

Organizational discipline must be instituted by management and must be supported by the whole organization. Attempting to legislate discipline by making rules for the organization to follow does not work. Trying to impose it with some technological enforcement mechanism such as a data dictionary is a sure-fire bet to fail.

Other reasons for the lack of data integration lie in the inherent organizational resistance to it, despite its being in the long-term best interests of the company.

4.12 RESISTANCE TO DATA INTEGRATION

Resistance to integration comes at different levels in the organization. Usually, most programmers, designers, data processing management, and operational management resist data integration, at least initially. Programmers who resist integration do not appreciate a data administrator saying that the way to get the job done is not to begin to write code immediately but to research existing systems to see if the same code has been written or if the data exists in a different form elsewhere. Furthermore, a programmer does not like being forced to leave his or her house in such order that the code he or she has developed, and its processing of data, can be shared at a later point in time, because this extra effort reduces the programmer's efficiency as measured on the immediate project.

Data processing management resists integration because it requires a level of organizational control that had not been mandated previously. This means that some managers must give up a degree of local control for global considerations, and they are usually very loathe to do that. Data integration requires discipline, and most data processing shops are notorious for their lack of discipline.

Operational management (i.e., the operations of the company, not computer operations) generally resists data integration because of a lack of trust of other operational components. For example, one department may choose to construct a system identical in processing and content of data to another department's just because one department does not trust the other to take responsibility for crucial data.

Thus, to be successful, data integration *must* be understood and supported at a high level. The irony is that each rationale for resistance has some basis in fact, but each organizational unit that resists is sacrificing long-term gain for a short-term benefit. If a company allows resistance to short-circuit the efforts of data administration (or whoever is concerned with data integration), it will never realize the benefits of integrated data.

Part of the basis for resistance to data integration is that data is not viewed globally. Each user, each programmer, and each designer is concerned only with the immediate subset of data with which he or she is working. Furthermore, there is such an emphasis on quick results that little or no attention is paid to how the data *will* or *can* be used or viewed in the future, as opposed to how it is viewed or used today. Another basic resistance to data integration is operational distrust, as has been discussed. Still another fundamental reason for resistance is the inability or unwillingness to abstract data to its lowest, most fundamental level. When data is frivolously designed or shaped by designers with only functional specifications in mind, the designers probably are not aware of the pitfalls of *not* understanding data at its most fundamental level. It is no wonder that the result of not abstracting data is usually poor integration.

There is one other great cause for resistance to data integration, and that is the difficulty in retrofitting integration onto existing systems. Even where *all* the other reasons for resistance have been nullified, there remains the nasty problem of living with existing, unintegrated systems.

4.13 APPROACHES TO DATA INTEGRATION

Despite all of the sources of resistance, the rewards of data integration are so large that it is worth the effort. What, then, are some basic approaches to achieving data integration?

- Management understanding and commitment—at the *highest* level. Without management understanding and commitment, there is no possibility of success.
- Long-term plan and short-term plan. The data administration group (or whoever is responsible for data integration) must not become so involved in long-term benefits that it does not produce short-term results as well, or data administration will find itself in a very awkward position organizationally (in terms of justification of their existence).
- Data integration should be achieved through marketing the benefits, not by a mandate. When mandated, resistance only goes below the surface and reappears in a different, usually more obstinate form.
- Recognize resistance when it occurs and confront it, rather than avoiding it. Recognize that it exists at many levels.
- Allow data administration to operate at the point of the system life cycle of greatest effectiveness, which is between the feasibility study and the layout of system requirements. Not letting data administration influence systems at this point almost precludes the need for a data administration function, because it renders the need for data administration ineffectual.
- Understand the benefits of data modeling and use modeling techniques on major systems.

4.14 TOOLS FOR ACHIEVING SUCCESS

Some of the tools the data administrator shall have in order to lead an organization to integrated systems are:

- *Data dictionary (or automated documentation).* A data dictionary, in some forms, is desirable in the short term, mandatory in the long term.
- *Design review methodology.* This allows data administration to participate in design *and* have rights of approval, especially for the architectural review (refer to Chapter 19 and to Inmon and Friedman's *Design Review Methodology for a Data Base Environment*).
- *Data modeling.* This tool refers to the knowledge and techniques of normalization, canonical data structures, and the abstraction of data from requirements into its lowest, most basic form.
- *Organizational change and planning.* Data administration should act in the capacity of a traffic director (see Chapters 23 and 24).

REFERENCES

Date, C. J., *An Introduction to Data Base Systems*, Addison–Wesley Publishing Company, Inc., Reading, Mass., 1975.

Inmon, W. H., *Effective Data Base Design*, Prentice-Hall, Inc., Englewood Cliffs, N.J., 1980, Chaps. 5 and 6.

Inmon, W. H., and L. J. Friedman, *Design Review Methodology for a Data Base Environment*, Prentice-Hall, Inc., Englewood Cliffs, N.J., 1981, Chaps. 6, 7, and 8.

Sanders, D. H., and S. J. Birkin, *Computers and Management in a Changing Society*, McGraw-Hill Book Company, New York, 1980.

CASE STUDY

The Alamosa Aluminum Company has been building aluminum parts and frames for 25 years. They have had automated systems for the past 10 years, but automation has extended only to personnel and payroll. Recently, management has been greatly interested in streamlining the mainstream business of the company. To this end, they are embarking on automating the manufacturing process—from refining aluminum ore to building parts and frames. The intent of the designers is to build a system based on the user's needs. The requirements of the system are laid out by the user, and from those requirements the designers began to specify the system. The system is to track aluminum in its different manufacturing stages— as it is stored (or piled) prior to refinement, as it is refined into raw metal, as it is put into raw product form, and as it is stored after it is put into final product form. The intent of the system is to track material through these various phases. Once the aluminum is sold or shipped as a final product, the user no longer needs the data about the aluminum, so that information is deleted from the system.

The system designer has built an intricate set of data bases to accomplish the user's function. There is a data base for piled material, one for raw metal material, one for raw products, and one for final products. Each data base is connected by a series of pointers. All programs access all data bases. In the segment for each data base, the following basic information can be found: grade of material, amount of material, location stored, location shipped from, date of storage, temperature requirements, special stacking, and time in process. Even though most of the data is common throughout the data bases, the format (semantics) of the data differs from one data base to the next.

The processing against the data is fairly heavy. In the 24-hour processing cycle, the nightly update runs a full 7 hours. The data is then extracted (another hour and a half) and then becomes available for on-line scans and access for the next 12 hours. On occasion, there is special reporting or month-end handling that literally fills up the 24-hour cycle.

The system has been up and running for two years. One day the federal government issues a statement that sulfur diethyloxide (SO^2C) is dangerous to employees' health. Sulfur diethyloxide is used in the processing of one grade of aluminum. If management had taken snapshots of the data periodically and saved the snapshots, they would have been able to determine which personnel had been exposed to the toxic chemical. However, no such records exist since the data is discarded once it cycles through the system. The union is threatening to take a class-action suit against Alamosa Aluminum if Alomosa does not furnish the union with a list of all personnel who have been exposed.

Another problem has arisen. Through new technology, there are now sub-grades of aluminum as it goes from ore to finished product. This has meant that a change must be made to every segment definition. This has affected *every* program in the system, which is a big effort to correct. Furthermore, there are new sets of problems in that the data definition change was made to all currently running production programs, but a whole series of programs were overlooked—those that were to be run at year end. When the year-end processing was to begin (at which point machine time was tight anyway) a massive conversion effort was undertaken under the worst of deadline pressures.

The amount of machine resources consumed by the system has also come into question. A system programmer claims that if the data existed in a single data base under a single definition and that the data stayed in a single place while its status changed, the I/O usage would be cut down by 75%! However, given the current state of the design, there is very little that can be done to tune the system.

One day the piled material data base comes down, and it takes three days to be fixed. Because all programs access all data bases, the entire system is shut down. The departments that access only the raw product form of data are very upset because they claim that they should be able to access their data even if piled material is bad. The data base administrator thinks they have a good point.

As subgrades of aluminum are implemented in the update program and are used operationally in the company, it is noted that nightly update time is going from 7 hours to 9½ hours on occasion.

Comment on the Following

1. Does the aluminum tracking system work? Does it work well? List five major ways in which it could work better.

2. Archiving of data was not seen as a user requirement, so it is no one's fault in particular that the data for SO^2C was not available.

3. User requirements did not mention subgrading, so the designer is not to blame for the maintenance mess that was created.

4. Piled data is really different from the other kinds of data, so it makes sense to put the data in separate data bases.

5. The amount of processing consumed by subgraded data could not be foreseen, so it is not the user's or designer's fault that the overnight processing is beginning to creep over the nightly processing window.

6. Even though the data elements are the same from one data base to the next, there is no good reason to define them uniformly.

7. Since programs often need to use all data bases, it is necessary for the system to come to a halt when one data base comes down.

8. How would you rate the system design? Good? Bad? What can be done now? At what point could the system problems have been solved inexpensively? Are *any* of the system deficiencies necessary in light of good design practices?

MULTIPLE-CHOICE QUESTIONS

1. User A has built a system. User B is preparing to build a system. Eighty-five percent or so of the data that user B needs already exists in user A's system. The suggestion is made to integrate the data, but user B does not trust user A. Furthermore, user B has his own sizable budget and claims that he will build his own system even if he has to build his own computer department.

    A. The reasons for lack of data integration usually are not technical reasons.

B. User B may well be justified.

C. Upper management must decide this issue. Upper management is spending money at the macro level in allowing this practice to happen.

D. If user B has his own budget and can afford to build his own computer department, there is little that can be done to coerce him to integrate systems.

E. Even if 85% of the data exist in user A's domain, if the designers of user A's system did not plan for multiple uses of the data, user B may be *forced* to build his own system.

2. A company reports bottom-line profits to the president of the company monthly. One system analyzes the profits by state. Another system analyzes the same data, but by division of the company. Still a third system analyzes the data by product line. When the reports differ by only $2,000,000, the accounting department is pleased. In theory, the bottom-line amounts should be identical—down to the penny.

A. Data reconciliation is much less of a problem with integrated systems.

B. When large systems begin with a base set of numbers and do much complicated processing, it is not surprising that the end result is not reconcilable. There actually may be valid reasons why the data should *not* be reconcilable.

C. One concrete measurement of the value of integrated systems that can be reconciled is the minimization of the need for accountants whose sole purpose is to reconcile reports.

D. Another justification for integrated systems is the potential reduction of the amount of processing being done.

E. Some data may be reconcilable only at a basic level, not at a summary level.

EXERCISES AND ESSAYS

1. Describe 10 ways in which systems can be made "fail-soft."

2. What can be done about the political forces that work against data integration? How can the costs of unintegrated systems be quantified?

3. What techniques and philosophies can be employed to build systems that will lay a foundation for future use as opposed to building systems that meet only the immediate set of requirements?

4. Why is data integration called a "passive" activity? Why must it be achieved over time?

5. Why is representation of status structurally such a poor practice? Is it

ever necessary? Is it intuitive? What are the long-term costs in terms of performance? Flexibility? How much more difficult is it to build systems that represent status structurally?

6. Is there ever going to be a need *not* to change the semantics of data? Why? How should this shape the design philosophy?

7. Performance and availability ultimately are negatively affected by a designer who has not adequately prepared for exclusive control of data. Why?

8. When is the least expensive time to solve the problems associated with data in a system?

V

Availability
□□

The availability of data, together with performance and flexibility, is one of the great issues facing managers. The issue of availability is generally associated with on-line systems, but in some cases applies to other types of systems. From the user's perspective, availability is the amount of time the system is usable versus the amount of time the user desires the system to be usable. The ultimate in availability, of course, is 24 hours a day, 7 days a week, 365 days a year.*

Some shops attempt to maintain this level of availability; few shops presently have a business need that warrants this amount of data availability. The time for a manager to learn about the issues of availability is *before* an on-line system comes down and causes a crisis. Once the system is down, there is little the manager can do but react to the crisis. Effective managers *plan* for their systems to come down, so that when they do have problems it is not a crisis and the response is not simply in a reaction mode.

5.1 SYSTEM FAILURES

When a system is unavailable, the user could care less *why* the system is down. All the user knows is that the system *is* down and he or she wants it back up. The perspective of the data processing manager on the unavailability of systems is different, however. Data processing management cares a great deal *how* and *why* a system goes down and exactly *what* it takes to bring it back up as well as *how long* it takes to bring it back up. There are four general classifications of failure:

- Hardware (mainframe, network, terminal, etc.) failure
- SCP (system control program/operating system) failure

*With today's hardware and software technology, a true 100% availability for large multipurpose machines is possible only theoretically.

- DBMS (data base management system/data communications software) failure
- Application failure

Each of these types of failure has its own characteristics and peculiarities.

- *Hardware failure.* Generally speaking, the hardware vendor is quite anxious to make sure that hardware uptime is high. The responsibility for high uptime lies between the vendor and the hardware engineers of the company. Relative to other types of failures, hardware availability problems are very low. However, when hardware availability is not very high, there is little a company can do except complain or replace the equipment.
- *SCP failure.* Again, the software vendor is usually very responsive to errors actually caused by the SCP. There often is a very fine line in determining whether the problem is the vendor's or the client's. If the error is the client's and only manifests itself in the SCP, the vendor is not quite so anxious to become involved. Errors are then resolved between the vendor and the systems programming staff of the client company. Relative to other types of software failures, SCP failures are rare, making the SCP a reliable tool. Even when SCP errors do occur, a problem bypass can often be implemented quickly so that processing is not severely affected.
- *DBMS failure.* As in the case of the SCP, the vendor is anxious to assist whenever the error is truly the fault of the vendor and occurs in the DBMS. In general, the DBMS is not quite as reliable as the SCP, but is nevertheless a very reliable piece of software. The greater frequency of DBMS failures over SCP failures may be attributable to the increased number of options that the client can exercise in using the DBMS.
- *Application failure.* The correction of application errors is in the domain of the client. The vendor may assist (usually on a marketing or a contract basis) but is not responsible for application fixes. Compared to SCP and DBMS software, application errors are by far the biggest cause of data unavailability.

Fairly universally, the pattern of error correction proceeds as follows:

1. Determine the nature of the error and its criticality.
2. Determine where the error should be fixed.
3. Fix the error as soon as possible.
4. If a fix is not quickly forthcoming, circumvent the error, document it, and allow the error to be worked on in a noncritical mode.

The whole point of the procedure is to keep the data (hence, the system) unavailable for as short a time as possible. Only in the worst cases do long outages occur, and that rare case occurs when the nature of the error is critical, when the error cannot be isolated and/or fixed, when the error cannot be circumvented, and when the symptoms (not the causes) cannot be treated. In any other case, at least *part* of the data and the system is available to the user.

5.2 COMMON DANGERS TO AVAILABILITY

There are three common situations that cause data to become unavailable. They are data reorganizations, recovery situations, and occurrences of data being used exclusively.

Data reorganization commonly occurs for two reasons. Data needs to be "internally" reordered or the structure of the data needs to be changed. These circumstances are shown in Figure 5.1. The internal reordering of data is necessary because attempting to access the records in the logical order of occurrence causes much unnecessary system overhead. The restructuring or redefinition occurs because the designer needs to make a fundamental alteration of the physical form of the data. In any event, while reorganization is occurring, the data is not available for any other kind of processing. Reorganizations can usually be planned and run on a scheduled basis. The manager who allows systems to be built under the assumption that reorganizations will never be needed causes much unnecessary work and awkward processing when reorganization *does* take place. Reorganization of data is a fact of life.

On the other hand, recovery cannot be scheduled because it must be run on an "as needed" basis; that is, the nature of recovery is always to be in a reaction mode. When a recovery program is running, data is unavailable for other kinds of processing, as in the case of reorganization. Running recovery procedures is like exercising a muscle: the more it is done, the easier and more automatic the process becomes. Much of the time spent in recovery is spent in analyzing the situation, determining which procedures should be run, and then executing those procedures. While all of this operaator activity (think time) is going on, the system is unavailable. Practicing recovery procedures will reduce the analytical time and allow operators to become familiar with the specifics of the data, the systems, and what recovery vehicles are available to them. This does not mean that a shop should damage its data so that it can run recovery procedures. It does mean that a shop should practice recovery procedures long before they are needed. The time to learn how to do recovery is *not* at the moment when recovery actually needs to be run. Recovery procedures should be set in place as one of the first acts of the designer, early in the implementation phase.

The third type of activity that can make data unavailable is the running of programs that require extended exclusive usage of the data (i.e., those

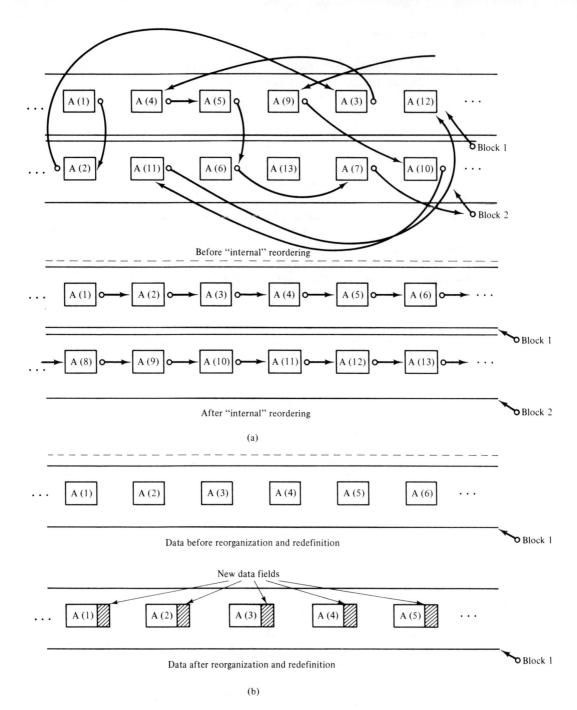

Before "internal" reordering

After "internal" reordering

(a)

Data before reorganization and redefinition

New data fields

Data after reorganization and redefinition

(b)

Figure 5.1 Data reorganization: (a) internal reordering; (b) change in data structure.

64

programs that prevent other programs from accessing the data while they are running). Long batch update runs are in this category. When a shop develops the application system, it must be aware of the implications to the issue of availability of programs that will tie up the data for long periods of time.

The problem with processes that use data exclusively (and this includes reorganization and recovery) is not that they exist (because they are *necessary* functions) but the fact that they take a long time to run. In general, these processes operate on data on a basis of physical units (i.e., data sets, files, etc.) of data. This means if there is a relatively large amount of data in the physical unit, the process will take a relatively long time to run. Thus the amount of data in a physical unit on which these processes operate becomes a real and limiting factor. In fact, the issue of data size in many instances is synonymous with the issue of availability. There are ways to manage large amounts of data and keep availability high. The common techniques are discussed in Chapter 7 of the author's book *Effective Data Base Design.*

5.3 DESIGN PRACTICES

From the types of failures presented, it is seen that the most likely failure to occur is that of an application failure. With this type of failure a company is on its own (i.e., the vendor is normally not anxious to become involved with this kind of error). This exposure leads the careful observer to the conclusion that the application should be designed so that when failure occurs, a minimum amount of the application is affected. In essence it is desirable to have a "fail soft" system to the greatest degree possible. This ultimately translates into a high degree of user availability. Interestingly, the approaches to system design have a great deal to do with whether a system will fail "hard" or "soft," and since the greatest exposure is within the application, it makes sense to pay more than casual attention to design concepts that can greatly enhance availability.

The design philosophy for the greatest availability is to build systems that are as disjunctive and unrelated internally as possible. Each processing unit and physical unit of data is broken into as fine a unit as is feasible, and there are as few relationships as possible between any two or more units.

As an example of disjunction, consider the very simple case of a data base, as shown in Figure 5.2. In this case data A(l) to A(n) are stored in the same data base. Upon insertion of A(m) [somewhere between A(l) and A(n)], an error occurs because A(m-1) is physically destroyed, as shown in Figure 5.3. Now the entire data base must be recovered, since it has bad data and the data exists (nondisjunctively) in a single physical unit of data. While recovery is occurring, A(l) through A(m-2) and A(m) through A(n) are not available, even though they are perfectly all right.

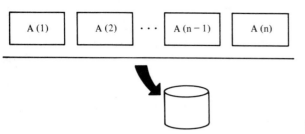

Figure 5.2 Data base showing disjunction.

Figure 5.3 Insertion of $A(m)$ causing destruction of $A(m\text{-}1)$.

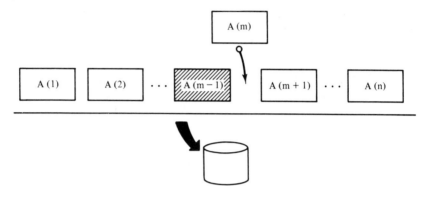

The designer could have introduced a simple degree of disjunctiveness in the design, as shown by Figure 5.4. Here the same data as was in original data base is broken into separate physical units of data. Now when A(m-1) is broken, only the data residing in the physical unit of data need be restored, not all of A(l) to A(n).

Another example of beneficial system disjunctiveness is illustrated by the effect of combining multiple functions into the same transaction, as shown by Figure 5.5. Transaction A is made up of four related yet distinct functions, A, B, C, and D. The programmer for function C has made an error that occurs under certain conditions. One day transaction A is running and an error condition is encountered under function C. The entire transaction comes to a halt until C can be corrected (Figure 5.6). If the functions had been designed disjunctively so that each function was its own transaction, then when function C has an error, there is no impact on A, B, and D (Figure 5.7). The same breakup of function into separate units applies to programs as well as transaction design.

As a third rather simple example of the benefits of disjunctiveness, consider two applications that share a common data base, say an audit data base. This data base configuration is shown by Figure 5.8. The access to any data base in personnel or accounting must first be logged on the audit data base, for each execution; that is, the first activity of any transaction is to

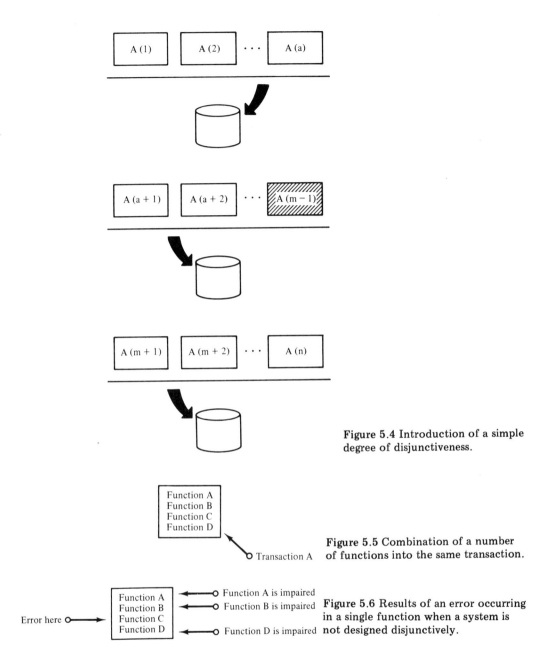

Figure 5.4 Introduction of a simple degree of disjunctiveness.

Figure 5.5 Combination of a number of functions into the same transaction.

Figure 5.6 Results of an error occurring in a single function when a system is not designed disjunctively.

log a record onto the audit data base, then continue the flow of processing. One day a special accounting program is set up and run many times during the day. Late in the afternoon, the audit data base fills up and must be recovered, and more space needs to be reallocated. This is shown in Figure 5.9. The problem is that the personnel application is affected even though it

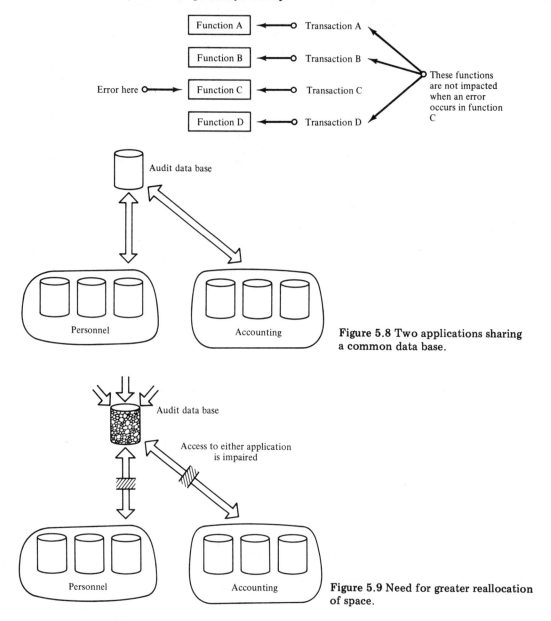

Figure 5.7 Results of an error occuring in a single function when a system is designed disjunctively.

Function A ← Transaction A

Function B ← Transaction B

Error here → Function C ← Transaction C

Function D ← Transaction D

These functions are not impacted when an error occurs in function C

Audit data base

Personnel

Accounting

Figure 5.8 Two applications sharing a common data base.

Audit data base

Access to either application is impaired

Personnel

Accounting

Figure 5.9 Need for greater reallocation of space.

had nothing to do with the problem. Had the audit data base been created disjunctively so that a separate audit data base existed for each application, the personnel application would not have been affected at all (Figure 5.10).

68

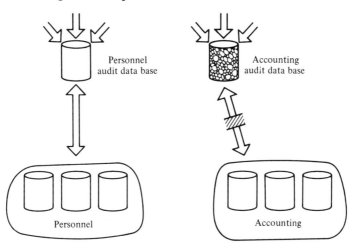
Figure 5.10 Separate audit base for each function.

Note that this degree of disjunctiveness *does not* necessarily contradict the good principles of data integration. This specific issue as it relates to data integration was discussed in Chapter 4. It is also very interesting to note that splitting work loads across a number of machines (as discussed in Chapter 13) agrees 100% with the disjunctive approach to system design.

The preceding three examples serve to illustrate just how nicely disjunctive system design works toward the goal of "fail soft" systems. It is worth noting that the time to design disjunctiveness into a system is *not* when the problem of availability manifests itself, but at the initial point of system design. The alert manager circumvents *many* crises by building disjunctive systems. The dollar value of the disjunctive approach is hard to measure, but is nevertheless very valuable.

5.4 USER DOWNTIME SPECIFICATIONS

One of the fundamental criteria that should be specified by the user as part of his or her requirements relates to the acceptable limits of planned and unplanned downtime. This should be stated explicitly at the very start of the project. The designer should then use his or her estimates of the size of the data base to estimate roughly reorganization and recovery time (and any other time in which the data base must be used exclusively). This estimate can be done in many ways. Three common practices are:

- *Prototyping the data base, then doing a reorganization and/or recovery.* A full data base may prove to be too much data to be actually prototyped, so extrapolation of the processing requirements based on the processing of a subset of the data may yield a suitable estimate.

69

- *Comparison to existing data base reorganization and recovery times.* This is a complex matter because there are many variables that have an impact on reorganization or recovery that may not be obvious at first glance, and that may be quite different from one system to the next. Care should be taken here.

- *Paper-and-pencil method.* This method can be fairly accurate if done by experienced analysts thoroughly familiar with the internals of the DBMS and the specifics of the data base. For inexperienced analysts, this method probably will not yield a very accurate estimate.

5.5 OTHER AVAILABILITY ISSUES

Most sophisticated data communication (DC) systems give the user a number of ways of enhancing the availability posture. There are usually many levels and techniques of recovery and backup of data, depending on the sensitivity of the data. It should be kept in mind that the more fail-soft a system becomes, in general the more overhead is involved. The ultimate, of course, is running systems in duplication, which is very expensive, but does provide a high degree of availability.

Whatever the stance a company takes on recovery and reorganization of data, the user should keep in mind that at some point the system will be unavailable, and that, in the worst (but not unlikely) case, previous on-line activity may be lost. Hopefully, unplanned downtime and lost data are to be rare events; in any case, they are a fact of life. To that end, users should plan their strategy to continue their operations whenever either or both of those eventualities occur. If downtime and lost data become regular events, the alert manager should deeply investigate the roots of the problem. As in the other cases of system design where preparation and forethought are necessary, formulating a strategy during the first occurrence of a disaster is too late.

A final issue is that of archival availability. When data is archived, at least two factors should be considered: what can be done in the event of the physical loss or permanent damage of data, and how can the definition of the data be carried forward through time? Quite often data that is archived is simply written off to a tape file. The problem is that over time it is likely that at least some (or all) of the data residing on tape will become unavailable due to physical aging of the tape (or other reasons, such as a mistaken write-over on a tape of some other data). The analyst should consider the loss of this data at the onset of archival, not at the time when the data is needed but is permanently lost.

The other consideration of archived data is that of storage of the definition of the data. It makes no sense to store data without keeping its semantic and content descriptions with it, because over time, the definitions and meaning of the data are sure to change, thus rendering earlier definitions meaningless without a description of what was current at the time the data was archived.

REFERENCES

Inmon, W. H., *Effective Data Base Design*, Prentice-Hall, Inc., Englewood Cliffs, N.J., 1980.

Inmon, W. H., and L. J. Friedman, *Design Review Methodology for a Data Base Environment*, Prentice–Hall, Inc., Englewood Cliffs, N.J., 1981.

CASE STUDY

The Texas Rawhide and Steer Company is operating their first large on-line system. They have built smaller systems in the past, but nothing that is as closely related to the business of the company as the point-of-sale on-line system.

The point-of-sale system is rather intricate and involved. The designer has constructed transactions that perform a great many functions. For example, a *simple* transaction will:

1. Verify the Master Charge or Visa account number.
2. Determine whether the customer has given bad checks previously.
3. Credit the store with a sale and prepare a balance ledger at the end of the day for each machine.
4. Automatically lower the inventory of the item sold.
5. Cross-reference the sales personnel with a register to help prevent theft.
6. Store information about time of day and day of week for further sales and marketing analysis.
7. Calculate change.

To accomplish these functions, eight data bases are accessed. Because of the large volume of business, the data bases are not small. Furthermore, the data is tightly connected—by the design of transactions and by the design of the data bases.

From the outset, management has been very proud of its technical achievement. The designers that had served them well in batch appear to have made an easy transition to the on-line environment. There has been one detractor. A systems expert on the data base administration staff has alerted management to the fact that when the system goes down, it may stay down a long time. Management has been assured by the vendor of the software that failure of a data base is a rare thing and probably will never happen. Furthermore, the vendor supplies recovery routines and software for reorganization of the data. Even with the vendor's software, the systems expert warns that it would be wise to at least estimate the amount of projected downtime.

Since progress is being made on systems development and there is no immediate danger posed to management, the concerns of the systems expert are set aside. The designer of the system resents the interference of the DBA and management supports the applications designer because the designer has a long track record of successful development.

After 10 months of development, the system goes live. In short order the data bases are fully loaded. The system operates fine until one day—about four months after the system is brought up—a power surge occurs. Nothing is noticed at the time, but what has happened is that an internal buffer is lost. This does not turn up until seven weeks later when a program goes to access data that should have been in the data base, but instead was lost during the power surge. At this point the data base is rendered useless and must be recovered.

The vendor's recovery utilities are run, but because there is no backlog of experience in running them, there are several wasted iterations. In all, it takes 36 hours to correct the data base. In the meantime, the entire point-of-sale system is unavailable. Needless to say, the user is *very* upset because the cash flow of the company is greatly hampered, record keeping is hindered, and in general, the user is greatly alarmed that the same thing may happen again.

After the crisis is over, management investigates the alternatives. They are:

1. Trust the system not to fail again.
2. Rely on vendor-supplied software to recover the system.
3. Urge operations to speed up the recovery process.
4. Restructure the data bases and rewrite the transactions.   ∎

Comment on the Following

1. The system is basically reliable and will not fail very often.
2. The vendor-supplied software works and is adequate.
3. Operations should be able to speed up significantly the recovery process.
4. A system rewrite will require many personnel, take more time, and will disappoint the user.
5. The system is most likely to fail at the worst possible time (at the time of greatest stress).
6. At this point, management has only unrealistic or undesirable options.

Management could have kept itself from being painted into a corner only at the moment of initial system design.

MULTIPLE-CHOICE QUESTIONS

1. A large data base needs to be reorganized. The reorganization will take at least 20 hours. The user must have the data base available seven days a week. However, next Christmas, there will be a week in which the data base can be reorganized.
    A. Unduly long reorganizations are a sign that a shop needs better technicians.
    B. Reorganizations are not as critical to recovery because they can be scheduled, whereas recovery is not normally scheduled.
    C. Internal data organization is the only reason reorganization must be done.
    D. With a really sharp set of systems programmers, the time needed for reorganization can be cut down to a reasonable amount.
    E. Waiting until Christmas for reorganization is an acceptable alternative.

*2. A manager determines that the system to be built is going to involve a large amount of data. She understands that availability is a problem and so instructs the designers to prepare for that aspect of system design.
    A. The designers are careful not to tie the data too closely together with such things as pointers.
    B. The designers build transactions that access only one or two data bases.
    C. The data is physically broken up by key range so that the same amount of data exist but it exists in different physical units.
    D. The point of design is the appropriate time to address the problems of availability. Retrofitting a high degree of availability into a system is difficult to do.
    E. In the case where a truly high degree of availability is desired, duplicate systems may be run and maintained.

3. A user is entering data into his terminal at 2:00 P.M. in the afternoon. He has been using his on-line system all day. At 2:05 P.M., his terminal goes blank and does not respond to the keyboard.
    A. The user may have to reenter all of his data since the beginning of the day unless proper recovery utilities are run.
    B. The system stoppage may have resulted from many factors—a machine failure, a software failure, an applications bug, and so on.

C. The user is stymied unless there is an alternate system or a manual system that he can run on.

D. Response time is not an issue in the light of system unavailability.

E. At this point it is not clear how long the system will be unavailable or what damage has been suffered.

EXERCISES AND ESSAYS

1. When is the appropriate time to address the issues of availability?

2. After a system is up and running, what can be done to enhance availability?

*3. Is data base splitting always difficult to implement after the fact?

*4. What are the advantages and disadvantages of writing private software to do recovery and/or reorganization?

5. Is it a good or a bad idea to divide update and access functions in transaction design with regard to the issue of availability?

6. Do multiple physical data bases (which might enhance system availability) necessarily imply a lack of data integration?

7. Is it *ever* safe to design a system under the assumptions that the data base will not need to be recovered or reorganized?

VI

Standard Work Unit

□□□

At first glance a manager may mistake the standard work unit concept for a scurrilous or deeply technical concept that has little impact on management. On the contrary, the standard work unit concept is the *single most important* concept for the manager to understand, and is best understood on a commonsense level, not a technical level. The standard work unit concept is *the* key to building on-line performance into an application.

The concept of the standard work unit is one of the cornerstones of success in the world of on-line processing. Applications built under the standard work unit are those that (1) minimize the critical resources used for each execution of an online transaction, and (2) uniformly apply the discipline of controlling resource consumption against all transactions in the on-line environment. For an in-depth discussion of the standard work unit concept, refer to Chapter 12 in *Design Review Methodology for a Data Base Environment* (by Inmon and Friedman).

The standard work unit concept applies to a much broader environment than just IMS DB/DC. The concept almost directly applies to CICS and in principal to nearly all on-line environments. In an IMS environment (as in other environments) one of the most expensive operations is I/O. I/Os are expensive for two reasons. The first (and most important) is that an I/O transfers execution control from a very fast electronic device (the computer) to a relatively slow mechanical device (a disk or tape reader). The difference in speeds is like the difference in the speeds of an airplane and a bicycle.

Thus the very fast electronic device is put into a state of waiting by the slowness of the mechanical device (which is looking for data, retrieving it, and transferring it back to the electronic device so that processing can continue). The second reason I/O is expensive is that it requires the execution of considerable instructions. Not surprisingly, the standard work unit addresses the number of calls the programmer issues in an online transaction, which indirectly influences the number of I/Os. There is not a perfect match between calls to a DBMS and I/Os done, as shown by Figure 6.1.

In Figure 6.1 it is seen that two call patterns (the same number of calls to the DBMS) generate quite different I/O characteristics, based on the type

Call pattern 1		System Activity	I/Os generated
1.	Get unique	Random retrieval	1
2.	Get unique	Random retrieval	1
3.	Get unique	Random retrieval	1
4.	Get unique	Random retrieval	1
5.	Get unique	Random retrieval	1
6.	Get unique	Random retrieval	1
7.	Get unique	Random retrieval	1
8.	Get unique	Random retrieval	1
9.	Get unique	Random retrieval	1
10.	Get unique	Random retrieval	1
		Total	10

Call pattern 2		System activity	I/Os generated
1.	Get unique	Random retrieval	1
2.	Get next	Sequential retrieval	0
3.	Get next	Sequential retrieval	0
4.	Get next	Sequential retrieval	0
5.	Get next	Sequential retrieval	0
6.	Get next	Sequential retrieval	0
7.	Get next	Sequential retrieval	0
8.	Get next	Sequential retrieval	0
9.	Get next	Sequential retrieval	0
10.	Get next	Sequential retrieval	0
		Total	1

Figure 6.1 I/O characteristics of two call patterns.

of call and pattern of calls. This illustrates that there is not a perfect correlation between number of calls issued by the programmer and the amount of I/O done. There is, however, a *general* correlation between the two in the sense that a maximum of n calls produces a maximum of $n + m$ I/Os. There are technicians who will be quick to point out that certain calls will cause all or part of the entire data base to be scanned—and m in this case is large or unpredictable. Unless the programmer is a beginner or the designer is unaware of the danger of those types of calls, the *normal* case is for m to be a reasonable number. It is also noted that due to buffer handling and other internal efficiencies, n calls may well produce many fewer than n I/Os.

The other major parameters addressed by the standard work unit (in IMS) are on-line load time (i.e., the time the program takes to be loaded into the computer into an executable state) and message size going up and down the line. Load time into the on-line region (in IMS—where transactions or programs must go to be executed) can be minimized by keeping application load module size (i.e., the size of the program in its machine executable form) small. Sending smaller messages to the on-line region, then back to the terminal, is another way on-line system performance can be optimized.

The particular parameters chosen for the standard work unit in IMS may or may not have applicability to other DBMS. The point is that there *will* be a standard work unit for other DBMS, depending on the specifics of the architecture. To determine what the parameters should be, the designer should:

1. Identify what precious resources should be protected. These may be the number of I/Os a transaction does, length of region occupancy (how long a transaction stays in the on-line region), uses of certain media, modes of operation, protection features, and so on. In short, the designer should identify all impediments to the smooth flow of transactions through the on-line system. These impediments are normally where queues will form.

2. Prioritize the precious resources selected in the first step. Determine which resources are critical to protect, important to protect, and nice to protect if convenient.

3. Based on the results of the second step, the designer must determine what options or features of the DBMS should be used or should be avoided and what options or features of the DBMS must be used with discipline and specifically what that discipline should be. The enforcement of discipline may be administrative (e.g., though design reviews) or automatic (e.g., though modification of the language interface, intercepting and negating an "outlawed" activity).

6.1 IMPORTANCE OF THE STANDARD WORK UNIT CONCEPT

The standard work unit (SWU) concept is one of the cornerstones of success in the on-line environment. It is at the very heart of satisfactory, longterm online performance, and performance is *always* visible— good or bad—in the on-line environment because it is always visible to the user. There are other very important implications of the SWU concept, all of which are positive.

One of the most positive benefits of the SWU is that it allows the on-line system to undergo a reasonably orderly and predictable growth. Predictability of growth is enhanced in that the capacity planner looks upon each of the transactions as being equal—no allowances have to be made for giant transactions that play havoc with system flow and cause internal queues to form. Capacity can be measured in the simple terms of number of transactions per unit of time as opposed to measuring the number of transactions and the transaction mix. The predictability of capacity enhances an organization's ability to operate in an "act" mode, rather than in a "react" mode.

Orderly growth comes about by creating an environment that can be tuned. In the face of the SWU the tuner can base tuning decisions on operational and business criticality, not on prioritizations that serve to insulate high-resource consumers from normal transactions. When the tuner must use the tools of tuning for reasons other than business functions, the prior-

ities of tuning are influenced improperly. The data processing manager is
adhering to the needs of data processing, not business, in this case. This
automatically places data processing management in a reaction mode.

Another long-range aspect of building systems under the SWU is that
they tend to be more easily divisible than systems built otherwise. This is a
by-product of the designer having deliberately split function into small
units. Therefore the work load can be split into small, discrete, disjoint functions. The hardware planner is likely to have more options available when he
or she needs them in the face of applications built under the SWU than if
applications are not built under the SWU. Chapter 13 addresses the issue of
system divisibility and hardware in greater depth.

One last very obvious and very real benefit of the SWU is that systems
built under the concept undergo fewer code changes over time for the purpose of tuning the system. Performance is built into on-line systems at the
point of design. Trying to tune performance into a system or muscle performance into a system through bigger and faster hardware is futile, expensive, and frustrating in the long run. Thus systems not designed with
performance in mind must be changed over time simply to achieve satisfactory performance. Systems written under the SWU concept (as well as
any other discipline) will have to be changed over time, but not for reasons
of performance.

6.2 SWU IN THE EARLY PHASES OF DESIGN

One of the criticisms of the SWU concept is that the measurements of ac-
ceptability are in terms of the final product of the developer; that is, the
SWU is often quantified in terms of load module sizes, calls to the DBMS,
message size, and so on. The problem with this form of measurement is that
the program must already be coded to determine if it fits the SWU or not.
If it does not fit, it is expensive to go back and rework the offending program. Thus one argument against the SWU is that it is measured too late in
the game to determine the effectiveness of the design being produced.

Such is not the case *at all*! It is true that the *final* parameters of the
SWU are measured in very concrete terms (in fact, the SWU *must* be objective to be effective), but the alert designer should not and need not begin to
think about the SWU at the pre-implementation point of development. The
alert designer should think about and prepare for the SWU at the initial
architecting of the system.

Preparations for building a system under the SWU concept may begin
after (1) the data elements and how they are to be grouped has been determined, and (2) a rough idea of the processing that is to occur is settled.
This sketch of the processing requirements will be in "black box" form—
the inputs identified, the outputs identified, but none of the details of how

input is transformed to output necessarily specified. Note that many details, such as native access methods, block size, and data element size, do *not* need to be specified for the designer to determine if the system will fit within the confines of a predetermined SWU. The points the designer *should* look for are:

1. *Data-driven processes.* Transactions or programs whose resource consumption depends on the amount or configuration of the data on which it operates. A simple example of a data-driven process is one that accesses all occurrences of a certain type of data. The calls to the DBMS (and indirectly the I/Os done) depend on how many occurrences of data there are in existence. The same program will use different amounts of resources for different numbers of occurrences of data. Such a program is a candidate to violate the standard work unit. Refer to Chapter 12 in *Design Review Methodology for a Data Base Environment* for an example of data-driven processes.

2. *Multifunction processes.* These transactions or programs are of the "do everything at once" variety. *Many* business functions will be able to be done by the transaction. All of the activity of data (creation, deletion, and change) will be done for many data elements which may well cross functional lines. In the worst case the elements manipulated by a transaction will relate to more than one business function, such as accounting, inventory control, storerooms inventory, etc. When the designer identifies processes that fit this description, there is a *strong* chance that ultimately the process will violate the SWU parameters.

3. *Overspecified processes.* These processes are very similar to multifunctional processes except that they relate to a large amount of processing, but for a limited business function. In this case the problem is not too much work spread over many areas but too much work concentrated in a single process. As an example, consider a process that will search a million occurrences of data, averaging or totaling some figure. It is not difficult to see that many I/Os will probably be required, and that if the design of the process is unaltered, the process will violate SWU parameters at a later time.

4. *Calculation-intensive* processes. In a business environment this type of process is *very* rare but must be included for the sake of completeness. In this case a process is specified that uses a moderate amount of I/O, but then settles into a calculation-intensive mode, not unlike the number-crunching processors typical of scientific data processing. If the designer has specified such a process, he or she should be alert to the fact that while the transaction is going into its deep calculation mode, other processes may need to use resources being reserved for the process in execution.

If the designer identifies and prepares for these four candidates for violation of the SWU concept early, by the time the process is coded the chances for serious violation of the SWU parameters are slim.

6.3 SWU AND BUSINESS FUNCTION

One of the common excuses for not using the SWU concept is the adherence
to "business functions." This argument is typical of shops just going to the
on-line environment or shops that do not have a fully mature on-line system.
The argument for "business functions" goes like this—the designer must
mimic in the on-line environment those processes that form the backbone
of the designer's system requirements, and in mimicking those processes the
SWU parameters are openly violated. As an example, consider an insurance
transaction that requires much information: the name of the policyholder,
policy number, residence, age, sex, job title, prior record of insurability, and
so on. A simple-minded (batch-oriented) approach to building a policy
(which is the "business function") would be to enter the data all at once,
doing some minor editing, then processing the fully described policy against
the data base, doing more edits, verifications, rate calculations, and so on.
After this large process is completed, a policy is issued or statements are
given as to why the policy cannot be issued.

The business function approach is to build the process (transaction or
transactions) mimicking the way the policy is currently being built by hand
or in batch. The problem is, in an on-line environment the processing required violates the SWU in many places and, under a full transaction load,
will lead to *long* response times for *all* the users of the system.

Does this mean that there is a conflict between "business function" and
the SWU concept? Not at all. There is a conflict only if the designers are
inexperienced or unimaginative. Taking the example of the insurance policy,
there are *many* ways to implement the process of building a policy that will
exist quite adequately under the SWU parameters. When the argument is
made for business functions over SWU, the proponents of business function
probably do not realize that they are ultimately forgoing response time,
(which certainly is an implied part of business functions!). The problem is
that it is intuitively appealing to implement what the business functions look
like in the batch environment since they can be handled that way rather
easily in the on-line environment. The irony is that building and implementing batch-type processing on-line is fairly easy, but running batch processes
online clogs up the entire online system. Just because batch business
functions *can* be built on-line does not mean they *should* be built on-line.

Some of the techniques that can be used to fulfill business functions
and still exist within the confines of the SWU parameters are:

1. *Process iterations.* Whenever the designer must handle a data-driven
process or an overspecified process, one technique is to break the lengthy
process into multiple iterations. Each iteration lives within the confines of
the SWU parameters. At the end of an iteration the process relinquishes
control so that other processes are not "frozen out" from resources used

by the process in execution. This iteration of a process is shown by Figure 6.2.

Figure 6.2 Iterated approach toward implementing processes under the SWU concept.

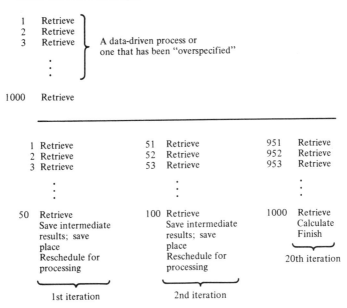

There is no question that iterating a process uses *more total* system resources than not iterating a process. The point is that the *average* amount of time a resource is frozen is small and uniform.

2. *Changing modes of operation.* Another technique the designer has at his or her disposal is that of changing modes of operation. This means that when an online process is entered for execution that will violate one or more of the SWU parameters, the operator entering the request is sent a reply telling him or her to expect the request to be satisfied in a different mode. The request is then channeled off to a different mode of operation, such as the batch environment.   Figure 6.3 illustrates this process. By changing modes of operation the on-line system does not have to suffer from resource insensitive transactions.

3. *Redefinition of business functions.* The most fundamental change the designer can make (which is probably the most effective one also) is to redefine the business function requirements so that they will fit under the SWU concept. This is probably the most difficult solution, as it requires people to alter their concepts of how the system is to be used. In the long run, as the user becomes more experienced with on-line systems, this reshaping of thinking is fairly easy to do. However, in the initial stages of online development, it is usually very difficult to do.

Figure 6.3 Changing modes of operation.

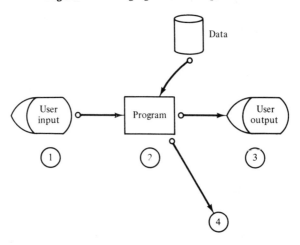

1. The user enters a request.

2. The program determines that the request will violate the SWU. This determination is made by analysis of the data on which the request will operate, by the parameters of the request, or by some other mechanism.

3. A message is sent to the user not to expect normal output. This reply to the user is very quick.

4. The request is rerouted for execution in one of the following modes:
(a) batch mode controlled on-line;
(b) batch mode;
(c) rescheduled for execution at a noncritical time.

It may help to redefine business function by thinking like an airline reservation clerk. Airline clerks do a large amount of function on a large system, but they do their function a step at a time. They enter some data, wait for a reply, enter some more data, wait for the next reply and so forth. In all, they enter much and complex data, but they do it a little bit at a time. And they consistently experience adequate response time.

In restructuring the concept of business functions to fit the on-line environment, the designer is not going to ask the user to reduce or give up *any* business functions. Instead, the designer is really asking the user to re-shape the ways the business functions are to be accommodated. Figure 6.4 shows an example of how a typical business function can be divided.

6.4 ORGANIZATIONAL ASPECTS OF THE SWU CONCEPT

Although the SWU was originally developed as a major solution to the problems of performance, it has some interesting side benefits that probably were not intended by originators of the concept. One of the most unstable

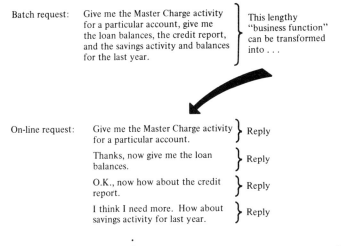

Batch request: Give me the Master Charge activity for a particular account, give me the loan balances, the credit report, and the savings activity and balances for the last year.

This lengthy "business function" can be transformed into . . .

On-line request: Give me the Master Charge activity for a particular account. } Reply

Thanks, now give me the loan balances. } Reply

O.K., now how about the credit report. } Reply

I think I need more. How about savings activity for last year. } Reply

Figure 6.4 Breaking down a typical business function.

organizational relationships is that between applications and data base administration. The role of applications is to take user requests and translate them into a system. When the user is happy, the applications group has done its job.

The primary role of the data base administrator is to protect the on-line resources so that systems running under it will yield the best response times and will be available when they are supposed to be available. There is a major difference in the perspectives of applications and data base administration. Applications administration view their universe as if their user were the most important thing in that universe. Data base administration views its universe as if the on-line system were most important.

Application designers build systems to satisfy the business function of their user and data base administration designs systems to optimize the usage of on-line resources. The problem is that one aspect or the other can be optimized in system design, but not both. Unfortunately, once the system designed by applications goes on-line, the DBMS will *not* consider that system to be the most important one under its control (unless it is the *only* one under its control).

Unfortunately, the effects of this democracy under the DBMS are not obvious until the on-line system is running under a full transaction load, which may be *years* after the application system(s) has been programmed. Thus it is politically easy to opt for dominance in design by applications in the short run. Allowing applications to overrule data base administration in the long run will lead to major dissatisfaction with on-line systems. The major dissatisfaction will ironically come from the user, who does not like being saddled with unnecessarily long response times.

Figure 6.5 SWU parameters.

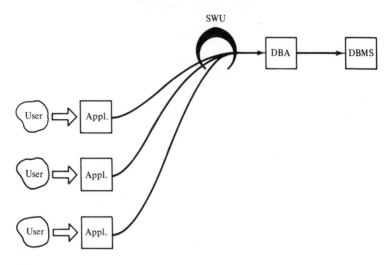

The SWU concept goes a long way in balancing the functions of applications and data base administration as far as performance goes. This is depicted by Figure 6.5.

In Figure 6.5 the SWU parameters are shown as objectively defining the interface between applications and data base administration. The parameters only directly address issues of performance but that is a very big issue. The applications group knows it can satisfy data base administration by staying within the SWU parameters. Furthermore, it has been shown that there need not be any loss of business functions. The data base administration group ceases to have a great interest in the design done by applications as far as the issue of performance is concerned, as long as the design meets SWU parameters. By meeting those parameters, the data base administrator protects what goes into the on-line system.

6.5 SWU AND MODULARITY

There is a connection between the SWU concept and the concept of program modularity. Undoubtedly, the relationship between the two is coincidental, but the fact is that systems built under the SWU concept also enjoy many of the benefits of modularity. Without going into the theory and notions of system modularity, a few of the major benefits of a system built under the SWU concept will be discussed that do not relate particularly to performance but that do relate to modularity.

One advantage is the ability to add on to a system built under the SWU. Consider Figure 6.6, where the same business function is realized in two

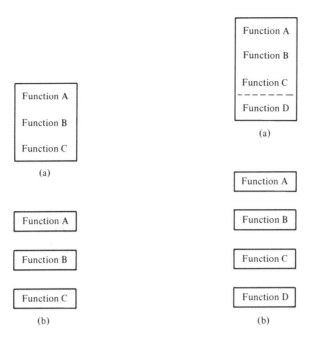

Figure 6.6 Same business function realized (a) as a non-SWU transaction, and (b) under the SWU concept.

Figure 6.7 Addition of function D to functions A, B, and C: (a) as a non-SWU transaction, and (b) under the SWU concept.

ways: under the SWU concept and not under the SWU concept. When a new function, function D, is added, it has little or no impact on functions A, B, and C when they are built under the SWU concept. If there is a necessary interface, the interface is realized explicitly—through the issuance of a transaction, a written output to a data base or conversational work area, or some such mechanism. However, when functions A, B, and C are not built under the SWU, there arise all sorts of complications and potential for complications. At the very minimum, functions A, B, and C will be affected during changes being made to source code. But the biggest danger exists where A, B, and C must interface with D. The interface can be accomplished in a myriad of ways, many of which are not straightforward or easily understood. By going to the SWU concepts, the interface between functions must at least be explicit and formalized. Figure 6.7 illustrates the addition of function D to A, B, and C.

Since transactions are divided into small, disjoint groups in the SWU environment, it is fairly easy to measure progress as a system is being developed. This is done simply by keeping track of which transactions have been programmed and tested and which have not. Such is normally not the case in the non-SWU environment, where programs typically are "95%" complete, but seldom 100% complete. Figure 6.8 depicts the differences

85

Figure 6.8 Differences in measuring completeness of a project: (a) system progress in a SWU environment; (b) development progress in a non-SWU environment.

Transactions to be programmed	Transactions completed	Percent complete
Tx A Tx B Tx C	Tx A, Tx E, Tx F	50
Tx D Tx E Tx F		

(a)

Transaction to be programmed	Percent complete	Programmer estimates
TX A		1. Main body of code is done.
		2. Most of functions A, E, and F are done.
		3. Some of C and B are done.
	95	4. D has been started.

Function A	Function B
Function C	Function D
Function E	Function F

in measuring the completeness of a project in the SWU environment and not in the SWU environment.

Another advantage of projects developed under the SWU concept is that they can be easily phased, whereas in a non-SWU environment, phasing of projects is a more complex proposition. Figure 6.9 depicts the phasing of projects in both environments.

Phasing of projects is easier in a SWU mode because transactions are separated at the source level and because they are disjoint or minimally related at the load module level. Adding a new set of functions in the SWU environments causes an absolute minimum of interruption of ongoing processing.

One final major advantage of projects designed and built under the SWU concept is that they are able to be subdivided among a number of computers. This facility is very important in terms of the ability to cope with long-range growth.

6.6 CHANGING THE SWU PARAMETERS OVER TIME

One of the major factors influencing the selection of the SWU parameters is the assumption that I/Os need to be minimized because of the relative speeds

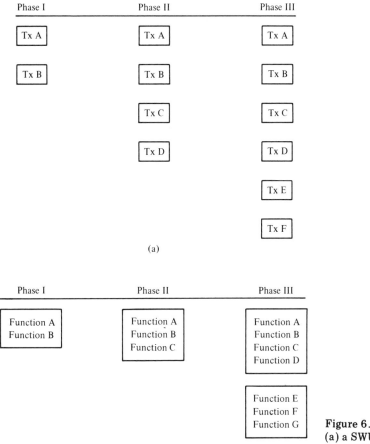

Figure 6.9 Phasing of a project in (a) a SWU environment, and (b) a non-SWU environment.

of electronic devices versus mechanical devices. Given the current configurations of hardware, system control programs, and DBMS, this is a fairly valid assumption. However, if advances are made such that I/Os are *not* the major factor (or are not the *only* major factor) relating to performance (which they are currently), the need for SWU parameters would not diminish, only the need to reevaluate what the critical resources are, and what new parameters can be set to protect those resources.

6.7 PERFORMANCE WITHOUT THE SWU CONCEPT

Not all installations use the SWU concept in the building of their on-line systems. The SWU concept is not intuitively obvious. It requires organizational discipline and insight. It often means making politically unpopular decisions for long-term benefit. For these reasons not every shop that goes on-line uses the SWU concept. What do these shops do to address the issue of performance?

One common ploy is to buy more hardware—a faster machine, more memory, more channels, and so on. This approach is fairly effective but it is unnecessarily expensive and has limitations that are reached in a finite amount of time. Another approach is to tune the system very finely. This produces rather good results the first time it is done, but only marginal improvements thereafter. Furthermore, any tuning effort is relative to the immediate environment and configuration. The instant the environment of a well-tuned system changes, the tuning effort will need to be repeated. Transaction volume may change, data base size or organization may change, a new release of the SCP or DBMS may alter certain fundamental activities, and so on. Any of these changes (and plenty more) warrant a new tuning effort. For this reason the effects of tuning are necessarily temporary.

Another approach to performance is to attack poor performers on a piecemeal basis. Once the on-line system is brought up and transactions begin to flow, monitoring can be done to determine which transactions are using the most resources. Those transactions can then be modified. If the modification (at the source code level) was small, this approach to achieving performance *may* work. Unfortunately, an analysis of what needs to be modified to achieve performance usually indicates that large, sweeping changes need to be made, not just a few changes in the offending transaction, but in entire data base designs and consequently in other transactions. As a general strategy to achieving performance, selective reworking of transactions has a limited effectiveness. Ironically, if applied religiously, over time this approach produces systems that look as if they were originally designed under the SWU concept.

Another strategy to achieve performance is to determine which transactions are the guilty ones and to isolate them as much as possible. In the best case this means putting them onto an entirely separate system. This is seldom possible because even if the transactions can be isolated, the data and network on which the transactions operate probably will *not* be able to be isolated. The second option is to use tuning parameters of the system to remove the offending transactions off into a low-priority part of the machine, where they will do the least damage. The latter scheme works fairly well until the system comes into heavy use, at which point tuning options are not an effective way to isolate transactions. Unfortunately, this problem turns up when the designer can least afford it— at the point of maximum system transaction stress.

A close examination of the options available to the shop not running in the SWU environment should convince the designer that performance *must* be achieved at the point of design. Trying to retrofit performance is a very expensive and frustrating activity.

6.8 OTHER PERSPECTIVES OF PERFORMANCE

One of the reasons the SWU is not particularly intuitive is that the time spent in the on-line region is relatively short. A very basic model of the way a single transaction flows through the system is shown in Figure 6.10. In this figure it is seen that transactions are queued prior to going down the

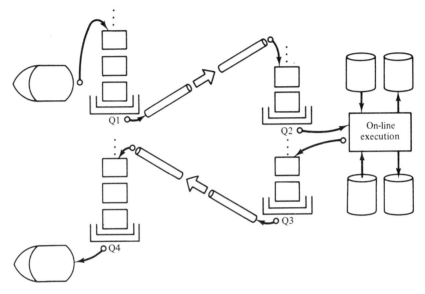

Q1:   transactions queue in anticipation of going down the line.
Q2:   transactions queue to await execution.
Q3:   transactions queue upon output of execution.
Q4:   output queue waiting to be displayed.

Figure 6.10 Basic model of a single transaction flowing through a system.

line (Q1); once they reach the central processor they are queued prior to execution (Q2); they then execute, and output is placed on Q3, awaiting transportation to the final destination; and finally the output is queued at the final destination, prior to actual display (Q4). If an analysis is done for a *single* "normal" flow of a transaction (i.e. where no abnormally long waits occur), it will be seen that a transaction spends most of its time going to and from the computer (i.e., going up and down the line). Relatively little time is spent in execution. This perspective may lead the observer to conclude that performance should be optimized by concentrating attention on line time. To some extent this is true, and this is reflected by the SWU attention to message size going up and down the line.

There is an important distinction to be made, however. Looking at a *single* transaction profile can be very misleading because an important point is missed. The point is that there normally are *many* lines and only *one* processor. Thus Q1 and Q4 are *not* particularly important relative to Q2 and Q3. Even Q3 is not important if the output can be distributed to a number of output queues. Q1, Q3, and Q4, which all relate to line transmission time, are not (relatively) as important as Q2, since there can be multiple physical occurrences of them. However, *all* transactions must pass through Q2, so it is the single most important queue. The events that will make Q2 grow long are the activity that occurs in the on-line system—thus the emphasis of the SWU on the activity that occurs in on-line controller. This is true in spite of the relatively short amount of time spent in the on-line controller by any given transaction. Line time, as long as it is, can be spread across many physical lines; on-line control time is concentrated in one place.

6.9 SUMMARY

The manager who attempts to live without the SWU in the on-line environment ultimately costs his or her company a great deal of money. Experiences indicate that performance is put into the system at the point of design and the SWU is the way in which performance is designed. In the on-line environment, business functions are achieved *through* the SWU, not in spite of it. For the competent designer there is no conflict between business functions and the SWU.

REFERENCES

Control of the Data Base Environment, McDonnell Douglas Automation, Manual GP76-6261-2.

Inmon, W. H., *Effective Data Base Design*, Prentice-Hall, Inc., Englewood Cliffs, N.J., 1980.

Inmon, W. H., *On-Line Data Base Design: Standard Work Unit Concept*, Amdahl Technical Topic T1008.0-01B.

Inmon, W. H., and L. J. Friedman, *Design Review Methodology for a Data Base Environment*, Prentice-Hall, Inc., Englewood Cliffs, N.J., 1981.

Sallee, Michael R., Larry Bristol, Harry Hartman, and Mike McKenna, "Capacity Planning for IMS/VS Systems," *Guide 47.0*—Chicago, Session M-13 (with work by John Green).

CASE STUDY

The California Department of Motor Vehicles operates an on-line system for officers as they approach vehicles that have been stopped, are abandoned, or are otherwise under investigation. It is very important for an officer to know that a car that is being approached has been marked as dangerous or under suspicion.

The officers radio the license number of the car to a central dispatcher, who in turn enters the number into a terminal that is attached to a central computer in Fresno. The terminal reply gives a lot of information—whether the car is potentially "dangerous," the owner of the car, the address of the owner of the car, insurance information, prior ticket information for the owner of the car, past accidents (if any), the prior owner of the car (if the car has changed ownership in the last two years), and other miscellaneous information.

The system operates 24 hours a day, 7 days a week. The average number of accesses each day are about 75,000. There is a peak period between 6:30 and 8:30 A.M. and 4:30 to 7:30 P.M. each weekday. The average response time is 15 seconds, but periodically there are moments when response time goes to 3 or 4 minutes. These periods have increased in the past few months, as all California vehicles, including those from the San Diego and Redding regional offices, are loaded onto the system. Conversion to the existing system has taken about two years.

Because there are occasionally 3- or 4-minute delays, there has been some criticism of the system. It can be very dangerous for an officer to wait that long when the car he is investigating in fact holds a dangerous occupant. The Policemen's Union is registering a claim against management saying that the system is dangerous to officers when it malfunctions or slows down. The union has been selectively monitoring response time. In the first few months the system was up (when only the Sacramento and Fresno regional offices were on the system), there was adequate response time—3 to 5 seconds.

Then Los Angeles was hooked up together with San Francisco and response time went to 12 seconds on the average, with occasional waits of up to 10 minutes. The data processing manager was contacted and an expert in tuning on-line systems was brought in. Response time then dropped to 8 to 9 seconds, with occasional 1- to 2-minute delays.

In the meantime, other on-line systems were being brought up using the same on-line system. More regional offices were cut over and response time soared—to an average of 30 seconds, with occasional waits up to 15 minutes. The users began to view the system as a liability, not an asset. The tuning expert was brought back in and response time was brought back down to 10 to 11 seconds. (A faster computer was purchased, but response time dropped only marginally.) The union is threatening a suit and will probably have legitimate grounds should an officer who has not been alerted in a reasonable time by the system be injured or killed in pursuing a car that is marked "dangerous." The system exhibits the worse response time during the peak period of processing—at the very time that response is most critical.

BACKGROUND INFORMATION

The system has been designed around business functions and needs. Prior to the system, there was a batch system in which weekly reports were distributed to regional offices. As officers called in, the reports were consulted. This was a laborious and slow process for the most part. The system designer has translated this report into an on-line set of screens. Since the user is accustomed to having the information at his disposal, that information is translated into his business function, even though the user has never before had to operate an on-line system.

The problem is that the on-line information is gathered by searching many files—the driver's license file, the insurance file, the wreck file, the "hot-car" file, and so forth. In the beginning, a member of the systems staff worried that it was not wise in the on-line environment to access too much data in any one transaction. The designer of the system (who had built many successful batch systems) argued that there was an overriding need for a business function. Since applications had always supplied the needs of the user, management and the user backed the designer, not the systems staff.   ■

Comment on the Following

1. An intensive and long-term tuning effort should be made to ensure adequate performance.
2. Faster equipment should be purchased to enhance performance.
3. Since the existing work load appears to be too much for the current hardware, consideration should be given to splitting the work over a number of machines.
4. A rewrite of the application should be considered. This can be done in two ways: a rewrite from scratch or a rewrite of the system in piecemeal fashion.
5. Since the existing system is a poor performer, it does not make much difference how new systems are constructed.

MULTIPLE-CHOICE QUESTIONS

1. System A is running on a machine and has consistently delivered a 3-second response time, with occasional waits of up to 30 seconds. System B is in the final stages of implementation and is just being cut over to the on-line environment. System B has been designed around business functions and this means an almost literal conversion of a batch mode of thinking to an on-line format. As system B begins to run in the production environment, the response time of system A goes to 7.5 seconds, with occasional waits of up to 2.5 minutes.

    A. The jump in response time of system A is coincidental. Outside factors should be investigated.

    B. System B should not be put into the same on-line environment as system A.

    C. Within most on-line environments, there are techniques and facilities that can be used to match batch processes run on-line.

    D. A massive tuning effort should be undertaken for system B.

    E. There really is not much difference between an average 3-second and a 7.5 second response time.

2. The Aardvark (AA) system is being designed. The designer is firmly convinced that the system should be built under the standard work unit concept. He strongly suggests that the large amount of business function that is to be done be broken up into small units. On the other hand, the user will not compromise the way he envisions his system, although he has never operated in an on-line environment. The user's view is that he has been using a system for years and all the on-line environment will do for him is to allow the identical system to be translated onto a screen, rather than appearing as a report. The user feels that it is his right to dictate the specifics of the system since he is paying the bill.

    A. Breaking up the system into small functional units that ultimately achieve all the user wants is an excellent way to live with the standard work unit concept.

    B. Addressing performance this early in the system is entirely appropriate.

    C. The user is used to data processing servicing his needs without any further discussion.

    D. Batch systems can usually be recreated or simulated on-line. This is nearly always a poor practice.

    E. Translating reports to screens is a symptom of batch design that is being translated into the on-line environment.

*3. In DBMSI—the industry standard for full functional DBMS—the performance considerations center around I/Os, critical resources (such as region occupancy), and queues of transactions. At national computer conventions it is widely stated that DBMSI is difficult to use and poor response is a normal expectation. A new DBMS—NIFTY—has been released that is purportedly superior to DBMSI. NIFTY is claimed to be easy to use, always performs well, allows a designer to do all that he or she wishes, and so on. Many executives spend time at the NIFTY booth reading the promotional literature.

    A. DBMSI is necessarily a poor performer.

B. If DBMSI did not have I/O as a performance constraint, it would not be a poor performer.

C. There is no need for a standard work unit in the NIFTY environment.

D. In evaluating DBMSI versus NIFTY, the most important feature to evaluate is total achieveable throughput as opposed to integrity and backup features.

E. In NIFTY, I/O is not a problem with regard to performance.

EXERCISES AND ESSAYS

1. Discuss ways to implement the standard work unit in an existing environment that is currently not operating under the standard work unit concept.

2. It has been said that "IMS runs at the speed of the slowest transaction." How does this relate to the standard work unit concept?

3. Should the user know about the standard work unit and its consequences, or is that topic entirely in the domain of data processing?

4. Is the standard work unit a concern of data processing management? Of management of users of data processing services? Is the standard work unit concept entirely a technical subject? Just how important is the standard work unit concept to the on-line environment? How important is the successful operation of the on-line environment to a company?

5. Can performance be retrofitted into an on-line system? Can the standard work unit be retrofitted? Must transactions be redesigned? Must data be redesigned? What is the impact of redesigning data and transactions? Can data be redesigned on a piecemeal basis?

VII

Capacity Planning

□□□

There are three major approaches to capacity planning: the "threshold of pain" approach, the "bits and bytes" approach, and the "analytical" approach. Each evolved from the other and as such each represents a new level of refinement. This chapter discusses what they are, how they evolved, their strengths and weaknesses, and issues relevant to managing capacity in an environment of complex, explosive, and often unpredictable growth.

7.1 THRESHOLD OF PAIN APPROACH

In the threshold of pain approach to capacity planning (which can be termed a "nonapproach"), nothing actively is done to determine current levels of capacity or to project future needs. The way management learns that there is a capacity problem is to listen to the level of complaints. When the hue and cry becomes loud enough, management realizes that there must be a capacity problem somewhere in the data processing environment. The only really good thing that can be said for the threshold of pain approach to capacity planning is that it does not require a large staff, since there is *no one* charged with the task. There are *many* serious drawbacks to this approach.

The first drawback is that a company is *always* in a reaction mode, never a planning mode. This mode of operation—the reaction mode—is bad enough in itself, but even worse, the point at which a company discovers it needs resources is the moment of peak process utilization, when those resources are most important and are not available. Another ramification of not planning capacity is that a company is not in a position to make the "best" decision for the acquisition of new resources. The only decision the company can make is that which will most quickly ease the pain being felt. The "best" decision will undoubtedly have financial, technological, and logistical aspects, but a company in a reaction mode can operate *only* from a stance of expediency. Another major drawback to the threshold of pain approach is that lead times may be required in the acquisition of major equipment such that there may be no real immediate solution to the problem.

Perhaps the worst drawback of this approach is that the business considerations of the company (as opposed to the data processing considerations) are not considered at all (or at least in the proper perspective). The focus is so set on the immediate data processing problems that there is no opportunity to consider the full horizon of criteria that should have a bearing on the acquisition of new equipment.

7.2 BITS AND BYTES APPROACH

The next progression beyond the threshold of pain approach is the bits and bytes approach. In the threshold of pain approach, data processing management waits until conditions become so bad that they can no longer be ignored. That pain is unnecessary in an environment where the current level of activity is measured in anticipation of reaching the threshold of pain. The bits and bytes approach takes its name from the very technical way in which the current level of activity is measured. The emphasis here is on the measurement of current activity in very concrete numbers, usually many types of numbers that are very technically detailed. Both hardware and software are monitored and measured. By measuring current activity and comparing it to previous activity, it is possible to predict (using a linear projection) when the threshold of pain will be reached and thus anticipate it, and avoid many of the problems associated with the expeditious acquisition of major equipment. When the anticipatory projection is done properly, it allows a company the margin to make such major decisions as to lease or purchase in the face of announced and expected technological developments.

This approach works to a fair degree for throughput-oriented systems but not so well for response-oriented systems. Response-oriented systems have more variables and complexities, with peak and slack periods of processing, so that capacity projections are much more open to interpretation. The major problem with the bits and bytes approach is that it really only tells a company where it stands today (which is certainly better than the threshold of pain approach). The projections made into the future tend to be very haphazard because they are based on a linear model, which usually does not lead to accurate conclusions.

As a final note, the bits and bytes approach to capacity planning at least gives a company a technical justification for the acquisition of hardware. The main strength of this approach is that a company at least knows where it stands with regard to today's processing.

7.3 ANALYTICAL APPROACH

The analytical approach to capacity planning attempts to build on the two previous approaches in that the first approach (threshold of pain) waits for problems to occur, the second approach (bits and bytes) measures where a company is at and can at least tell a company where it stands today, and the third approach (the analytical approach) projects where a company will be. It is true that the bits and bytes approach can be used for projection, but the projections using that approach are based on the extension of existing data (usually linear) rather than on any impact of a projected workload. Using the analytical approach, the corporation is able to be more objective, at least insofar as the *business* needs of the corporation are able to be represented more easily.

There are basically two types of analytical approaches to capacity planning: the simulation model and queuing model. In the simulation model, the projected work load is profiled and the actual I/O operations are run and measured. In the queuing model approach, the workload is profiled, but the I/O operations are not actually executed; only the *effects* of the I/O operations are determined. The difference between the two approaches, then, is that in one case (the simulation case) the calls of the profiled system are actually done, and in the other case (the queuing model case) the calls are not done, but the *effect* of the calls is calculated.

7.4 PITFALLS

Despite the elegant tools for doing capacity analysis, there are some major problems of which the manager should be aware. The major pitfalls are:

- *Not taking into account the business needs of the corporation.* Capacity planning can become a self-serving exercise for data processing. In this sense data processing is viewed as something other than a corporate function. A simple example of this pitfall is not taking into account the *business* long-term plan of the corporation. The viewpoint of the capacity planner in this mode is that the long-term plan is a *data processing* long-term plan, not a corporate long-term plan.
- *Analysis done to too great a level of detail.* Because of the technical nature of much of capacity planning, it is easy to generate many, many numbers, so many that the overall picture ends up getting lost in the mountains of detail being generated.
- *No feedback mechanisms.* The typical capacity planning cycle is to prepare a plan, discuss it, acquire new equipment, and discard the plan. In very few cases is the plan scrutinized after the fact, so that inaccuracies and errors can be identified and thus avoided. Very few managers are held accountable for their capacity planning activities after the fact, even when there are gross errors. This means that the capacity planning activity ultimately will not be taken seriously and that managers who make gross

errors will not have the opportunity to learn from their mistakes. The feedback loop is incomplete.

- *Not allowing the end user to participate at a meaningful level.* This leads to a lack of credibility of inputs. Often there are very good external measures that can serve as valid input, such as orders of raw materials for the foreseeable future, and expansion plans. The capacity plan can be only as good as the input on which it is based.

Perhaps the worst abuse of capacity planning is when the exercise is used as a justification for self-centered activity. This is a fairly easy thing to do when (1) data processing controls all the inputs, and (2) data processing controls the technical environment in which capacity planning is done. Is it any wonder, then, that the results will come out to the satisfaction of data processing? Furthermore, when there is no accountability attached to the process, why should data processing care if the results are biased as data processing wants to see them? As long as the manager in charge of the capacity planning exercise does not have to answer later for the results, why not make the exercise self-serving to data processing?

7.5 MONITORING THE COMPUTER SYSTEM

Fundamental to any planning is monitoring the activity that is happening in a shop. The manager should understand at least two basic facts about monitoring: (1) there is an overhead associated with using a monitor (i.e., a certain percentage of system resources will be dedicated to the monitor and nothing else), and (2) monitoring is necessary to determine long-term trends and changes. This means that it is wise to choose the *proper* amount of monitoring activity. Too much full-time monitoring will use too many system resources unnecessarily, and too little full-time monitoring will allow important information to go unnoticed.

There are basically two types of monitors: those that should be run full time, and those that should be run only on special occasions. These monitors exist for both hardware and software. Essentially, the dividing line between the two types of monitors is drawn by the resources they consume. The low-overhead, basic activity monitoring that is run all the time is used to determine when problems occur and to give a clue as to the nature of the problem. The high-overhead type of monitoring is usually run only during problem periods, to help in problem solving. On occasion, this high-overhead monitor can be run during a "normal" period merely to provide a statistically objective basis for what is normal.

7.6 CAPACITY PLANNING AND SYSTEM TYPES

Certain types of systems lend themselves readily to capacity planning and other types of systems are somewhat impervious to a planning effort. The systems that are easy to plan capacity for are batch, throughput-oriented systems. Systems for which capacity is not so easy to plan are response-oriented systems, input-driven applications, and new systems that lack track records.

One reason (certainly not the only one) response-oriented systems are difficult to plan capacity for is the fact that there are normally "peaks" and "valleys" of work load. In a "valley" it may be desirable to have no more than 80% utilization of the machine, so that there will be enough power left for peak-period processing. To the uninitiated this 20% unused capacity may signal that more capacity is *not* required. Thus a level of subjectivity is created. Response-oriented systems must be sized for peaks if they are to be usable.

Perhaps the hardest systems of all for which to plan capacity are systems where there is usually a wide discrepancy in resource utilization from one configuration to the next. TSO and NCSS are systems of this variety. As an example of the difficulty, in one shop there may be 30 TSO users logged on and active, using 50% of a machine, whereas in another configuration there may be 10 users logged on using 95% of the machine. The real measure is not how many users are logged on, but what the users are doing, and this will vary with time! Thus the amount of capacity used is very difficult to predict.

There are some solutions to this dilemma. The first is to limit the resources that a high-consumption user can get to. This means that a "hog" will receive fewer resources and will ultimately have longer throughput time while executing than will a more efficient resource user. There are some sophisticated software techniques at the SCP level that can effect this resource redistribution based on level of consumption.

Another way to effect this equitable distribution of resources is to install a "charge-back" scheme. In this scheme, users are charged for the resources they use and billed on a weekly, monthly, and so on, basis. The problem here is that they are billed in "internal" money, and budget overruns of this type are usually not taken seriously. Only when the resource being charged for is in critical demand, so much so that the corporation really cares how that resource is used, do charge-back schemes work. Many shops have charge-back systems; few pay any attention to it.

Still another technique for equitable distribution of resources is implementation of the standard work unit concept. This is done at a design and administrative level. It has been thoroughly discussed in the literature and is discussed in depth in Chapter 6.

7.7 VENDOR-SUPPLIED ESTIMATES

In nearly every case, a hardware vendor will be happy to lead or actually conduct a capacity-planning study. It is naturally in the best marketing interests of a hardware company to pay serious attention to this problem. In general, vendor-supplied estimates can suffer from the same problems as a shop doing its own capacity planning. Not properly accounting for the long-term business plan of the company, getting too involved at the detailed level, and not particularly worrying about the long-term feedback are problems (although vendors are a bit more wary of providing a flatly incorrect estimate than employees internal to the corporation).

There are, however, some distinct advantages to allowing the vendor to provide capacity planning services. The vendor usually has ample technical expertise. The vendor may have sophisticated software not otherwise available to the client. The vendor may be aware of future directions and can subtly steer the client in a wise direction without compromising the announcement of new capabilities. The vendor is usually able to get a more accurate measure more quickly because of its expertise. So there can be some significant advantages to having a vendor participate in the capacity-planning process.

The client should keep in mind that, when a vendor does participate in the capacity-planning process, there will naturally be an inclination to present the results in as favorable a light as possible toward the vendor's products. The very least that happens is that the future needs of the company are disclosed to the vendor. So it is seen, quite naturally, that there is a trade-off for vendor expertise. Vendor objectivity should be a serious concern.

7.8 COMMONLY OVERRUN RESOURCES

The resources that typically are overrun are the CPU, channels, memory, disk, and teleprocessing facilities. Growth is so explosive that it tends to go in all directions at once, so the critical resource at any time really depends on various factors, such as relative costs, the lead times involved, and the changes in technology. It is interesting to note the great difference technology can make in costs and capabilities. In the early days of computing, core was expensive and difficult to come by, and it became one of the limiting factors of the computing environment. In today's world, memory is much less expensive, is not particularly difficult to acquire, and is thus *not* a limiting factor, certainly not as it once was. It is interesting to note that the drop in the price of memory was brought about by new technology. Thus it can be said that critical resources at any moment are determined by many factors.

7.9 FITTING CAPACITY PLANNING INTO THE ORGANIZATION

Traditionally, the capacity planning function is placed entirely within the data processing department. This is a natural placement due to the technical aspects of capacity planning. Often, the technical expertise for capacity planning was allocated to other projects and capacity planning became a "back-burner" project. When this happened, the organization easily fell into the threshold of pain mode of operation. One of the major problems with putting the capacity planning function in the data processing department is that the business needs of the company may not be represented properly or at all, as has been discussed.

It has been suggested that the capacity planning function be placed outside data processing, in a position to serve both data processing and the business planning function of the organization. This would allow the capacity planning function to have a global perspective, rather than such a parochial view of the world. This perspective has been likened to that of the data administrator. In this position, the capacity planner has greater corporate exposure and as such has more influence, fewer day-to-day concerns, and more of an opportunity to learn from past errors, which can only be a healthy proposition.

REFERENCES

Best/1 Computer System Capacity Planning, BGS Systems, Inc., Lincoln, Ma., 1978.

Best/1 User's Guide, BE78-020-1, BG Systems, Inc., Lincoln, Ma., 1978.

Teleprocessing Network Simulator Release 5.0: General Information Manual, IBM Manual GH20-1907-3.

Van Duyn, Ted, "SURF: Managing IMS/VS with TPNS," *Guide 52*, May 13, 1981.

CASE STUDY

The St. Louis Door and Gateway Company is experiencing great growth as a company. This growth quickly translates into growth in computer utilization, which is compounded by a trend toward automation that is really coincidental with the growth the company is experiencing. New systems and new uses of systems are the daily experience.

St. Louis Door and Gateway currently owns a medium-size processor from the familiar product line of a vendor. The makeup of the work load currently is batch and some TSO (Time Sharing Option). On-line is being considered, but is not a factor presently.

Management is interested in how much capacity is left in the machine and how long it will last. Approximately 50% of the machine is being consumed currently. The manager in charge of capacity planning drops in on the head of applications software and inquires about plans for the future. The chat lasts about 10 minutes and the manager in charge of capacity planning writes a memo that it is her opinion that there is enough capacity left for the next 15 months or so. This is based on her conversation and a "general feeling" about things.

The vendor offers to undertake a more formalized effort, but it is felt that there is no pressing need. About the time the projected capacity memo is written, systems programming undertakes a project that will make occasional heavy use of TSO. Also, within the existing applications there is a spurt of activity that has not been anticipated. Originally, two divisions were cut over as a pilot for usage of a new system. However, the pilot was so successful that 10 more divisions are being cut over when only three were scheduled. This means that there is almost a doubling of the use of existing systems. Batch runs that formerly took 2 hours now take 4 and 5 hours. Also, as TSO is used more frequently, programmers are beginning to discover the capabilities of it and are beginning to do more exotic things.

Five months after the projections on utilization have been done, operations begins to experience difficulty in getting all the processing done that needs to be done. TSO frequently takes up large amounts of resources, batch jobs occasionally run longer than anticipated, and operations is faced with the unenviable task of determining what should and should not be run. Usually, test jobs are the first to go and this upsets the development programmers. Problems really begin to crop up when an entire night's worth of processing of one of the major applications must be rerun because the wrong input tapes were hung at the start of the job stream and not caught until the final reports were scanned.

Management grows concerned and charges the manager who originally wrote the projection memo to consider hardware acquisitions. The original projection memo is never referred to by anyone; in fact, it has been forgotten. The vendor is more than happy to talk about an upgrade or the purchase of another machine. The only problem is that there is a three-month lead time required for the next machine. A third party brings to management's attention that it can install an upgraded computer next week if management is willing to meet the premium terms of the company that currently owns the computer.   ∎

Comment on the Following

1. Some growth patterns can simply not be anticipated.
2. Waiting to the last moment to acquire something as major as a large computer can be expensive in many ways. What are they?
3. The manager in charge of projecting growth and capacity has done a slipshod job that has harmed the company. How should she be handled?
4. The vendor offered to do a capacity study. What bias may the vendor have? What valid input could the vendor have offered?

5. What is the impact of *not* acquiring more equipment?

6. Should the original projection memo be scrutinized after the fact? Is it important not to make the same mistake again? How can that mistake be avoided?

7. Other than money unnecessarily spent, what are the problems of being *forced* into hardware acquisitions rather than making acquisitions by choice?

MULTIPLE-CHOICE QUESTIONS

1. Management has decided that capacity planning is a necessary and useful activity. Several system programmers are hired to plan a comprehensive study of what the current position is on all hardware—mainframe, communications, and storage media. The study goes to a very low level of detail. Much attention is spent on detail, tuning, and hardware and software architecture.

   A. There is a real danger that the amount of detail may swamp the capacity planning effort.

   B. With all the emphasis being placed on current utilizations, the fact is that future utilization and acquisition is the major issue, and that fact may be lost.

   C. There may be some very beneficial side benefits by focusing the study at the low level of detail.

   D. The technical material that will come out of the study may not be appropriate for high-level management discussion. It may only cloud the issues.

   E. There is little or no mention made of the business plans of the company. The focus is almost entirely on data processing plans.

2. Management has decided to form a permanent function for capacity planning. It has decided to locate the new organization under the head of systems programming. The two people currently in the group are system programmers.

   A. This is a good place to locate this function in the company.

   B. Since the job of capacity planning is technical, it makes sense to have systems programmers staffing the function.

   C. Placed where it is, the group will probably have a broad perspective of the job of capacity planning.

   D. The permanent function should not be mixed with other, ongoing duties.

   E. Capacity planning is not an ongoing function.

EXERCISES AND ESSAYS

1. Describe the tools for capacity planning. Can growth be extrapolated? What if growth cannot be extrapolated?
2. What safety measures can be taken in the event of an inaccurate plan? What is the cost of those measures?
3. Describe the various considerations (at the highest level) that should be made by the capacity planner. Then describe the personnel that are needed to staff that function. Where should those personnel be placed in the organization? What is the cost of not planning capacity? In the worst case?

VIII

Productivity

□□

8.1 ISSUES OF PRODUCTIVITY

The explosive growth of the use of computers and the growth in the ways computers can be used have produced a universal demand for more and better application systems. This demand can be measured by the backlog of applications to be developed and by the growth in the total amount of computer power being consumed. The growth is not limited to large scale users of computers, but is uniform across the spectrum of machine sizes.

The primary limiting factor in satisfying this growth is the human factor—the analysts, designers, programmers, and technicians who produce systems. The demand for their services increases faster than their ability to produce systems. Thus, growth is the primary motivating force behind the emphasis that is placed on productivity. Greater productivity means more throughput from the limiting factor—the human one.

An indirect limiting factor is the computer itself. If the computer were not as primitive as it is, human manipulation of the computer might be accomplished at a higher, more productive level. Since computers are directed (or programmed) in a very primitive fashion, the level of commands given to the computer are very basic and low. This is at the same time an advantage and a disadvantage. It is an advantage in that the programmer has at his disposal all the tools needed to direct the computer to do all sorts of tasks; it is a disadvantage in that the instructions are at such a basic level that directing the computer is cumbersome, usually complex, and very intolerant of errors. It is the low level of control required, however, that gives the programmer and designer all the options needed to accomplish the varied tasks that can be done with the computer, so there is a good case to be made for directing computer resources at a low level.

The issues of productivity are intimately related to the issues of the best usage of human resources. Human resource management at the micro level involves tasks such as paying attention to the tools humans use to produce code, i.e., the actual production of code. The macro level of human resource management addresses such issues as the general direction of systems and strategies for achieving success. The differences between the micro level and macro level may be made clearer by an analogy. Suppose an Army general wants to study the effectiveness of his soldiers. At the micro level he can inspect guns, backpacks, helmets, uniforms, etc.— all the tools his men have. This is one perspective of how effective they will be. On the other hand at the macro level, the general can study such things as: On what front are soldiers most effectively deployed? Where should they be fighting (and not fighting)? Where will unification of forces produce the best effect? Etc. Using human resources wisely in data processing, at both the *micro* and at the *macro* level, is the key to productivity.

Some seemingly unrelated issues, such as system quality and reasonableness of user requests, ultimately have a great deal to do with productivity. Other issues, such as organizational attitudes and methodologies, also have much to do with productivity, as well as the usage of the traditional tools such as specialized software and design techniques. Whatever reduces the backlog of user requests will be viewed as a productivity aid.

8.2 OBSTACLES TO PRODUCTIVITY

One of the major obstacles to productivity is the very nature of computerized systems themselves. Programs (the heart of the application) are very sensitive to the form and content of the data on which they operate. When the data changes, programs must be changed, and this means human intervention and manipulation. Furthermore, it is the nature of data to change its content and form, since the physical form of data is nothing more than a representation of the data as it logically exists in the user's environment, and the logical form of the data in the user's environment, given enough time, is *always* changing. Systems, then, are sensitive to change, and change is always occurring.

The only variation in change from application to application is the *rate* of change. This sensitivity of programs to the form and content of the data is referred to as data dependence, and this phenomenon indirectly impacts productivity (to a *very* large degree) in that systems, once architected, are not very easy to change. Of course, the careful designer employs all the best design practices to ensure the highest degree of *data elasticity*, but even then, systems are still somewhat data dependent. Were they not as data dependent as they are, productivity would not be nearly the issue that it is.

8.3 UNREALISTIC USER REQUESTS

Another "macro" factor indirectly contributing to the issue of productivity is "unrealistic user requests." Given that most shops have a large backlog of "to do" lists, the consensus of opinion is that the backlog could be greatly reduced if the requests were all reasonable. For example, suppose the backlog was made up of nothing but requests that were technically feasible, cost justified, were rational (given the environment in which they were requested), and were prioritized according to importance. The problem is that many user requests are not "reasonable." The best thing that can happen to such requests is that management (or someone) will quickly ferret them out and remove them. The worst thing that can happen is that the system (or request) is actually built and the user learns the hard way that his or her request is not reasonable.

To some degree the user can hardly be blamed for submitting unreasonable requests, especially for on-line systems. Several factors account for this. On the one hand the user is attempting to realize the full promise of automation and the computer development team is doing what it can to appease the user, so it is not surprising the user's plans are ambitious. Secondly, the user is oftentimes operating from a standpoint of ignorance, that is, the user really does not know what to expect, nor how to envision the system. He has no parameters or constraints on which to gauge his requests and, as such, has no idea what is reasonable or not.

The user should understand that on-line systems are expensive to build and operate. The user should not build online systems when the power of online systems is not needed. If the user has a backlog of experience or even a reasonable framework to relate to, then the requests made tend to be quite rational. In the absence of a backlog or framework, unrealistic expectations are not surprising. One of the roles of the successful applications designer is to provide the education the user needs in terms of system cost effectiveness.

8.4 SYSTEM QUALITY AND PRODUCTIVITY

System quality has a *great* deal to do with productivity, although the effort necessary to achieve quality may lead an observer to the opposite conclusion. The importance of quality is underlined by widespread growth of the phenomena of "post implementation" development and design. This phenomena occurs as a product of the rush to meet deadlines, or in some cases, as the result of not understanding the components of quality of system design. What happens is that program code, *any code*, is put up to satisfy deadlines. After the code is written and pressure is off, the next phase of the project is making the code actually work (and work efficiently), which often means rearchitecting some or major parts of the application. In some cases this "post implementation" development may consume as much as *five to ten* times the original resources as did the original development effort. It is this wasteful consumption of resources that stifles productivity.

The point is: If system quality were put in the system in the first place, there would be *no need* for a large "post implementation" development effort, thus freeing major human resources for more useful work such as cutting into the backlog of work to be done. In this light, there is a very definite relationship between system quality and productivity. It is interesting to note that *system quality is most difficult to attain in the on-line environment*, most easy to attain in the batch environment.

8.5 MANAGEMENT DECISIONS AND PRODUCTIVITY

In the same sense that system quality relates to productivity (at a macro level), so does management understanding of the issues of productivity and leadership. A proper understanding of issues and an enlightened direction by management can lead, at the macro level, to a high degree of productivity, whereas a lack of understanding of issues and improper direction by management at this level *will* lead to great unproductivity.

This point is best explained in the understanding of tradeoffs the designer makes and management's recognition and handling of those tradeoffs. For example, if management is not aware of the tradeoffs between performance and flexibility, it is likely that those tradeoffs will not be properly balanced and that the tradeoffs will be decided by default; for example, due to lack of recognition of these basic issues, designers will make choices without realizing compromises are being made. In the average case (and, of course, in the extreme) this lack of perception may lead to whole magnitudes of unnecessary work.

Another way in which management influences productivity occurs when management is aware of the tradeoffs of design and development but opts solely for performance because the results are more visible, more readily attainable, and more politically expedient. When a system is optimized for performance, it often is difficult to change. The manager may be buying user satisfaction today at the expense of long-term dissatisfaction with the reaction time of the data processing development group when it comes time to change the system. In this fashion, management greatly impacts productivity by ultimately increasing the work load for the development staff.

8.6 SYSTEM SPLINTERING

Intimately associated with the issue of the data dependence is the issue of integrated systems, or the converse, which can be termed "splintered systems" or unintegrated systems. This issue, too, is at the macro level. When systems are integrated, changes and program maintenance can be done with a minimum of energy because the impact of changes affects a minimum amount of data (which results in a minimum amount of program changes).

This means fewer human resources are required and are free to do other activities, thus indirectly enhancing productivity. When systems are splintered, changes become: 1) more complex to implement, 2) more voluminous to implement, and 3) more prone to error. This is true because a given change must physically be implemented in more than a single place. Because of this work and complexity, more human resources are required, thus indirectly negatively impacting productivity.

8.7 OTHER INDIRECT FACTORS

There are other indirect factors that impact productivity at the macro level. It has been shown that system quality relates quite directly to the issue of productivity. An interesting side issue is that the very definition of system quality has changed over time. As systems become more sophisticated and powerful, so does the definition of system quality.

In batch system, quality of design could be measured by two major criteria: 1) How quickly was the application developed? and 2) How accurate is the application? Any batch system that was quickly done and met the specifications was deemed to have quality.

However, as systems grew in sophistication and were built for more powerful environments, the criteria for quality was upgraded. An on-line system which only was quickly constructed and "met" user requirements was hardly of high quality if it did not also *perform* well, was not *available* when needed, and was not unduly difficult to *change*. Thus system quality is a moving target, and since system quality is indirectly a big factor in productivity, system sophistication is likewise a big factor in the issue of productivity.

8.8 MEASURING PRODUCTIVITY

At first glance it appears that productivity is a fairly easy thing to measure. One very basic measure is lines of code produced. There are however some major difficulties in measuring lines of code produced and using that as a barometer of productivity.

If lines of code produced are to be used as a measure, then the following is the *least of the considerations* which must be accounted for:

1. *Languages.* Some languages lend themselves to more lines of code than other languages. Some factors are standard prologue for each program, restrictions on number of statements to be placed on a line, the syntax of the language itself, the length of the operands, the power of the operators, the level of the language, and the existence or lack of automatic code genera-

tion mechanisms. In analyzing productivity based on lines of code, is a programmer working in a language that lends itself to much "verbosity" more productive than a programmer working in a language that is more concise? Probably not, but using a *pure* measure of lines of code may erroneously lead to that conclusion. Lines of code comparison across languages is a *very difficult thing* from which to draw conclusions.

2. *Automatic Code Generation.* If number of lines of code is to be measured, what should be done about code generated from a data dictionary, a copylib,* or other such mechanism? On one hand it seems unfair to count multiple lines of source code that were generated by a few statements from the programmer. On the other hand, totally disregarding the code easily produced likewise seems unfair. Comparing the productivity of a programmer who generated 1000 lines of "raw" code versus a programmer who generated 1000 lines of code, 500 of which were automatically generated, is a very odd comparison. The programmer producing 1000 "raw" lines of code may be a very *hard* worker, but the programmer producing 500 lines of generated code may be a very *smart* worker. The issue of automatic code generation should be explicitly resolved *before* productivity comparisons are made.

3. *Comments.* Should comments in the program count? If the answer is no, the programmers who want to excel in productivity will be rewarded by including a minimum of documentation. If yes, then the lazy programmer who writes 10 lines of "working" code and 100 lines of documentation will excel. This issue should be resolved.

4. *Changes.* If a programmer finds a bug and takes out 10 lines of code, replacing it with one correct line of code, is that programmer doing "negative" work? Certainly not, but the measure of productivity indicates otherwise.

5. *Coding Styles.* Some programmers produce a program in 200 lines of code. Another programmer will produce the exact functional equivalent, in 300 lines of code. Is the second programmer more productive?

6. *Skeleton Programs.* Some programmers carry around with them skeleton programs that can be automatically generated. The programmer then "fills in the gaps" and quickly has results. Should the code that is generated from the skeleton be counted as productive lines of code?

7. *Programming Aids.* TSO and VM/CMS are two programming aids that can greatly enhance the speed at which code can be generated. If a programmer in a TSO environment produces 25 lines of code an hour, is he more productive than a programmer in a non-TSO or CMS environment who produces 10 lines of code an hour?

---

*Copylib is a library that a programmer refers to and references code which is then copied from the library to the programmer's source text.

The questions listed above have alerted the reader to be *very* careful in comparing lines of code production. All of the above specific problems should be resolved before any comparison is made, otherwise the conclusions drawn from the comparison may be very misleading.

8.9 OTHER ISSUES

Even if the basic issues of lines of code measurement are resolved (and they must be for any meaningful measure of work), there are other important issues that should be resolved. What exactly should be measured against the total system lines of code? Exactly whose work should be counted into the lines of code produced? The analyst? The programmer? The operator? The designer? How far back into the project should work that ultimately led to the lines of code be counted?

Suppose a company states that a project has achieved a rate of 10 lines of code per hour of work and another company claims a rate of 5 lines of code per hour. Is the first company more productive than the second? Not necessarily. If the 10 lines of code per hour included *only* the programmer's time, and the 5 lines of code per hour included analysis, design, testing, implementation (as well as programming), then the 5 lines of code per hour probably represents a *much more* productive environment than the 10 lines of code. If comparison is to be made across projects, great care must be taken to ensure that the same activities are being accounted for, otherwise the relative numbers can be misleading.

8.10 OTHER MEASURES

At this point, it is apparent that measuring lines of code is fraught with inequities. To rectify this situation, some shops count other tangible outputs as measures of productivity, such as number of programs and/or transactions produced. Just as counting lines of code is filled with inequities, so is counting number of programs. Some of the problems with this approach are that some programs are much longer and complex than other programs, some designers produce specifications for many more programs than other designers, and approaches to design in batch are very different from approaches to design in the on-line environment.

The whole issue of measuring lines of code or counting complete programs comes from the batch environment. In the batch environment success is measured by speed and accuracy of coding. While speed and accuracy of coding are important in the on-line environment, they are by no means the only measure of success. System response time, system availability, and flexibility are all equal parameters of success in the on-line environment. In light of the *total* parameters of success, lines of code produced or programs written is not necessarily a meaningful number for on-line systems.

8.11 TOOLS FOR PRODUCTIVITY

Constructing application systems would be truly onerous if it were not for the tools which exist that ease the burden of the designer and the programmer. If programs were all written at the assembly level, for instance, development time would unquestionably be much longer than it is. In a very basic way, the standard high-level language compiler—COBOL, PL-1, FORTRAN, etc.—is a productivity tool taken for granted throughout the industry.

Another very basic productivity tool is the Data Base Management System (DBMS), such as IMS, TOTAL, IDMS, etc. The DBMS allows the designer and programmer to concentrate on the major issues of design without being fettered by all the details needed to manage such diverse subjects as physical structuring, placement, and organization of data, logical structuring of data, teleprocessing monitoring, and system control programs. The programmer interfaces with the DBMS in very basic terms— such as GET, DELETE, INSERT, and is essentially free to concentrate on other important issues—such as data independence, system performance, system availability, and flexibility. Without a DBMS the programmer and designer would be deeply entwined in details that greatly impede the speed with which development can proceed.

Another tool for productivity is automatic code generation. Automatic code generators come in many forms. One of the simplest is a "copylib." Using a copylib, a programmer only codes a single line. Before the program is compiled, the copylib is passed against the programmer's source text and appropriate messages to copylib are picked up, interpreted, and source code from copylib is merged into the programmer's source code. Typically data layouts and subroutines are found in copylibs, along with other commonly accessed code. Figure 8.1 depicts the workings of copylib.

Another form of the copylib concept is the "macro" concept. The chief difference between the copylib approach and the "macro" approach is the level of languages on which they operate. Copylib usually operates on high-level languages such as COBOL or PL-1, while "macros" usually operate on assembly code. There are other minor distinctions in the actual implementation of copylib and "macros."

8.12 OTHER CODE GENERATORS

Another common code generation technique occurs as a subset of the functions of data dictionary. One of the functions of data dictionary is

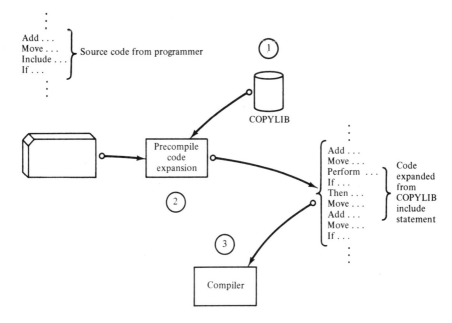

1. The programmer codes certain statements recognizable to the COPYLIB code expansion program. In this case "Include . . ." refers to some text that resides in COPYLIB.

2. The programmers source code is run through the COPYLIB code expansion program. The reference signaled by "Include . . ." is located in COPYLIB and source code is then generated and is inserted into the programmer's source code.

3. The expanded source text is sent to the compiler for the next step of processing.

Figure 8.1 How a COPYLIB works.

generating source to a copylib. The difference in copylib and data diction-ary lies in all the other functions data dictionary provides that a copylib does not provide. Some of those functions typically are: data cross referencing, data definitions of more than just data layouts, unification of data defini-tions, and many more such functions, which are either totally missing or only provided as an incidental feature of a copylib facility.

Another form of code generation occurs in the storage and automatic reproduction of code not used for programming but used for auxiliary pur-poses. Such an example is in screen definition. Figure 8.2 shows a type of control code that will enable the computer to 1) format a screen, and 2) interpret the user's information entered on the screen.

There are three basic techniques to produce this code. They are:

1. The programmer actually writes the code.

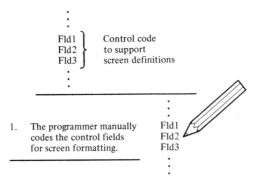

Figure 8.2 Type of control code.

2. The designer formats the screen and feeds that information to a program that produces the code.

3. The designer sits at a terminal, formats the screen interactively, and when an acceptable format is designed, sends the format to a program that produces the proper control information. Figure 8.3 illustrates these three modes of producing the control fields.

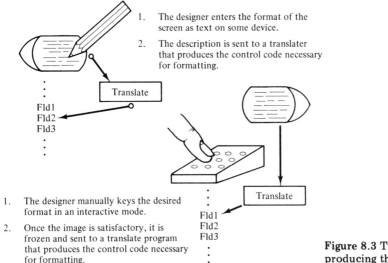

Figure 8.3 Three modes of producing the control fields.

A few points can be made concerning this basic control field translation process. The higher level the human interaction, the greater the productivity. The designer sitting at a terminal interactively producing the screens is much faster than the coder building screens control field by control field. The lower the level of human interaction, the more control, but also, the more work to produce the same effort. Suppose a designer wants to do something at a terminal which can be done but is not supported by the "translate" pro-

114

gram. The designer must rely on hand coding to accomplish this unsupported activity.

Another form of code generation occurs when programs are initially generated using a skeleton program. Figure 8.4 shows this process. The skeleton program concept is nothing more than an extension of the copy-lib concept, with more whistles and bells.

8.13 CODE MANAGEMENT FACILITIES

Other aids for programmer productivity include such "code management" facilities as IBM's TSO (Time Sharing Option) and IBM's VM/CMS (Virtual Memory/Conversational Monitoring System). Using these facilities, a programmer can interactively enter code onto a library, edit it, reproduce whole other sections of code, and perform such tasks as compilation and in some cases, testing of the code. Using facilities like TSO or CMS can greatly speed the rate at which code can be generated. The programmer dispenses with much manual activity and replaces it with immediate hands-on accessibility of code.

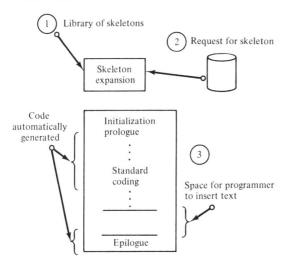

1. The programmer enters a request for a certain "skeleton" program.
2. The "skeleton" library is searched and the request is located.
3. The skeleton expansion program takes the skeleton, embellishes it, and produces standardized code that the programmer would otherwise have had to produce by hand.

Figure 8.4 Skeleton program.

8.14 HIGH-LEVEL LANGUAGES

Another productivity aid is high-level languages. The language level referred to here is not at the COBOL or PL-1 level, but higher—principally query languages. An example of such query languages are IBM's SQL or Informatic's Mark IV. These high-level languages allow the users to access much data and perform many activities with a minimum of coding. This ratio of processing power versus lines of code required greatly enhances the productivity posture of the languages. This power is not without its drawbacks. Simply because the languages can do so much means that there is a potential for inefficient or unnecessary execution of code. The designer should be aware of the tradeoffs in selecting a high-level language.

8.15 SYSTEM PROTOTYPING

Another approach to productivity is through system prototyping. Software supporting this kind of activity is IBM's ADF (Application Development Facility). The theory behind prototyping systems is that users do not really know what to expect when they initially specify a system. Giving them a complete system is wasteful because much will be changed once the system is in a usable form and the users perceive the full potential. The designer using prototypes builds a realistic looking model of the system insofar as the external characteristics are concerned. Once the user is satisfied with the system, a firm set of requirements can be laid down. From those requirements the production version of the system can be constructed.

There is a danger that the user will want to start using the prototype system as if it were the full production system. The problem is that many prototype systems are supported by an architecture that is unsuitable for a full production environment. For example, suppose the prototype system can manage up to 5,000 transactions a day, but any more than that cause a bottleneck. In the case where the user wants to run 100,000 transactions a day the prototype would prove to be unsatisfactory, *despite* the fact that *externally* the prototype and the production system are identical.

CASE STUDY

The Santa Fe Trail and Ticket Sales Company does a large business as a retailer and wholesaler of entertainment events throughout New Mexico, Arizona, Colorado, and Oklahoma. What started as a small business blossomed as the population and industry shifted from the northern states to the Sun Belt. From the beginning, Santa Fe had automated systems. As the company has grown, its computing facilities and automated systems have grown. Part of the success of the company is attributed to its timeliness of information, and this is a direct result of the sophistication of the data processing department.

For the past two years, there has been a backlog of requests for systems and changes to systems that have been stacking up faster than data processing can deliver. This is surprising in light of the fact that the data processing development staff has gone from 15 developers 2 years ago to 60 developers today. The backlog of requests is rising much faster than the requests can be serviced. An interesting sidelight is the rise in maintenance activity. Three years ago maintenance comprised about 20% of the activity in the shop. Today, the ratio is 55% and management has the feeling that the ratio will go higher.

Another interesting note is that system rewrites have become an annoying habit. This has been true as systems have grown more complex and as new users are brought into the world of automation. Interestingly, the first two on-line systems were discarded, wasting a total of 15 person/years of effort.

Management of data processing has always enjoyed a sterling reputation at Santa Fe. Because users are not being serviced as they have been in the past, data processing's reputation is beginning to tarnish a little and this upsets data processing management. The director of data processing has read an article in a trade journal proclaiming gains in productivity that are remarkable. One development expert claimed a coding rate of 50 lines per hour. Management estimates that, at this rate, the backlog of user requests would disappear in half a year.

An investigation is made into possible ways to increase productivity. The following represents the findings:

1. *Acquisitions and use of a new high-level language called ALLSTAR.* ALLSTAR gives the programmer power to write many functions in a small amount of code. The problem is that the language is so high level that there are some fundamental things the programmer cannot do that he or she needs to do on occasion, such as abort the application or write a message to the console operator.

2. *Acquisition and use of a development tool such as TSO or VM/CMS.* There is little doubt that these tools would enhance productivity, but there is concern as to their costs. The major problem is not the cost of software, but the hardware—the terminals, lines, and computers that are required.

3. *Development methodologies.* These methodologies hold promise for faster, cleaner development and for an easier maintenance profile. The problem is that they are aimed at sequential systems development and focus on coding almost exclusively. The cost of acquisition is the price of sending people to class and/or to have a consultant come in and install the methodology.

The director of data processing's next-door neighbor is a college professor in computer science. During a work-related conversation one night, the professor offers the opinion that the tools being considered will probably help productivity, but may not be addressing the most germane areas. He suggests that addressing problems such as system quality and maintenance techniques may be more appropriate.   ∎

Comment on the Following

1. Describe the levels of productivity—micro and macro—as they are manifested at Santa Fe.
2. Are the costs of TSO and VM/CMS the only ones there are? What happens when developers become dependent on TSO and TSO goes down? What other pitfalls are there?
3. The maintenance ratio has climbed from 20% to 55% in 3 years. Will it go higher? What factors will make it go higher?
4. Should the user expect development service levels to remain constant over several years?
5. Is it possible that whole new technologies and approaches can be used to reduce the backlog of requests? Roughly outline two or three of them. Why doesn't management consider them?
6. Would it be useful for management to begin a scheme to determine how many lines of code are being produced in Santa Fe's shop?

MULTIPLE-CHOICE QUESTIONS

1. A new director of computer development has been hired. She is an efficiency expert at getting systems developed quickly. She has worked for four companies in the past five years. She is charged with getting a project development moving that has been in a design stage for awhile. It is an on-line project. In the interest of speed of development, project deadlines are moved up. The top priority of development is the speed of development.
    A. Because development time is the problem confronting management now, they want to optimize it. When the system goes into production, they will want the system optimized on performance. When the system goes down, they will want it optimized on availability. And so forth.
    B. On occasion, a project flounders because of lack of leadership. Putting a "take-charge" person in a responsible position can be a very productive thing to do.

    C. The future seeds of success of many important aspects of the system are being laid now. It may be a serious mistake to neglect them or not give them proper attention.

    D. The efficiency expert probably never sticks around a company long enough to learn the true effects of her approach.

    E. On-line projects offer great dangers when speed of development is optimized compared to other kinds of systems.

2. Management undertakes an analysis of the backlog of user requests for systems. Some requests are mandatory, some requests are important, some would be nice to have, and some requests should not be honored.

    A. Educating users as to what should be expected can reduce the backlog of requests by causing unnecessary and unreasonable requests not to be queued.

    B. If systems were integrated, the impact of users' requests to change systems would be much less.

    C. Ignoring unreasonable user requests is not an effective way to reduce the backlog of requests.

    D. The most expensive way to educate users as to the reasonableness of a request is to actually build the system for the users, then allow them to make up their minds.

    E. If there were a way to reasonably educate users without using a great deal of human or computer resources, what way would prepare the user psychologically for asking for reasonable requests?

EXERCISES AND ESSAYS

1. If lines of code are to be used as a measure of productivity, what activities should be included in the hours spent to produce that code? How can those hours be measured? If comparisons of productivity are to be made based on lines of code, how can the comparison allow for differences between activities that are or are not included in the measurement?

2. What is the relationship between system quality and productivity? System quality and maintenance? Where is system quality built into the system?

3. List as many ways as you can to educate the user as to the reasonableness of requests. What is the cost of each of these ways?

4. List the different ways in which TSO and/or VM/CMS costs a company that uses them. List the benefits. How can the benefits be measured? When do the advantages outweigh the disadvantages? Vice versa?

5. What levels of management need to be concerned with productivity? In what ways? Is productivity a concern of non-data processing management? How can management learn about the relevant issues?

IX

Security

□□

Security is one of the major issues facing managers in today's data processing world. Like so many other issues, the real need for security is not felt until the results of lack of security are felt—after the fact. Managers can, however, learn from the problems of other shops; that is, the lapses in security do not have to be experienced personally. Security must be planned to be effective and timely. The greater the level of security, the greater the cost, and in the data processing environment there are usually multiple levels and types of security. Exactly what costs are justified and what costs are not depends on the sensitivity of the system being secured.

9.1 SECURITY—FROM WHOM?

The first type of security lapse to be considered is that of the inadvertent user of a system. In this case a user is, entirely by accident, accessing or modifying data that should not be available to him or her. By definition there is no malice in an inadvertent breach of security. Even so, inadvertent security lapses can cause problems with system integrity and the proper use of the system. This type of security breakdown is the most common. The impact is usually bothersome rather than destructive. Occasionally, the inadvertent security lapse becomes a temptation to the user and turns into an intentional security breakdown.

The second type of security break is advertent. In this case a user deliberately sets out to access or modify data that he or she should not be able to access. The motivation is not innocent. The user typically attempts to modify data for personal gain, to learn facts that he or she is not authorized to know, to bypass charging procedures, or some other intention not in the company's best interest.

The third type of security lapse comes from what can be termed a "peripheral" user of a system. The peripheral user is not particularly interested in the programs or data of the system being secured, but is interested in using computer resources under the guise of exercising some part of the system.

The fourth major type of security lapse arises through application loopholes that have been built into the system accidentally or otherwise. As an example, consider what happens in the Social Security System when someone dies. If the system is not updated, checks still continue to come (and are endorsed by the culprit). At a later time the culprit notifies the system that the recipient of the checks has expired. Cheating of this nature is very difficult to audit because of the system itself. This type of abuse presents a whole new dimension to the manager installing security controls and procedures.

9.2 LEVELS OF SECURITY

The first level of data processing security is physical. Physical security protects the system by not allowing physical access to the equipment needed to manipulate the system. This level of security is typified by locked doors, guarded entrances and exits, and limited access to buildings and equipment. This is a necessary level of security but is *far from adequate* by itself.

The next level of security is at the system level. Large computer systems run under a hierarchy of software systems. The usual flow of control is as follows: the operating system software communicates directly with the computer, the DBMS software communicates with the operating system, the DC monitor software communicates with the DBMS and operating system, and finally, the application programs communicate with the DBMS and/or DC monitor. There is a high degree of interwoven activity, and security can be maintained at all or any of those levels.

The most basic level of security is at the operating system level. Because the operating system is at the core of the running of the computer, it has access to facilities that other software components do not have access to, making it a natural target for unauthorized entry into a system. Corresponding to the privileges of the operating system software are its own internal security measures. A very careful balance should be made between the degree of security needed and the overhead of maintaining security at this level. This balance is most critical because the operating system runs at such a fundamental level, and a miscalculation of resources expended can affect adversely everything that runs on the machine.

The next level of security is at the subsystem software level—the DBMS and/or DC monitor level. Like the operating system, these pieces of software have their own internal security features. The difference between the security features at the system and subsystem level is that subsystem security is a bit more localized to its own immediate needs; that is, operating system security is at a general level and subsystem security is at a more specific level. As with operation system security, subsystem software security involves overhead. Typical subsystem security features are terminal password protection, protected operator commands, protected data (by data base, data record level, and data element level), and schema/subschema delineation of data.

The next level of security is application-created security. If the security features employed down to this level of software are not adequate, the designer can always build special features into the application. Before the designer builds security features, he or she should be aware that, in general, the greater the security, the worse the performance and flexibility of the system. As an example, suppose that a designer specifies data encryption into his or her application (which is a common security measure). In this case, before the data is written as output, it is run through a piece of code that "garbles" it. This step is called *encoding*. Upon retrieval of the data, the garbling process is reversed (called *decoding*). This ensures that someone stumbling onto the data, accidentally or otherwise, needs the garbling algorithm to make sense of it.

This process is expensive in that the encoding and decoding process uses extra computer resources and thus affects performance. Furthermore, the encoding/decoding algorithm *forces* every access of the data to go through the process. But there are other implications as well. Flexibility is impaired, because any change in the data must take into account the algorithm that does the encoding/decoding. The issue of flexibility is affected further by the use of the data. If the data is sitting on a tape or disk in encoded form, it *will not* be available for access to such software as a report writer or other software that does automatic retrieval, unless the encode/decode algorithm is implemented somewhere in that software—and that often is not an easy or natural thing to do. Thus there are a whole series of considerations to be made when a designer begins to implement special security features at the application level.

In addition to encryption, password/authorization schemes are commonly written as an application feature. Another application technique to enforce security is that of separation of processing. In this case, entire data bases which are to be secured are kept separate, physically or logically, from all other data bases. Only on special occasions are the secured data bases accessed, and then only by special programs. By introducing this level of separation of processing, the secured data bases are kept safe from a normal operating processing activity.

This concept can be extended to the operation of a system. Many security-conscious shops feel that having multiple hands do critical work is a sound philosophy. This is similar to having two keys to open a lock and making sure different people control each key. One problem with this approach is that it costs more in manpower and often slows whatever process is being protected because of the added level of bureaucracy.

9.3 BREAKING SECURITY

There are at least three major ways in which security is broken. The first is technically. In this case, the security barriers are overcome technically. Very often the dishonest technician enters a system indirectly then uses his entry for personal gain. As an example, suppose that a DBMS contains a list of terminals and associated passwords, and that the DBMS protects the list quite adequately. It is possible, through the operating system software, to locate that data and bypass the security measures of the DBMS to determine the actual values.

The second way that security is broken is "personally." Even if a system has many levels of technical security, as long as there *is* a way to access sensitive data and as long as *somebody* knows how to get through the technical barriers to get to the data, the security of the system can be violated by making personal contact with the person who knows how to use the system and learning what that person knows. The fact is that you cannot entirely protect against an "inside" breach of security—some people, somewhere, simply have to be trusted, and if they weaken or fail, all other security measures are useless.

The third major way in which security is broken is when the designer purposefully creates "private" code or sections of the system. In this case the designer has instigated features that only he or she knows about, so that later the designer can break security.

As an example, consider the horse player who is a programmer and has established his routines as part of the heavily secured accounting system. The programmer does not care about the accounting system. He only cares that he can get access to computer resources through the accounting system to run his calculations for the next day's races.

Whatever security measures are implemented, there should be a justification for them based on the following criteria:

- How sensitive is the data? What is the worst that can happen if the data is misused? Abused? What is the probability that it will be abused?
- How much money does the system make or save for the company? What is the cost of the security features?
- What security features can be implemented later?

9.4 AUDITING SYSTEMS

Auditing of systems is a passive security measure. It is not a deterrent in an active or direct sense, in that it tracks only what has happened. By itself it will not deter someone from violating security at the moment of violation.

However, in the sense that a person knows his or her activity will be audited, auditing is a passive deterrent to system abuse.

There are several approaches to auditing that are useful in security systems. The first is through the regular logging of all system activity. Logging occurs at the operating system level, at the subsystem level, and can be implemented at the application level. Logging involves very large volumes of activity and it is usually a major problem to manage the huge amount of data that has been collected to determine what is meaningful. However, audit data bases or files can be scanned for exceptional situations without scrutinizing every detail on the file or data base.

A second approach to auditing is to select one or more sensitive places and audit all the activity that passes through them (as opposed to all activity that passes through the system). These audits may make use of hardware monitors or software monitors. They differ from an audit of system logging functions in that the system logging function is regularly done for *all* system activity, whereas monitoring of the media is usually done only for activity flowing through the device(s) or process(es) selected. Depending on exactly what is monitored and where, the output may include much extraneous data. For example, suppose that line traffic is being monitored. All the messages up and down the line are collected. It may be that there is a highly unusual activity under scrutiny, but it will probably be buried within much very normal activity. Thus it is desirable, if at all possible, to be able to select the data that will be monitored.

The third approach to auditing—critical-point auditing—can appear in many forms. It is characterized by a scrutiny of critical system points and times. On a predetermined basis, certain crucial points in the system are audited. This may mean a physical check of who is using what devices, a special program that analyzes data selectively, or a monitor of several critical points of the system at a critical time. This approach to auditing differs from the previous in that monitoring of the media is usually done over a relatively long period of time for all activity that flows through a particular point of the media, whereas critical-point auditing measures data over a short time span and may even be done interactively, given the right set of technical tools.

9.5 DISASTER PLANNING

Closely related to the issue of security is the issue of disaster planning. Every data processing shop should periodically assess the consequences of a major and permanent loss of data, programs, systems, and equipment. The loss could be caused by fire, earthquake, vandalism, or other reasons. Given the sophistication and fragility of many parts of the data processing environment, it is obvious that data processing may become a company's Achilles' heel.

The usual strategy to prepare for disaster is removal of copies of critical assets to a physically separate site. This means data, systems, documentation, and anything else that is vital to the running of the company's data processing system. The removal of data and programs must be done periodically, as the content changes.

It is worthwhile on occasion to practice recovery procedures from the off-site facilities. How often this recovery practice should take place depends on the relative risks involved. Certainly, the wrong time to do the first recovery is in the advent of a real disaster. The feasibility of any plan is always suspect until it is exercised.

REFERENCES

DoLotta, T. A., M. I. Bernstein, R. S. Dickson, Jr., N. A. France, B. A. Rosenblatt, D. M. Smith, and T. B. Steel, Jr., *Data Processing in 1980–1985*, Wiley-Interscience, New York, 1976.

Hoffman, L. J., *Modern Methods for Computer Security and Privacy*, Prentice-Hall, Inc., Englewood Cliffs, N.J., 1977.

Lecht, Charles, *Waves of Change*, Advanced Computer Techniques Corporation, New York, 1977.

Lientz, Bennet, and Burton Swanson, *Software Maintenance Management*, Addison-Wesley Publishing Company, Inc., Reading, Mass., 1980.

Smith, Robert, *Privacy—How To Protect What's Left of It*, Anchor Press/Doubleday, Garden City, N.Y., 1979.

Yearsley, R. B., and G. M. R. Graham, *Handbook of Computer Management*, Gower Press, Epping, Essex, England, 1973.

CASE STUDY

The New York High Rise Rental Association has been in business for the past 35 years. Their primary function is to manage commercial rentals throughout Manhattan. The business blossomed so much that they computerized their first system six years ago. Since then, they have built many applications—billing, payroll, accounts payable, accounts receivable, and so on. Management has not been particularly concerned with computer security. The computer room is secured physically and the payroll data base has certain checks and balances that make management feel that everything is in order.

A new system—inventory and storage—is being built. Because it does not have anything to do with cash flow directly, there is very little concern for security. The emphasis instead is on quick construction of the sequential system.

Unbeknown to management, one of the programmers has a job on the side. The programmer runs a newspaper delivery service and must bill his customers and keep track of accounts due. Since the programmer is in charge of one entire block of programs, he inserts code that will allow him to perform his moonlighting functions as a regular part of the inventory and storage system. He is able to disguise the input so that it is virtually indistinguishable from any other input and he routes this output to a special printer. He arranges to have two sets of source code, so that to detect a problem an inspector would have to go to the actual machine code that the computer executes. For several months now the moonlighting business has blossomed.

Several months after the inventory and storage system has been implemented, the maintenance costs take an unexplained rise. When this goes on for three months in a row, management becomes suspicious and calls in an outside auditing firm. After much analysis of records, it is noted that New York High Rise is paying for maintenance goods never received.

A trace through New York's systems (which is a very complex and tedious process) shows that someone is receipting the delivery of goods never received and placing the acknowledgment in the inventory and storage system. From there, the acknowledgment triggers a payment in the accounts payable system. At this point, management has lost about $250,000 in unexplained losses and $25,000 in special auditing costs. Management wishes now that it had paid closer attention to the security requirements of the inventory and storage system.

Comment on the Following

1. The primary goal of security is to focus on how the company might be defrauded.
2. There are many aspects of security.
3. There are many levels of security.
4. Auditing is only a passive restraint.
5. In some cases, the security risks are so great that financial loss cannot be calculated.
6. Retrofitting security into a system is easier to do than retrofitting performance or availability. Still, the best time to build security into a system is at the point of design.
7. Every security feature costs money. The potential gain should be evaluated against the cost.
8. The latent problem of the moonlighting programmer has yet not surfaced.

MULTIPLE-CHOICE QUESTIONS

1. The systems designer is very concerned with security. He has designed passwords to get into data and onto terminals. He has encrypted the data internally. He has broken sensitive functions into a series of steps that must be done by several people. He has instigated a procedure to change passwords on a frequent and random basis.

   A. Even with all security measures taken, a clever and determined outsider could still get into the system.

   B. The security measures taken are sure to have a negative effect—to some degree—on the operationality and performance of the system.

   C. The risks should be balanced against the probability of unauthorized use of the system and its cost.

   D. Even with all of the security measures noted above, there is nothing that prevents the development programmer from building private, unspecified code.

   E. It is worthwhile monitoring such activities as unsuccessful password entries to determine if a pattern develops.

*2. A designer has specified that a data base be encrypted. The data base has variable-length records defined in it. Much space is saved and data is secure, but a problem arises when an error occurs in the disk on which the data resides. The problem is that some normal recovery methods will not work on the variable-length, encrypted data.

   A. Query languages will not work on the data unless the encryption/decryption algorithms are used in the query language.

   B. Raw scans of the data will be very difficult to interpret.

   C. Normally used utilities may have to be altered to access the secured data.

   D. The worst that can happen is that entire sections of the data base may be lost. The designer should weigh the chance of that loss against the extra security of having the data encrypted.

   E. Even data encryption can be broken, so there is still a potential security problem, however unlikely it is.

EXERCISES AND ESSAYS

1. Describe the various levels of security. Give three or four examples of security at each level. Describe what it would take to break through the various security measures.

2. Why can security measures be retrofitted more easily than other attributes, such as performance or availability?

3. Are audit data bases in which every transaction logs its request prior to execution a good idea in general? For performance? For availability? For operational stability? For the programmer? What are the advantages? Disadvantages?

SPECIFIC
TOPICS

X

Selecting a DBMS

□□□

When the time comes to select a DBMS for a shop there are two basic choices: to purchase the software or to write the DBMS from scratch. When a shop builds its own DBMS the record shows few long term successes, so it is not surprising that most shops choose to buy software. The problems with "homemade" software usually stem from the fact that the result has a limited amount of function. The architects of the "homemade" DBMS usually have a set of criteria under which the software is built, and quite often those criteria are adequately met. The problem is not with the criteria under which the software *is* built but with the criteria under which the software *is not* built but *should have been* built. Because *all* criteria were not initially considered under which homemade software is constructed, such software ultimately has one or more severe limitations.

It is normal for a homemade DBMS to be fairly successful the first few times it is used. The problems arise when the homemade DBMS is required to do something other than what it was originally intended to do. This may mean handling a larger amount of data than originally intended, processing transactions at a higher arrival rate or at a higher volume than planned, recovering data efficiently, ensuring internal integrity of the processing, allowing data to be semantically altered, or allowing a different type of processing to occur. There are a seemingly endless set of criteria by which the DBMS must be measured and, if these criteria are not considered, it can cause real problems for the shop building the software when a limitation manifests itself. It is common for the architects of a homemade DBMS to have thought of *some* future needs, but usually not *all* future needs and this is the real weakness of homemade software. At some point well after the DBMS has been established (when it is normally too late to change the DBMS in any fundamental way), the problems caused by criteria missed by the software architects manifest themselves and general dissatisfaction results.

This does not mean that *every* "homemade" DBMS is a failure (or a "partial success" as data processing failures are often called). There are a few notable exceptions, but even in those successful cases the homegrown software has limitations and can seldom be extended to meet *all* the needs of the shop. Another problem arises with personnel who support and use the homegrown software. Quite a few people do not want to get into a situation where they are heavily experienced with a homegrown DBMS, because this greatly limits their own marketability.

10.1 PURCHASING A DBMS

The usual course a shop takes in acquiring a DBMS is to purchase software from a vendor. One obvious reason for this is to avoid the development costs and effort needed for a complex piece of software. Also, purchased software can be obtained immediately (or at least very quickly), so the lead time inherent to a development effort is cut drastically. There are other reasons why shops choose to purchase software.

If a DBMS is a commonly used product, there will be an available talent pool to draw on. A shop can hire designers and programmers with expertise (although such persons may command a premium price). Also, for a commonly used DBMS there will probably be supporting peripheral products, such as data base auditing utilities, teleprocessing monitors, statistical analysis packages, and testing facilities. A shop will not be faced with having to create the many auxiliary pieces of software from scratch. A DBMS that is commonly used will accommodate a shop when the shop needs to upgrade for a new generation of hardware and/or SCPs.

Another benefit to purchasing a DBMS is the availability of vendor personnel to aid in "fixit" situations. Whenever a software failure occurs in the DBMS, the vendor has a responsibility to see that it does a minimum amount of damage to the user if the problem lies in the software. Such is not the case, of course, when a shop creates its own DBMS. "Fixit" personnel must be made available at all times, whether their services are required or not, when a shop creates its own software. This ever-present need for personnel can present an undesirable overhead for a shop. Another benefit in purchasing software is in sharing experiences with other shops that have the same software. This is not possible, of course, when a shop builds its own DBMS.

10.2 SELECTING A DBMS

At first glance, selecting a DBMS appears to be an easy, straightforward task. Vendors are always happy to talk about their products. The DBMSs that are offered commercially generally have plenty of functions and can usually run on many classes of machines and under various operating systems (SCPs). There are surveys, magazine articles, and news articles that tout success stories of these DBMSs on a regular basis. Thus it appears that DBMS selection is an almost trivial task. That illusion would be shattered if the evaluator had just *ONE* good opportunity to investigate fully a case where a company was *forced* to migrate from one DBMS to another because of one or more shortcomings of the first DBMS selected. The traumatic experiences* that occur when a DBMS is improperly chosen would alert the evaluator that there is much more to DBMS selection than merely jotting down a few facts supplied by a vendor about one DBMS as opposed to another.

Certainly the evaluator must survey the DBMS products that are available, but dealing with most vendors is a tricky business. A favorite vendor ploy (and a legitimate one at that) is to find something that can be offered that other competing vendors cannot offer, and then to emphasize that difference very strongly. Relating that difference to the business of the evaluator's company further strengthens the vendor's point. The problem is that other competing vendors are doing the same thing to that vendor's product that he or she is doing to theirs, and what normally results is not an analysis of which DBMS is best for a given circumstance or for the long run, but which vendor personality can make the most convincing case, which may not be at all in the company's best interest.

Another tactic is for the vendor to supply the evaluator with references. The problem is that *no* vendor is going to supply references where serious problems have cropped up with the vendor's product, yet it is the cases where serious problems have occurred that will be the most interesting. There may be some value in checking vendor-supplied references, but the odds are excellent that the accounts will be glowing. This also applies to other vendors, so that the evaluator gets nothing but positive reports about *all* the DBMSs being evaluated. The fact of the matter is that it is *very* difficult to find experienced, knowledgeable, unbiased opinion.

10.3 OTHER SELECTION CRITERIA

If vendor contact can be misleading, what other avenues are open to the person evaluating software? One option is benchmarking. A benchmark is a measured execution of one or more samples of the work load typical of the shop being benchmarked. The first problem with benchmarking is that it is expensive and time consuming, but there are other problems as well. If the shop being benchmarked does not carefully select what is to be benchmarked, the results may be meaningless because the benchmark does not necessarily reflect anything significant about what is going on (or will be going on) in the shop. The work selected for benchmarking should be a representative sample of the customer's environment.

---

*These type of experiences are known in the data processing industry as "war stories."

A second pitfall is in the selection of requirements for benchmarking. By selecting an improper set of requirements, a benchmark can be terribly biased, so much so that the results of the benchmark are decided before the first run is executed. If an evaluator has a preference, he or she can bias the benchmark so much that the results are a foregone conclusion. In evaluating the results of a benchmark, care must be taken to ensure that bias is not inherent from the outset and that the requirements are in fact appropriate for the shop being benchmarked.

Finally, benchmarking results may be heavily influenced by competency of the vendor. One vendor may send inexperienced people to construct, run, and tune the work to be run on its software, whereas another vendor may supply very experienced people. The end result may be more of a comparison of the quality of the people running the benchmark than a measure of the relative merits of the software.

If talking with vendors can be misleading and benchmarking can be misleading, what other avenues of evaluation are open? Another option is to read market surveys. These surveys typically are put out by magazines, newspapers, and independent survey organizations. There is often very useful information in these media. On occasion material appears of very dubious validity. The evaluator searching for meaningful data on which to make a comparison would do well to look closely not just at the conclusions presented but how those conclusions were reached. Often the basis for the conclusions is much more interesting than the actual conclusions.

Consider a market survey and how it may be biased (either accidentally or otherwise). What did the survey ask? How was it worded? Who responded? Were they qualified to respond? Who was included? Who was excluded? How subjective was the survey? How objective? With just a little imagination the reader can see that surveys can be made to reflect a predetermined conclusion. In fact, it is difficult not to introduce some degree of prejudgment into surveys, polls, and so on. Therefore, the evaluator should weigh the results of surveys very cautiously.

Another phenomenon at work in influencing the results of surveys is that there is a tendency for the largest and most widely known software to present itself as the most exposed, most vulnerable product. Because a software product is widely used, there will be more occasions where the software has had problems under different circumstances. It is easy to concentrate on these problems and proclaim that less widely used software would have performed better. This *may* or *may not* be true. It is entirely possible that *any* software would have performed poorly under the same circumstances but the software most widely used just happened to be the product being used at that time and place. Thus the more widely used a product is, the easier it is to attack, especially in light of unknown quantities. This ability to "expose" commonly found software is a regular topic of discussion in the trade journals, and may be more the result of the immaturity of the industry than the weakness of the product being discussed.

Another source of information is the outside consultant. Although there are many knowledgeable consultants, care should be taken that a strongly biased consultant not influence a decision unduly.

The preceding discussion should have alerted the reader to the fact that it is indeed difficult to determine the relative merits of a DBMS.

10.4 REDIRECTING THE ANALYSIS

In general, most DBMS *can* do quite a few things. They can allow data to be represented in a number of ways; they can allow data to be accessed sequentially; they can allow data to be accessed and manipulated on-line; they can operate under different operating systems; and so forth. This means that when the evaluator is determining what a DBMS *can* do, the results will be that it *can* do just about anything desired. But so can almost any other DBMS. So the investigation should shift from "what a DBMS *can* do" to "what a DBMS *cannot* do," or "what a DBMS *cannot* do well."

The issue is not finding a DBMS that has capabilities but finding a DBMS that is best suited for the needs of the organization. For all of the *total* capabilities offered by a DBMS, usually only a subset of those capabilities are done easily and naturally. DBMS selection is more effectively done when focusing on the subset of capabilities performed well rather than on the total capabilities.

10.5 TOTAL SYSTEM NEEDS

Another pitfall in DBMS evaluation is that of using only the immediate requirements at hand for DBMS selection. The evaluation should look well down the road and anticipate the full set of requirements for the DBMS. As an example of the worst that can happen, a company sets out to select a DBMS. Part of the rationale for going data base is to satisfy the requirements on a new project—project A. A thorough analysis is done for project A and a set of requirements is drawn up for the DBMS. Based on the requirements, a DBMS is selected and work begins to progress.

Project A is built and one of two things happens. Either project A undergoes change and a new requirement is generated after the fact, or a new project—project B—comes on the scene with a new set of requirements. In either case, the DBMS evaluator is *lucky* if the changing requirements fit well within the environment of the DBMS. If the DBMS chosen to fit the initial set of requirements is inadequate, the shop is faced with making some nasty choices. The point is, in selecting a DBMS, the evaluator should emphasize and anticipate future requirements as well as the immediate set of requirements. Some of the reasons a DBMS may fail to provide long-term satisfaction are: the inability of the DBMS to handle large amounts of data, its inability to handle large numbers of transactions (for the data communications component of a full-function DBMS), its inability to sustain a high transaction rate, its inability to recover data gracefully, its inability to handle concurrent updates, and its inability to allow data to be redefined without much effort.

10.6 DATA BASE TRANSPORTABILITY

The evaluator would not have to be concerned with the future requirements as much as he or she is if it were not for the fact that, in general, data base applications are not transportable from one DBMS to another. This means that application code written for a DBMS usually stays with that DBMS. If there is a need to go to another DBMS, the application code must be re-written from scratch. Some code may be salvaged, but not much.

10.7 EVALUATING DBMS

If the goal is not so much to discover the capabilities of a DBMS, but to discover limitations, the evaluator should pay careful attention to the following:

1. *Maximum throughput.* What is the highest transaction arrival rate that can be processed without a queue building?
2. *Total throughput.* How many *total* transactions can be handled for a given period of time?
3. *Data base structuring.* What logical and physical structures can the DBMS support? What are the economies in choosing a given structure? The complexities?
4. *Data communications networking (for the DC component).* What network configurations are supported? Not supported?
5. *Flexibility.* How difficult is it to change data structures?
6. *System availability.* What expectations are reasonable for system up-time? How long will recovery take? Reorganization? Restructuring of data?
7. *Data base size.* What is the technically imposed maximum size of data that can be built? The pragmatic maximum?
8. *Personnel availability.* Are personnel available to staff, design, and programming positions? Can personnel be trained? Hired?

9. *Vendor.* What confidence is there in the vendor for support? Future enhancements? High-priority bug shooting? Responsiveness?

CASE STUDY

The Nebraska Corn Husking Company has had sequential systems for about six years now. Each year, the number of systems grows. In the past two years, that growth has been phenomenal. Management is aware of the fact that the systems being produced overlap a great deal and run on much redundant data. Management also realizes that in the current environment, data can be accessed only sequentially and there are many occasions where direct access to data would save much unnecessary processing.

The vice-president of finance (to whom the director of data processing reports) has read in a magazine that data base can cure many of the problems facing the Nebraska Corn Husking Company. The vice-president rejects the idea of building an in-house DBMS and sets out to evaluate the software that is available. He appoints a committee for the evaluation of DBMS to be headed by the DBA.

Two DBMS are being seriously considered: DBMSA from vendor A and DBMSB from vendor B. The review committee is making its decision in light of the first application to go up on the DBMS. That application will be batch, involves a small amount of data that is fairly complex in terms of its structuring, and entails about 10% updating and 90% inquiry.

Vendor A is called in to demonstrate the good qualities of DBMSA. DBMSA is based on a structuring of data that is unique and handles inquiries very efficiently. DBMSA is promised to have on-line capabilities next year. Currently, it operates only in batch. DBMSA has the reputation of being very easy to use, thus making possible quick construction of applications. After the meeting, the vendor privately takes the DBA and his wife to dinner in a very expensive restaurant.

Vendor B is also called in for evaluation of DBMSB. DBMSB is a full-function DBMS. It is used widely and operates in on-line and in batch. It can handle any imaginable amount of data. Plenty of independent software packages are available for tuning, monitoring, and so on. DBMSB is reputed to be difficult to use, but it is suspected that this reputation stems from the fact that it is widely and heavily used. The application that is first to go onto a DBMS at Nebraska Corn Husking is not optimal for DBMSB because DBMSB handles updates more easily than it handles inquiries. The salesman for DBMSB takes the vice-president and his wife out to dinner in the best country club in town.

The evaluation committee meets again and the vendor for DBMSA is recalled. The vendor points out how ideal her company's software will be for the application to go data base. She stresses the differences in the basic structuring of data between DBMSA and DBMSB. She points out industry surveys that discuss the weaknesses of DBMSB. She leaves giving five good references for her DBMS.

The evaluation committee ends up considering three alternatives:

1. Choose DBMSA. The software is easy to use, there have been few complaints in the industry about it, and it is ideal for the application to be put onto the data base. The DBA firmly supports this decision.

2. Choose DBMSB. This software offers great promise in the long term, even though it is not optimal for the application chosen for data base. The vice-president supports this decision.

3. Choose vendor A's software for the first application and convert to vendor B's software later if additional functions are needed.   ■

Comment on the Following

1. Converting application programs from one DBMS to another is a fairly straightforward thing to do. The calls must be reformatted and some logic may change, but that is all there is to it.

2. Taking a system written for batch and converting it on-line is easy to do.

3. The internal structural capabilities of a DBMS are one of the most important factors in comparing one DBMS to another.

4. On-line integrity and throughput should be at the top of the list in evaluating the software capabilities of a DBMS.

5. All or most batch systems eventually will be on-line.

6. The ease of use of a DBMS should be at the top of the list in evaluating a DBMS.

7. The reputation of the vendor and post sales support are only minor considerations in evaluating a DBMS.

8. If a DBMS has a practical limitation on the amount of data that it can handle, there is no problem as long as an application does not exceed that amount.

9. The "courting" of select people in the organization by vendors is unfair and unethical.

10. The long-term considerations of a DBMS are *much* more important than the short-term considerations.

MULTIPLE-CHOICE QUESTIONS

1. Three years ago management selected a DBMS based on what seemed to be a fair evaluation. Unfortunately, the DBMS cannot process on-line transactions as needed. Management must either "get the DBMS to work" or find another software package.
    A. At this point, all of management's options are painful.
    B. Even by making enough fuss, management cannot embarrass the vendor into "making the DBMS work."
    C. Duplexing the system (running two versions to reduce the necessary throughput) is not an option unless data can also be duplexed.
    D. Converting to another DBMS will probably involve a system rewrite.
    E. This predicament should have been foreseen.

*2. Management has formed a committee for DBMS evaluation. They have placed two systems programmers and an operation's supervisor on the committee. Not surprisingly, the committee's priorities for selection are heavily weighted toward the technical side of the software.
    A. Ease of installation should be a major concern.
    B. The periodic genning of the DBMS and the controls of the system's caretaker are extremely important.
    C. How the internal structure of the data is implemented is of great interest.
    D. The internal architecture of the DBMS should be the primary target of investigation.
    E. Randomization algorithms and the internal space utilization techniques rate as candidates for serious evaluation.

EXERCISES AND ESSAYS

1. Create a list of essentials and priorities for DBMS evaluation.
2. How does DBMS evaluation differ from software evaluation in general?
3. How can management that makes a poor decision concerning DBMS selection be made responsible for its decision?

XI

Selecting Projects for Data Base

□□

11.1 ADVANTAGES OF DATA BASE

Data base is a tool that can be used to create an environment for optimal use of data. Without data base, it is not particularly easy to retrieve data directly and still enjoy other benefits associated with data base, such as logical masking of data (i.e., the presentation of data in a form other than the form in which it is physically stored), data integrity, and data sharing across many applications. Prior to data base the system architect had to be quite sensitive to the details pertinent to how data was stored, the mechanisms of on-line accessing of data, and so on. The programmer had to build into programs many specifics for the handling of on-line data that made future program changes very difficult.

Data base freed the architect and the programmer of many of these details. The result was an enhanced or new capability for the end user. Direct-access storage devices could now be used in more than an indexed sequential manner.* Programmers had at their disposal new and more powerful ways to handle data. The programmer could be free of massive sorts, merges, and multifile match programs.

Another advantage of "going data base" was as a preparation to going on-line. Centralizing data under a single controller was an important preliminary step necessary to the control function that would be realized in the on-line environment. And ultimately, the on-line environment would lead to the most effective use of human time that the computer could accomplish. Thus going data base had its own merits and was a stepping stone to future benefits.

---

*Prior to data base, data that could be stored physically on direct-access storage was commonly accessed in an indexed sequential fashion. The storage mechanism allowed programmers to access data randomly (using the index) but it did not support the many features found in a full-function DBMS, and there were problems peculiar to the loading, deletion, and insertion of data in this access mode.

142

11.2 PROJECTS THAT FIT WELL IN THE DATA BASE CONCEPT

Some projects fit naturally with the data base concept and can realize immediate benefits. Typical good matches include the following:

1. Where there is a medium-size to large volume of data, data base is fairly well suited to handle a volume of data that would otherwise be awkward to handle. Certainly there are problems with large data bases, but those problems can nearly always be addressed at the design level. For very small amounts of data, it simply may not be worth the cost of construction to go to data base. As a general rule of thumb, the volumes of data that can be used to delineate large from medium from small are shown in Figure 11.1. The reader should note that these sizes are relative to a particular time and will undoubtedly change. Also, a spindle is taken to be a 3350-size device (a class of IBM direct access devices), capable of holding about 317 million (unblocked or unsized) bytes.

Large	Medium	Small
> 20 spindles	2 to 20 spindles	0 to 2 spindles
Average = 25+ spindles	Average = 4 spindles	Average = < 1 spindle

Figure 11.1 Data base sizes.

2. Where data is relatively stable, data represent values and structure found in one or more users' environment. Over time, every user's environment changes—the only difference is the degree and speed with which change occurs. As the user's environment changes, the data that represent that environment must also change, and this change is usually not an easy thing to accomplish. Thus data base best fits in environments where the fundamental nature of the user's data is fairly stable. As a rule of thumb, data base is best suited for systems where 5% or less of the fundamental data relationships and elements undergo redefinition in the time frame of two years or less. Where the rate of semantic change is higher than this, data base can be used, but the form of the data may prove to be difficult to change.

3. Where there is a need for high integrity or security, "going data base" can offer all sorts of external control over data that is not easily achieved otherwise. Data base can offer such features as encode/decode exits, monitoring of access and update control of concurrent access, restricted views of data, and so forth. Without data base, it is possible to achieve these functions, but not as easily or in a centralized manner.

4. Where on-line access is (or is going to be) needed, data base is normally the first step to on-line systems because of the capabilities of direct use of disk storage and because of integrity control. Without centralized integrity control, on-line sharing of data is meaningless. Central integrity control refers to on-line management of such occurrences as deadlock

detection,* concurrent updating of data, recoverability of data, and up-to-date currency of information. All of these features are central to the realization of data sharing.

5. Where a number of logical and physical views of the same data are needed, data base allows the programmer and the user to look at the same data in many fundamentally different ways—sequentially, directly, hierarchically, relationally, or as a network (all depending on the specifics of the DBMS and the application, of course). Data base allows a logical structuring of data to be superimposed over a physical structure that may or may not be similar. Data base also allows data and structures of data to be related to other data and structures of data. Applications can work in harmony with other applications whose view of the data is not the same in any way.

6. Where the updating of data is time sensitive, this situation nearly always lends itself to on-line data bases. In this case, absolute up-to-the-second accuracy of data is mandatory. Typical systems are ACP (Airline Control Program—reservation, flight information, etc.) applications and banking applications, where balances need to be instantaneously balanced. In this environment, data base is a necessary step to achieving success.

11.3 DATA BASE AND COST EFFECTIVENESS

Data base can be appropriate for all or some of the aforementioned reasons. The real determination as to whether data base is justified for an application is whether the cost of constructing the application and operating it is more or less than the payback of putting up the application. If costs are more than payback, there probably is good reason for not "going data base." The designer should look at other alternatives.

There is one possible exception to the cost justification of a data base application. On occasion an application is built as a pilot project or as a study, preparing the way for a more ambitious effort. In this case, the learning experience, not necessarily the usefulness of the project, justifies its existence.

11.4 WHERE DATA BASE IS NOT JUSTIFIED

When looking at all the advantages of data base, it is tempting to say that any project is a valid candidate for data base. The temptation is such that in

---

*Deadlock occurs when two programs are running at the same time. Program A controls data base A and cannot continue until it accesses data base B. At the same instant, program B controls data base B and is seeking to access data base A. It is also referred to as the "deadly embrace."

years past data base was hailed as a panacea—curing problems from programmer productivity to ultimate user satisfaction. Such is not the case; data base fits well in many places, but not in all places. Although data base does solve some problems, it is by no means a panacea. Some of the types of applications where data base is typically a poor fit are those in which:

1. The probable accessibility of the data is low. This may occur where large amounts of data are involved and only a limited amount of data will be accessed because of a low volume of activity or interest in the data. In either case, the data's usefulness must be weighed versus the cost of building and maintaining the data.

2. There are large amounts of data whose usage historically has been unpredictable or unknown. This type of system can be cast in the mold of a data base environment, but there is the danger that the particular logical or physical structure of data will be unsuitable. In this case, if data base is specified, it is prudent to create physically "normalized" structures, bringing data down to its "lowest common denominator" (refer to Chapters 13 to 15 in *Computer Data Base Organization* by James Martin). This may be costly in terms of physical implementation, but will give the system architect the most long-term flexibility.

3. There is no great need for integrity, security, or data sharing. In some systems there is not a pressing need for the features described earlier. Ordinary applications and operations outside data base provide all the necessary control; thus no extra features are required.

4. The fundamental data and data relationships are constantly and unpredictably changing in the user's environment. In this case it may be difficult to automate any or all of the user's needs, much less put them onto data base. Each change ultimately ripples through the definition of the data to the application code. As it does, a great deal of maintenance is required and the exposure to error grows.

5. There is little data and it is only of limited usefulness to a few people. In this case it may not be right to build a full-blown system. Something smaller and more limited in scope may be in order.

In short, the dividing line of what should or should not be data base is the comparison of the costs of data base versus the payback. Development costs refer to design costs and program testing and implementation costs. Operational costs refer to storage costs, execution costs, hardware overhead, and personnel required—both in the computer room and at the user's site(s) Payback comes by replacing old systems, reducing staffing requirements in the user's department, and providing timely information that allows the company to do its business more inexpensively or effectively.

11.5 DATA BASE HIERARCHY OF SYSTEMS

Within the realm of data base, there is a hierarchy of systems and storage. The amounts of data, the nature of the data, and the timeliness of the data all play a part in determining where an application fits in this hierarchy. This somewhat generalized hierarchy is depicted by Figure 11.2, where it is seen that the media (DASD, tape, incore storage, etc.) are more accessible the smaller the amount of data handled and the greater the probability of access of the data. Not coincidentally, there is a perfect correlation between

Type	Media	Probability of access	Cost of storage	Amount of data	Comments
On-line	Main storage/ DASD	High	High	Small to medium	Most complex environment; most difficult to build applications for
Batch	DASD	Medium	Medium	Medium to large	Not as many measures of success; less difficult to build applications for
Archival	DASD/ tape/ mass storage	Low	Low	Large to very large	Least difficult* to build applications for

* Archival systems can be considered the least difficult to build systems for because the time for retrieval and use of data is normally greater than the equivalent time in batch. There are other factors that complicate archival systems, such as making allowances for the change of definition and meaning of data over time, that may make them not so easy to construct.

Figure 11.2 Hierarchy of data base systems.

the cost of storage and the probability of access (i.e., the greater the cost of storage, the higher the probability of access). The complexity of building applications decreases as the need for data becomes less immediate. In selecting projects for data base, it behooves the analyst to ask not only if this project is a good candidate for data base, but also if this project *is* good for data base, what type of system is it best suited for? Figure 11.2 gives a thumbnail sketch of selection criteria.

11.6 DATA BASE SUBSYSTEMS (OR SPIN–OFFS)

In addition to the hierarchy of data base systems, there is a classification of applications that can be called data base subsystems. The term "subsystems" does *not* imply an element of inferiority or subservience; instead, it implies a different mode of operation and a different set of philosophies from a fully functional production on-line data base system. These subsystems are the tool by which "usable" systems are realized. Examples of the type of subsystem software products that support these subsystems are Query By Example (QBE), NOMAD, Focus, and Ramis.

For one reason or the other, these software systems are normally not found driving large on-line, fully functional production systems. Such reasons might be limited update capabilities, limited networking capabilities, resource utilization, or recovery/integrity considerations. Just because these systems usually are not driving fully functional on-line data base applications does not mean that they are not useful. On the contrary, they can be very useful — delivering at last some of the "management information system" capabilities promised so long ago. How, then, can they be used as a subsystem?

The real power of these subsystems is that they put the end user much closer to the data than he or she has ever been before. In some cases data processing is *entirely* removed from the processing loop. By putting the user close to the data, some of the backlog of demands for new facilities from the data processing department are eased. Because of this, subsystems (as presented in this book) are the key to usable systems and are *very* important in the next stage of evolution of data processing.

The normal way these subsystems are used is by "freezing" data in a production environment and extracting all or selected parts of the production data and reformatting the data into a usable form known to the subsystem. Thus the term "spin-off" applies to these subsystems. This process is depicted in Figure 11.3, where data is extracted from the production data

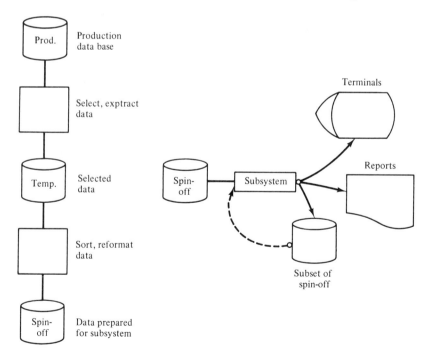

Figure 11.3 Spin-off process.

base and put into spin-off form. Once the spin-off data is created, the subsystem allows terminals to query the data, allows reports to be written, and allows further subsets to be created and used as input to the subsystem. Normally, updating is not part of the philosophy of data base subsystems, since the effects of updating will be negated the next time the spin-off is recreated from the major production data base. Where applications are run entirely under the subsystem, updating must of course be done.

One of the major utilities of data base subsystems is that they allow the user to look at data in many ways very easily. In a full-scale production data base system, the user is normally locked into viewing and using the data in the manner prescribed by the application programs that support the application (Figure 11.4). That view is not easily changed.

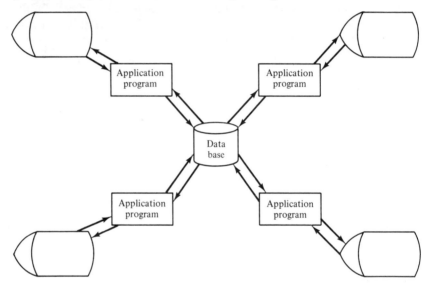

Figure 11.4 Full production data base system.

Such is not the case in a data base subsystem. The very nature of the data base subsystem is such that the program(s) that accesses the data is very easy to write and to change; thus users can change their views very easily. There is a typical pattern in using data base subsystems:

1. Extract data
2. Sort and reformat data
3. Run a report or query
4. Rethink needs
5. Reiterate the loop from step 2 until needs are satisfied

The user can sort, shape, or format the data in many ways very easily.

Furthermore, the user has little or no impact on the base production system. Only at the point of extraction is there an interruption in the activity of the base system. There is one drawback, of course, which is that the user is not working with an up-to-the-minute copy of the data since the data is correct only up to the point of the extract. These systems are used primarily for summarized decision making, where trends are more important than exact up-to-the-minute status (i.e., decision-making systems as opposed to operational systems). Figure 11.5 illustrates the relationship of primary systems to subsystems and the flow of data.

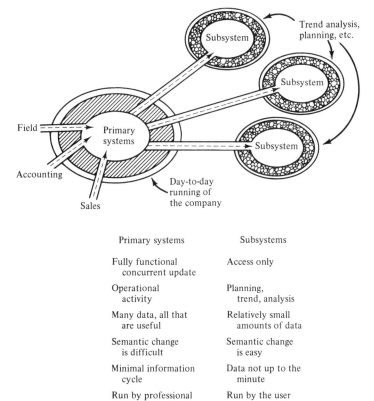

Primary systems	Subsystems
Fully functional concurrent update	Access only
Operational activity	Planning, trend, analysis
Many data, all that are useful	Relatively small amounts of data
Semantic change is difficult	Semantic change is easy
Minimal information cycle	Data not up to the minute
Run by professional DP	Run by the user
All data useful to company	Selected data useful to user

Figure 11.5 Relationship of primary systems to subsystems and flow of data.

11.7 CONTROLLING DATA

Is the domain of the data administrator restricted to data base systems? If so, what are the appropriate trade-offs? Normally, the function of data administration goes up to the point of extracting data for spin-off files.

Once the data is extracted, users of the data base subsystem can do what they want. In theory, this works well at the beginning of the use of data base subsystems, but over time, users may want more and more data and more and more function.

A rule of thumb for the control of data administration is to relinquish control at the point of the interface extract unless: (1) permanent files are being created to operate on each iteration of the extract, or (2) significant amounts of data are being processed that are similar or identical to other subsystem processing. If either of the above is occurring, the data administrator may want to step in and investigate. The danger is that redundant systems may be evolving.

Spinoff systems hold promise of being an increasingly important tool in the future. Certain major problems of data processing, such as productivity, are greatly enhanced by these systems and there are no great technological barriers to be overcome.

11.8 UNLOCKING THE POTENTIAL OF THE DATA BASE CONCEPT

It is a temptation to use a DBMS as just another file access method. When this is done (and it is very common) very few of the benefits of "going data base" will be realized. Realizing the benefits of data base is much more than simply selecting, purchasing, and implementing software. Data base software provides the *potential* for achieving many benefits. It is up to the application architects to use that potential.

As an example of some "myths" about data base, consider the following:

1. Data base makes data shareable. This is true only if the data has been designed with a broader perspective than the single set of requirements for one user for one system that immediately justify the data base. Data that is to be shared must be structured with sharing in mind; otherwise, it is only an accident when sharing can occur.

2. On-line systems will give quick access to date. This is true only if performance has been designed into the system. For example, if the application programmer scans an entire data base, just because the application is on-line, there will not be good performance.

3. Data base makes applications (code and programs) easy to change. Just as performance is realized only when designed into the application, flexibility is realized only when designed into the application. There is nothing magic about changing data definitions or the form of the data that can be achieved with data base.

4. On-line data base systems make data available whenever the user needs the data. In light of large data bases or interconnected data bases in

particular, availability becomes an issue. Periodically, data bases need certain utilitarian types of activity to be performed on them, such as restructuring, reorganization, or recovery. At these times the data will not be available to satisfy the needs of the user. However, careful design will minimize the pains of the user.

5. Data bases will integrate data systems. Data integration is much more than a technical issue. Technically, data base systems allow an organization to integrate data, but only if the organization has the discipline, maturity, and control to be integrated will integration occur.

REFERENCES

Date, C. J., *An Introduction to Data Base Management Systems*, 3rd ed., Addison-Wesley Publishing Company, Inc., Reading, Mass., 1981.

Martin, James, *Computer Data Base Organization*, 2nd ed., Prentice-Hall, Inc., Englewood Cliffs, N.J., 1977.

Query-By-Example: Terminal User's Guide, IBM Manual SH20-20780-0.

CASE STUDY

The Nashville National Insurance Company has been in the life insurance business since 1872. It began insuring automobiles, homes, and businesses in 1921 and has been growing at a steady rate for years. The company could not exist without records, and those records are stored primarily on magnetic tape. The first automated system was developed in 1958 and the first large computer was purchased in 1964. Since then, the accounting, planning, and actuarial functions have become heavily reliant on automation.

The president of Nashville National has been reading the computer industry's trade journals and is sold on the merits of data base. He understands that data base can centralize data, reduce the number of programs to be written and maintained, and can allow on-line access to data.

The tape files that exist contain data that go back to 1905. The actual files themselves are dated from 1964. There are approximately 100,000 files of tape. One problem is that the definition of the data has changed quite often, and unfortunately there is no good documentation of what files are which or what data fields are where.

The tapes are used occasionally for scans of data that go into massive summaries. On rare occasions, the tapes are scanned in search of a type of data that previously has not been analyzed. The actuarians do that kind of analysis.

The manager hires a consultant to take the organization into "data base."

After a few weeks of work at the shop, the consultant meets with management and makes the following somewhat surprising observations and recommendations:

1. The data in the tape files is rarely accessed. Even when it is accessed, it is for summary purposes.
2. The sheer volume of data precludes most of it being on-line. The consultant points out the cost of having data on-line.
3. Although most of the data does not need to be on-line, the consultant can see a need for:
   a. A summary data base where management can analyze data and alter its form. The data would be only at a high level.
   b. A "living sample" data base where a representative fraction of the data is stored. Statistical analyses are much easier to do on a sample, are much less expensive to do, and, done properly, are as accurate as if done against a live set of data.
4. Although all data does not need to be on-line, the non-data base portion should be standardized and indexed so that future analysis of the data is as free as possible from the changing form of the data.   ■

Comment on the Following

1. If management follows the consultant's advice, the company will be saved millions of dollars in unnecessary development costs.
2. It is *possible* to put National's data into a data base, even though it does not make sense to do so.
3. Management should be wary about long-term storage of data on tape because tape is not a good medium on which to age data.
4. Management may not be aware that data base brings on its own set of problems even though other problems can be solved by data base.
5. Management may not be aware that data base offers a potential for solving problems. Data base does not—by itself—solve problems.
6. The problem of the changing form of the data over time will occur with data base as it has with tapes.

MULTIPLE-CHOICE QUESTIONS

1. Mt. St. Helens Realty Company is keen on going data base. Giving customers on-line access to the different properties available appears to offer Mt. St. Helens a great advantage. However, there really is very little data, it is very nonuniform, and construction of the system would

be expensive. In fact, a computer expert points out that the cost of the equipment probably precludes such a system.

    A. The competitive advantage should be weighed against the cost of building the system.

    B. The characteristics of the data do not appear right for going data base.

    C. If there were more data, there is a possibility that this system would be a candidate for data base.

    D. Just because this system is not a candidate for data base does not mean that automation should not be used.

    E. The nonuniformity of the data will make it awkward to handle in a data base environment.

2. A company has seven sequential systems. The data run through the systems is very important to the operation of the company and is growing at a phenomenal rate. Management is preparing to build three more systems. The designer is beginning to get bogged down in the complexities of the existing system and how it will interface with the systems to be built.

    A. This environment appears to be ripe for data base.

    B. With data base, the data could easily be accessed randomly.

    C. Done properly, data base could simplify the interfaces of the data.

    D. Data base would allow the data to be accessed concurrently.

    E. Data base could serve as a vehicle for going to on-line systems.

EXERCISES AND ESSAYS

1. People tend to resist change. What can be done to lessen the resistance in a shop where the decision has been made to go data base?

2. Should the first application done in data base be critical to the shop?

3. What are the size limitations (too small or too large) for data base? What happens when data base is forced into an environment where it does not belong?

4. Why is the changing form of data a problem in data base? Will the user's environment ever remain static?

*5. What are the different phases of data base design? Where can mistakes be tolerated the most? The least?

6. What types of data bases are there? What environment is best for each type of data base?

7. What is wrong with using data base as just another file access method?

XII

The Transition from Batch to On-line

□□□

12.1 ONLINE ENVIRONMENT

The single most persistent problem facing managers in today's world of data processing is in bringing their organizations up to date with the capabilities of computerization. The first step is from manual systems to automated systems. That step is large and fraught with difficulties, but it is the next major step—going from automation to on-line systems—that is the most difficult. At least the step to on-line systems has seen more casualties, more wasted expense, and greater loss of morale than any other step.

Why is the transition from batch to on-line so difficult?

1. It appears to be easy, when in fact it is not.
2. It involves psychological and organizational change, as well as technical change.
3. The errors in the on-line environment are obvious, open, and very difficult to sweep under the rug.
4. The costs associated with on-line system construction and operation are high.
5. The scale of systems addressed in the on-line environment runs from large to colossal.
6. The complexities of the on-line environment that must be mastered are subtle and often latent.

For these reasons, managers going to the on-line environment are cautioned to read this chapter very carefully. For managers who are in the on-line environment and have more problems than they can handle, this chapter may provide some insight into why problems arose and how they can move to an action mode, rather than running from one crisis to another in a reaction mode.

12.2 EFFECTIVE USE OF USER'S TIME

Prior to computerization, many work-related tasks were repetitious, boring, and essentially demeaning to the human beings performing the tasks. The advent of computerization freed some people from those bonds. The very first uses of computers were in the batch mode and, unquestionably, if the computer were to be used in no other fashion, it would still be comparable to the modern "beast of burden."

The batch mode of computerization refers to the practice of collecting and holding work to be run on the computer and executing that work later, yielding the results after all work has been collected and executed. The batch user typically submits a "work sheet" or transaction that is keypunched (or submitted through data entry). The data is then run (overnight, once a week, etc.) and the results are available later.

The batch mode makes effective use of people's time in the sense that without batch processing the same work would have to be done manually, but in a larger sense, batch processing does not make optimal use of an individual's time. This is so because users must wait (typically overnight, sometimes longer) a significant amount of time to see the result of their activities. If those activities are important to their companies (financially, strategically, etc.), the delay caused by processing from the time the information is known (i.e., entered on the worksheet) until the time the information is usable can be quite expensive. The expense comes primarily in the form of users not being able to perform the next logical sequence of their work until the information is transacted by the computer. Other expense occurs by having personnel sitting idly waiting for the computer to complete the transacting of the activity. In addition, error correction may mean that a transaction will have to be resubmitted on the next processing cycle, delaying the completion of the business function even further.

These expenses can be reduced greatly or even eliminated with on-line systems. On-line systems enable users to enter, retrieve, and change data in a timely fashion so that the time lag associated with batch systems is reduced to nothing or to such a short period that the user perceives it to be nothing. Users can access and manipulate data without waiting for a prescribed time slot for activity. This timeliness of processing maximizes two things: the user's time and the speed of flow of information within a company.

To illustrate the importance of speed of flow of information in a company or industry, consider two institutions that heavily depend on on-line systems: airlines and banks. Airline reservations would be much less efficient and streamlined, both to the airlines and to the traveler, without on-line systems. The automatic teller services of a bank rely on on-line systems and would be a risky proposition (in terms of proper maintenance of balances, at the very least) without on-line systems. These are but two examples of how on-line systems can transform the environment of the worker and the level of service given to the customer.

The first technical step to achieving the on-line environment is usually "going data base," because data base centralizes the control of data and facilitates a degree of integrity that is difficult to attain without it. Also, data base eliminates the need to do all processing sequentially. Data base is a natural step toward achieving control of data at the data administration level. After the data base environment is established, the next step is the on-line environment. There are several standard on-line modes of operation:

1. Twenty-four-hour on-line operation
2. On-line operation with "batch windows"
3. Batch processing run in conjunction with and under control of the on-line environment

In 24-hour on-line operation, there is no batch window; that is, there is no time when the on-line system is regularly brought down so that batch jobs may be run. The 24-hour on-line environment is typical of companies running systems worldwide or for operations where the need for services can occur around the clock. The more typical on-line environment is the one where there is a batch window. In this environment, the on-line system is brought up at some prescribed time (usually early in the morning), stays up to service the workload of on-line activity during the day, and is brought down in the afternoon or evening after the need for on-line processing diminishes. At that time batch runs (sequential-type processing) can be made against the data base. This regularly scheduled break in on-line processing is called the batch window.

The third way of processing on-line data occurs through use of a hybrid mode of processing in which batch processing is run under the control of the on-line system. In this case, batch processing shares data concurrently with the on-line system. An example of this mode of processing is the IMS BMP (Batch Message Processor). Care must be taken in the mixing of these two fundamentally different modes of processing, because there are essential differences in the philosophies and uses of the two environments (e.g., sequential versus random access of data, large processing runs versus discrete processing units, etc.).

12.3 OTHER VARIATIONS

Within the two basic modes of processing (on-line and batch), there are variations in the way in which data is processed. Some shops do all updates in batch and use on-line facilities only for retrieval of data. This simplifies backup and recovery procedures but restricts the user in the degree of timeliness of the updating of data. Other shops run nothing but batch processes under the on-line controller, thus achieving a degree of data sharing not attainable in the pure batch environment. Still other shops run systems with a great deal of duplication of processing and data between the on-line and batch environments. This philosophy is expensive and prone to synchronization problems but can be used where backup and system availability are very important issues.

Figure 12.1 depicts non-data base environments. A non-data base environment is typified by a polyglot of processing, so much so that it is to the designer's advantage to isolate himself or herself as much as possible from other systems so as to create a world that can be understood and controlled. This leads to unintegrated systems and much unnecessary processing in the long run.

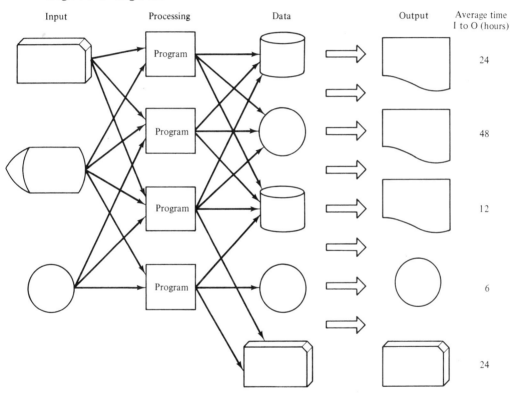

Non-Data Base Environment

Figure 12.1 Non-data base environment.

As a shop evolves to the data base environment, a new measure of control is added at the data level, as shown by Figure 12.2. Systems can now begin to be unified, if not in processing, at least in the common definition of data. (Note that the data base concept gives the designer the potential for achieving integrated data; it is up to the designer to achieve that poten-

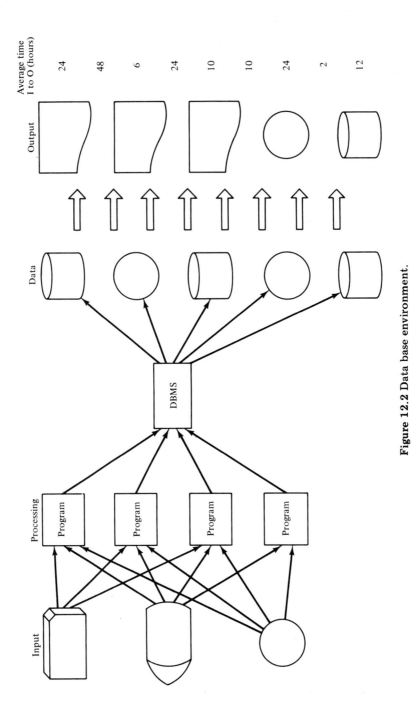

Figure 12.2 Data base environment.

tial.) In the data base environment, jobs do not have to process sequentially through a file, which cuts down on total processing time. However, the input of data and requests for processing activity must still be collected and run together (i.e., they must still be batched).

In the on-line environment processing is necessarily more integrated and the control of processing is more unified, as is the control of data, as shown in Figure 12.3. Again it is up to the designer to achieve the potential benefits of integration of processing; the on-line system does not somehow magically produce those benefits. This evolution of the potential control of data and processing is illustrated in Figures 12.1, 12.2, and 12.3.

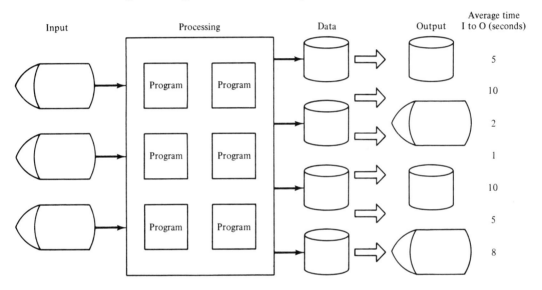

Figure 12.3 On-line data base environment.

12.4 PROBLEMS IN ACHIEVING ON-LINE POTENTIAL

There is no question that the on-line environment can make the best of a worker's time, a customer's time, and uses the computer in the most effective way for a majority of businesses. Furthermore, given an adequate budget for today's hardware and software, all the necessary tools for going to the on-line environment are at the fingertips of today's managers. What, then, is the difficulty in unlocking the potential of on-line processing? The problems range from the technical to the psychological and are many and are often insidious.

12.5 TECHNICAL PROBLEMS

The technical problems of the on-line environment arise chiefly in training programmers and designers in the usage of the new tools and the mechanics of constructing systems in the on-line world; in the generation of the on-line environment by the system programmer; in the planning, implementation, and control of the network that will use the on-line system; in the training of personnel to operate equipment on which the on-line system will run; and in coping with the flow of control of relevant events and activities that occur in the machine. Fortunately, the technical problems present managers with the least of their difficulties (although technical problems should never be taken lightly) because (1) the problems are concrete and (2) there exist other external technical resources on which the manager may rely.

These additional resources include hardware vendors (mainframe, peripheral, etc.), software vendors, training classes, consultants, and other commercially available expertise. People whose livelihood depends on overcoming the technical barriers to the use of their services and equipment (usually vendors) are more than happy to help in ironing out the technical problems related to successful use of their goods. Thus the manager may feel comfortable in the knowledge that whatever technical problems arise, there will be support and answers once the problem is narrowed down to a specific vendor or area of responsibility. Even though there is much to be learned and obstacles to be overcome in the way of technical expertise, management faces the biggest problems within its own organization.

12.6 PROBLEMS AT THE USER LEVEL

Perhaps the largest problem in the transition from batch to on-line lies in changing the attitudes of users when adjusting to the new environment. This resistance to change surfaces whenever people must learn something new and must alter a set pattern of operation. The irony is that the changes necessary to go to the on-line environment are central to the user doing a better, more effective, timely job. In fairness, it is difficult for users to imagine what their first on-line system will look like. Even the analyst discussing the new concepts and the way the system will operate puts a user at a disadvantage because on-line systems operate differently from any tool the user has seen previously.

This factor of dealing with the unknown increases the user's psychological resistance. Because of this resistance and doubt, it is not surprising that the initial on-line system usually undergoes much change from the time it is first implemented until it "settles" in its final form. The first implementation demonstrates to the user what the on-line system really is. Then the user is in a position of being able to envision the potential of the on-line environment.

One of the most successful techniques of overcoming psychological resistance is to put up a small but functional system in a short amount of time so that the user can envision the workings and mysteries of the on-line environment. By experiencing the workings of the on-line environment, the user begins to form an image of how larger, more fully functional systems would operate and be useful in his or her environment. Then, when the designer approaches the user about a new on-line system, the user has a framework with which to understand the system that is to be built. Without this framework, the designer's job is as much a selling job as it is a technical one.

12.7 PROBLEMS OF DESIGN

On-line systems pose special problems to the designer. Just as the user has problems orienting to the on-line environment, the applications designer is faced with similar problems, although at a different level. Unfortunately, for the most part system design in the on-line environment can *look* the same to the designer as system design in the batch environment. The basic design tools, with a few exceptions, are the same ones the designer has worked with for years. There are such familiar things as program specifications, user requirements, inputs, outputs, formats, decisions, retrievals, and updates. Certainly there are new considerations—such as the terminal network and screen formats—that must be mastered, but at first glance there appear to be few differences in the job of the designer in the on-line or in the batch environment. This impression is superficial, because beneath the surface there are *many major* differences between the environments.

The truth of the matter is that the job of the designer has drastically changed, and it is a major pitfall to think that it is a trivial task to convert design concepts from the batch to the on-line environment. Most designers are fooled at first by the similarity of the tools of the two environments; upon naively applying batch design techniques to a designer's first on-line system, the designer is rudely awakened at approximately the time the system goes under a full production load. At that time the designer is alerted to the fact that success in on-line design is measured by an entirely different set of criteria than in batch design. Following are typical measures of success in the two environments:

Batch	*On-line*
• How fast can the system be built?	• How fast does the system respond?
• Is user function satisfied?	• How long does the system stay down once it goes down?
	• How easy is the system to change?
	• How fast can the system be built?
	• Is user function satisfied?

In the on-line environment the same requirements exist for success as in the batch environment, with the addition of other requirements. *All* the requirements must be met in the on-line environment or the system will not be totally acceptable. All too often the designer in the on-line environment takes for granted the very issues that he or she should be concerned with. The (mistaken) attitude often is: "Response time will be good since the on-line environment runs on a very fast and powerful machine." The same sort of argument is voiced about availability: "The on-line system is going to be up; therefore, my application will also be up." And so forth.

After a sad experience or two, designers learn that the major parameters of success in the on-line environment cannot be taken for granted. Furthermore, if they are not consciously designed into the on-line system from the start, they will not somehow magically appear. These attributes do not lend themselves to be retrofitted after the fact. This means a shift in the role of the designer from the batch environment to the on-line environment. The designer is the central person around whom success or failure will occur. In the batch environment the job of the designer was important; however, the scope of the job was primarily to translate user requirements into a system using the tools of design. The scope is the same in the on-line environment, with one enormous distinction—if the design produced is of poor quality in the batch environment, more resources can at least render the system functional. This is shown by Figure 12.4

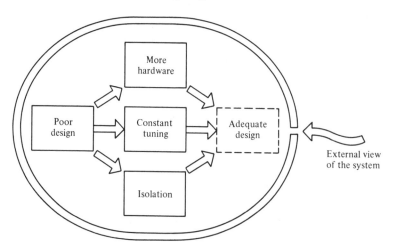

Figure 12.4 Batch environment.

However, in the on-line environment more and faster hardware can improve the system only marginally, and by their very nature, on-line applications cannot be isolated from each other, so all application systems sharing common resources suffer. Figure 12.5 illustrates the exposure of the on-line system application design.

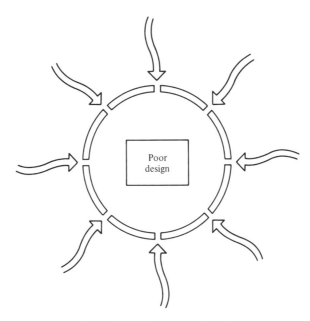

Figure 12.5 Exposure of on-line
system application design.

In a word, a poor design can be smothered with resources in batch, but it is exposed to the world in the on-line environment. In addition to the exposure given by the on-line environment, resource utilization is even more significant in that a poorly designed system will have a negative impact on more than itself; it affects the existing system as well. This is shown by Figure 12.6.

The emphasis on quality of system design in the on-line environment has never been so strong. In many cases there has been a long and painful lesson in realizing that the only real long-term solution to correcting a poor design in the on-line environment is to redesign and reconstruct the application system, and very few installations care for massive redevelopment efforts.

12.8 SHIFTING DESIGN PHILOSOPHIES

It is of interest to note just how much philosophical change a designer must go through in shifting from the batch to the on-line environment. The key to understanding the difficulty of making the shift is to understand the way in which work is accomplished in each environment. In the batch environment the major storage medium is tape. To build a successful batch system, the designer minimized the number of passes made by the tape. This meant

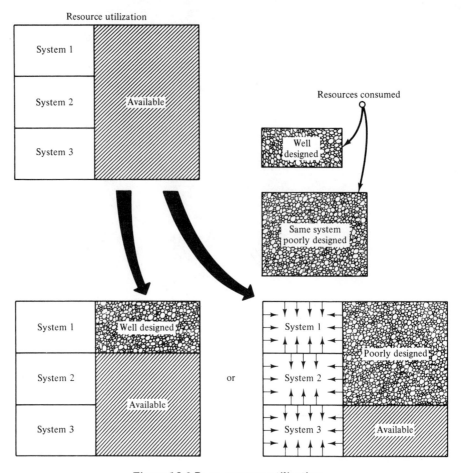

Figure 12.6 Poor resource utilization.

putting much data and diverse types of data on the same tape. It also meant doing as much processing as possible while the tape was being passed. Because of this processing philosophy, the sequential usage of data plays a *big* role in the sequencing of data, the structure of data, the contents of data, and the amount of data that is organized together.

When this philosophy of data design and transaction design is carried to the on-line environment, it is exactly the opposite of what it should be. There is no need to build "do-everything-at-once" processes because the data can be spread into smaller, more distinctive units. This is a result of the fact that the data can be accessed randomly and concurrently. However, designers not accustomed to thinking in this mode try to use batch design approaches and techniques in the on-line environment, much to the abuse of on-line facilities.

12.9 MANAGEMENT PROBLEMS

In addition to technical problems, user problems, and design problems, there are some problems at the management level in achieving a graceful transition from batch to on-line. The first (and probably most fundamental) change comes in the approach to building systems. The attitude of the batch developer was: *Can* I get the job done? How *quickly* can I get the job done? The attitude in the on-line environment should be: *Should* I get the job done? *How well* can I get the job done? This is not a play on words but a reflection of the fundamental shift of attitudes necessary to the successful management of building on-line systems.

In addition to the shifting of managerial attitudes, there probably needs to be a reidentification of complexities that the organization faces in the successful construction of on-line systems, and a subsequent shift in priorities. Management should:

1. Understand where the problems—technical, organizational, at the user level, and so on—are (at a fundamental level).
2. Understand the order of importance of the most critical aspects of the system (because there are limitations to what can be constructed).
3. Understand that trade-offs will be made, consciously or by default. Based on item 2 above, these decisions should be made consciously.
4. Understand the need to share installation-wide resources.

The reason management must change its attitudes and reevaluate how projects are to be managed is that all design will involve trade-offs and management must be aware of what is at stake in evaluating those trade-offs. Without that awareness management may opt for politically expedient solutions that will prove to be costly in the long run. The long-term cost will be in terms of on-line performance, poor system availability, unplanned hardware acquisition, expensive rewrites of system, and other costs of a very large magnitude.

Management must become aware of the temptation to treat design in the on-line environment as if it were a purely technical exercise; that is, there is a temptation to get wrapped in the technical aspects of on-line systems. There is no doubt that an organization must come to grips with the technical side of on-line systems; however, mastering technical solutions is only a part of achieving successful on-line data base systems.

12.10 TYPICAL TRANSITIONAL TRADEMARKS

When a shop first embarks on the design of an on-line system there are some typical holdover techniques from the batch environment. One of them is the "driver" program (Figure 12.7). The driver program is nothing more than a collector and director of transactions. Once transactions are collected and held for execution, at some point they are freed for execution under the auspices of a batch "do-everything" process that is controlled on-line. Such a technique is a simulation in the on-line environment of batching transactions. This technique can be found when installations are still uncomfortable with on-line update integrity features and are more secure with confining updates to a single program scheduled to run at a particular time. As transaction and data volumes increase, this technique becomes operationally awkward.

There is nothing wrong with this technique in the sense that it is technically difficult to implement. The problem is that it probably reflects a reluctance by the designer to convert fully to the on-line mode of operation.

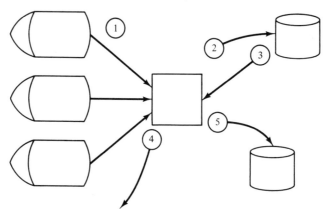

1. Transactions are collected by the driver program.
2. They are queued for later processing on a temporary storage device.
3. At an appointed time, the transactions are retrieved.
4. Then they are released for execution by another program, or
5. They are actually executed by the driver program.

Figure 12.7 Driver programs.

12.11 "DO EVERYTHING AT ONCE" DESIGN

Batch designers are used to working with reports and with minimizing the number of passes through a file needed to produce those reports. Translating that philosophy to the on-line environment produces packed screens to allow immediate use of all functions and immediate display of all data (in imitation of a page of a report) and transactions that literally accomplish functionally all that the application is to accomplish in a program or transaction. Although this philosophy can be accommodated, it is generally a mistake to do so for a variety of reasons, not the least of which is the performance of the on-line system (Figure 12.8).

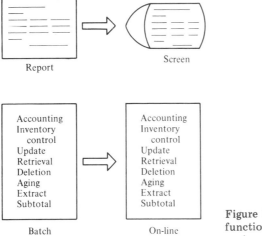

Figure 12.8 Translation of form and function from batch to on-line environment.

The problem of literal translation of form and function of what exists in the batch environment to an implementation in the on-line environment lies in the fact that performance, availability, flexibility, and long-range system divisibility are all negatively affected by the "do everything at once" philosophy in the on-line environment. The on-line environment greatly favors doing activity in small, disjunctive units, but this is not immediately apparent to the first-time on-line designer.

12.12 OVERUSE OF LISTS AND TABLES

It is typical to see an initial on-line design overuse lists and tables. There is nothing inherently wrong with lists and tables; in fact, in many cases these facilities provide the designer with a valuable tool for making functions and data as flexible as possible. However, overuse of tables and lists can cause unnecessary and awkward programmer logic and, in some cases, unnecessary system inflexibility. Such overuse indicates that the designer is thinking sequentially. One of the major strengths of the on-line, data base environment is an ability to get at data directly, not just sequentially. The designer would do well to begin to conceptualize the access of data directly rather than sequentially.

12.13 EXCESSIVE USE OF WORK OR HOLD DATA BASES

Another trait of the designer using on-line tools but still having an orientation to batch is overuse of "work" or "hold" data bases. It should be noted that there are very legitimate uses of these types of data bases, primarily, in pseudo-conversational processing and in some other types of applications. Work or hold data bases typically are used to collect data from different transactions and then, at some point, all accumulated processing is released and is applied to the data base. It is not unusual for work or hold data bases to be closely aligned with driver or collector programs, although by no means is this association necessary. Figure 12.9 illustrates the workings of hold data bases.

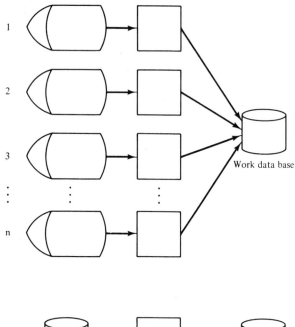

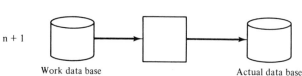

Work data base   Actual data base

Figure 12.9 "Work" or "hold" data base approach to system design. On-line activities 1, 2, 3, . . . , n transact against a work data base that accumulates activities and holds them in abeyance. At point n (determined by the operator of the system) the data is "safe" for actual transacting against the real data base.

The purpose of a hold data base is to tie together functionally different transaction processes and to ensure that a user does not try to use a data base that has not yet been edited, verified, and completed (in the sense of a large amount of business function). While a user is working on a lengthy transaction, the hold data base collects the interactions of individual transaction activities until the business function is ready to be applied to the on-line data base. This ensures that no "incomplete" activity is transacted and that the data is complete and available for reference to other users until it is updated. Many valid on-line systems are run under this philosophy. The problem is that the user is operating under a "mind set" of batch premises while using on-line tools; that is, the user thinks in terms of activity going against a record (batch) rather than individual functions being separately processed against data (on-line). The designer has compromised the on-line system by simulating batch thinking with on-line implementation.

12.14 UPDATE OFF-LINE/RETRIEVE ON-LINE PHILOSOPHY

Quite a few shops update in batch and retrieve data on-line. This technique enhances the availability and recoverability of data but does so at the expense of the timeliness and accuracy of the data. The data can only be as timely as the last batch update—and therein lies the limitation of this approach.

When the designer discards a whole mode of processing (on-line update) he or she gains some simplicity of operation but does so at the expense of full realization of the potential of the hardware and software at his or her disposal. This philosophy is not optimized in the long run to maximize the time of the users of the systems.

12.15 MASSIVE SHIFTING OF DATA

The on-line processing environment is normally not a good place to simulate batch processing techniques, although unfortunately it can be used for that. One of the real problems of on-line design is that batch techniques can usually be transferred easily from one environment to the other, at whatever cost to performance and flexibility on-line. One particular batch technique that can be deadly is the unnecessary moving of data en masse from record to record.

As an example, data is shifted from a "probationary" account record to an "active" account record when the status of the account changes. When the account becomes delinquent for some reason, the data is shifted to a probationary account record. Once the probationary data is cleared, the account is put back into an active record. After a period of inactivity, it is placed into an inactive record.

All of this movement of data is normal and usually efficient for non-data base systems but plays havoc with the work required of the programmer and performance in a data base environment. The programmer has to worry about deleting data in one place and inserting it elsewhere. The DBMS must manage the placement of data. The results are disk space that becomes poorly organized and fragmented, and I/O activity that is done needlessly. As a rule, in the on-line environment data should enter the system, be operated on, and be deleted from the same place. Massive shuffling of data is unnecessary and causes unneeded work.

12.16 "INTEGRATED" DATA

In the early days of data base, there arose the idea that "integrated" data was equivalent to collecting all of a company's data into a single physical data base. Perhaps this idea came about because a single physical data base did not require multiple definitions and therefore appeared to eliminate semantic redundancy. This idea also corresponded to the batch philosophy of conglomerating many different types of data. At any rate, one of the poorer practices in going to the data base concept or the on-line environment is constructing large, massive physical data bases. Such data bases (1) are difficult to tune, (2) are difficult to reorganize, (3) are difficult to restructure, (4) are difficult to handle in terms of flexibility, (5) make operations unnecessary difficult, and (6) are unnecessary.

The problem is that most necessary data base functions (such as reorganization, restructuring, and recovery) are achieved by programs that operate on units of physical data bases. This means that the execution of those functions depends on physical organization, not logical organization. The same data organized cohesively *logically* but disjunctively *physically* is relatively easy to manage. Without this physical division, data is very awkward to manipulate over time.

12.17 UNDERLYING ECONOMIES IN USING DBMS

A major initial flaw of system designers in going to the on-line environment is a lack of awareness of major issues of performance with regard to selecting DBMS options. This flaw usually occurs only in an installation's initial phases of design because designers soon become aware of the pitfalls they face once they begin to see firsthand the consequences of their decisions when the system is implemented.

The first time through the design process, the designer is usually delighted merely to have found *a* way to accomplish the design, much less an optimal way. To use an analogy, the jungle explorer sets out to discover a path through the underbrush to reach his destination. After much work, he figures out a path and then is so taken with his discovery that he never realizes that there are many paths, quite a few of which are better, faster, and easier. So it is when the designer first faces the task of translating user requirements into an on-line data base system.

The designer works diligently, constructs a plan that will accomplish the user function, then becomes wrapped up in his own design. The designer is stuck on the fact that his plan *will work* (i.e., he has found a path through the jungle), not on how *well* his plan will work (one mile from the arduous path discovered by the explorer it turns out that there is an Interstate where the explorer can hitch a ride). Once a designer lives through the full system life cycle (until the system reaches full production status), he discovers that there were other alternatives and that the name of the game is not merely to produce a workable design, but to produce the *best* design, and that in part this means having a full awareness of the underlying issues. In the batch environment it is usually not terribly obvious when the wrong set of options has been chosen. In the on-line environment it will *constantly* be obvious when a poor choice of options has been made.

12.18 GLOBAL DATA BASES

One of the fundamental misconceptions the batch designer may have in going to on-line environment concerns data integration, data control, and "global" data bases. Typically, the designer creates data bases that can be used across application boundaries. Examples are: terminal data bases, security data bases, tables data bases, control data bases, and audit data bases. There is nothing wrong with these kinds of data bases per se, except when the designer implements these data bases so that there is a single physical data base for all applications (e.g., an application shares a "terminal" data base with all other applications). This is done in the name of data integration, elimination of redundancy, or data control. The problem is that when the data base shared across multiple applications goes down, entire applications may become unavailable. Figure 12.10 shows a terminal data base that connects a number of applications.

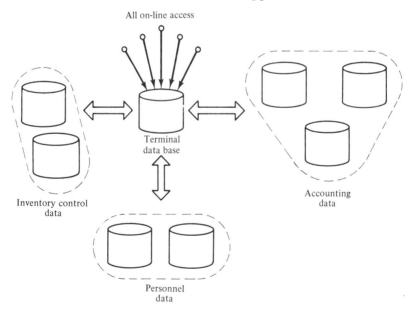

Figure 12.10 Terminal data base connecting a number of applications. The designer has specified that all transactions access the terminal data base before accessing a data base related to the application.

In Figure 12.11, the terminal data base is undergoing recovery and effectively shuts down all applications. The accounting and personnel users deservedly are upset because they are "innocent" of any error, yet they suffer because their applications are not available.

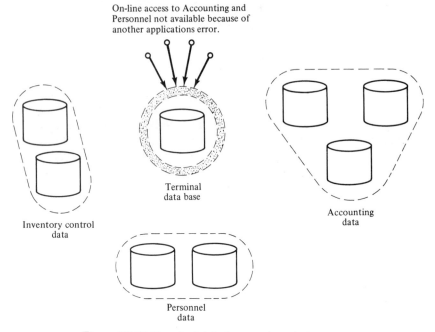

Figure 12.11 Terminal data base undergoing recovery.

In Figure 12.12, the terminal data base has been physically separated into units that service each application. When the inventory control application brings down its own terminal data base, there is no impact on the other applications using the terminal data base. [*Note:* Logically, the terminal data bases can be identical (and probably should be), as well as the programs that operate on them. The separation occurs at the physical data base level.]

As a separate but very important side issue, consider the problems of distributing processing and splitting data across a number of machines. This is often necessary when hardware capacity is saturated. "Global physical data bases" tie the hands of the manager struggling with growth.

As mentioned previously, splitting data bases into multiple physical copies does not necessarily mean losing control of the data administratively or creating an exposure to data redundancy.

12.19 LACK OF AWARENESS OF STANDARD WORK UNIT CONCEPT

Nearly all first-time on-line designers are unaware of the standard work unit

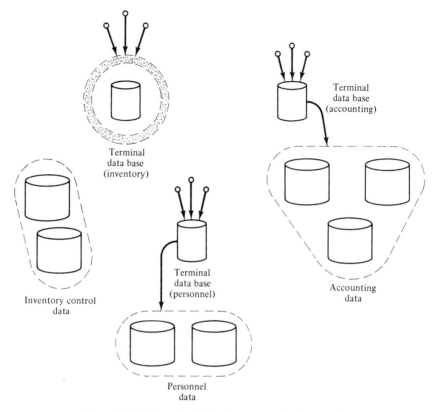

Figure 12.12 Terminal data base separated into units.

concept. So much effort is spent in learning the mechanics of on-line design that the designer is lucky or intuitively very talented if his or her first application fits within the parameters of the standard work unit. The standard work unit concept requires a different perspective on design than that normally associated with batch design, and it is usually through experience that the designer gains awareness of the importance of the standard work unit concept.

12.20 STRATEGY FOR SUCCESS

Understanding the problems of transition from batch to on-line is one thing; avoiding them is something else. The following list represents some ways in which organizations ease this transition.

1. Keep the first on-line system small, clean, and noncritical. Make it a prototype and use it as a learning experience. Do not worry about

having to throw it away—assume from the beginning that it will be thrown away.

2. Educate people at all levels—management, users, designers, programmers, operations. Instill an attitude of resource sharing throughout the organization.

3. Learn from other companies' mistakes. Communicate freely and do not be sensitive about discussing mistakes. Do not repeat avoidable errors.

4. Get technical and design input from a number of sources. Over a period of time, do not rely on the same group of people to make or influence critical decisions.

5. Closely involve users in the design process so that they have an opportunity to understand the effects of their requirements.

6. Beware of "clever" solutions to development and technological problems. Carefully evaluate the impact, trade-offs, and wisdom of "clever" solutions.

7. Do not attempt to use technology or software to solve administrative or organizational problems.

8. Implement the standard work unit philosophy. Use design review methodology in a consistent and effective fashion.

9. Formalize the interface between applications and data administration. Clearly define objectives, domains, responsibilities, and rights, especially in the area of data and transaction design.

REFERENCES

Dechow, Esther, and Don Lundberg, *IMS/VS Application Design Review Methodology*, IBM Manual G320-6009.

Inmon, W. H., *Effective Data Base Design*, Prentice-Hall, Inc., Englewood Cliffs, N.J., 1980.

Martin, James, *Programming Real-Time Computer Systems*, Prentice-Hall, Inc., Englewood Cliffs, N.J., 1965.

CASE STUDY

Houston Heat and Water is a large public utility. It is responsible for much of the water and electric services in and around southeast Texas. As Houston has grown and the cost of energy has risen, Houston Heat has grown exponentially.

The top management of Houston Heat has determined that it is time to upgrade its computer systems from batch to on-line. A large vendor has made a great effort to demonstrate just how effective the on-line environment can be in maximizing the use of people's time. The decision is made and in short order programmers and designers are sent off to class to learn how to use the tools of the on-line software.

Management and the systems staff lay out the following plan to get to the on-line environment:

1. Generate the on-line system—initial system definition.
2. Define and build data bases.
3. Specify and program transactions.
4. Begin to use the on-line system.

Things proceed in an orderly fashion. Users and their liaisons began to lay out how the users' business functions should look on-line. The initial business function to be converted is the order form for new service (heat or water) or a change in service. Currently, a clerk fills out a form and submits it for batch processing. The data includes name, address, type of connection needed, date of hookup, date of disconnection, phone, employer, bank reference, commercial/private, last address, number of persons in building or domicile, rating location, special considerations and conditions, tax base information, and other location customer can be reached at. The user is accustomed to handling this amount of material at one time in the current batch system.

The designer determines that all of this processing can be done on one screen by one transaction. The transaction can access up to six data bases. Some data bases, such as tax base information and rating location, require a full data base scan under some conditions.

The DBA reviews the design and claims that the design will not perform well on-line. The application designer states that the user must have his business function. The application designer states that she thinks the design can be implemented. The DBA says that is not the right approach.

Management supports the application designer because she (1) is delivering a system that meets user requirements and (2) has always delivered results for management in the past.

Management is reinforced in its judgment when the system is programmed and runs quite nicely for the first three months.   ■

Comment on the Following

1. On-line systems do not show their true operating characteristics until they are running under a full transaction workload, against a full amount of data, and are competing for precious resources with other systems under the on-line controller.

2. Management has a naive attitude about what it takes to go to the on-line environment.

3. Management has done very little to prepare programmers, designers, or users for the psychological shifting of gears necessary to going to the on-line environment.

4. User specifications often *can* be translated into the on-line environment, but *should not* be translated. The same function can be achieved with a different implementation.

5. The perspective of the DBA—a global one over all transactions that will be on-line—is necessary and is a departure from the traditional batch environment. The local perspective—that of the user and the designer—is still necessary, but should not be an overriding consideration.

6. One of the faults of some on-line system software is that it allows batch processes to be placed on-line.

MULTIPLE-CHOICE QUESTIONS

1. The way programmers and system developers are judged in batch is: (a) How quickly do they construct systems? and (b) Does the system meet the user's requirements? Management moves the organization to the on-line environment.

   A. The attitude "build it quickly now and tune in performance later" will not work in the on-line environment.

   B. The designers had better think at least as much about the availability of the system as they do speed of development.

   C. Speed of development is still a parameter of success in the on-line environment.

   D. Management will not really know whether the development effort has been successful until the system actually operates in a full production mode.

   E. The user, as well as the designer and programmer, needs to think in terms of the on-line environment.

2. The first on-line system management has chosen to construct is one that is very large and critical to the company's business.

   A. The importance of the system will force the designers to do a good job.

   B. By making the first effort a critical one, the designers will really impress the users with the capabilities of the on-line environment.

   C. The system, once implemented, can be tuned if there are any major problems.

      D. The designers can learn what they need to know about the on-line environment from courses or books.

      E. Speed of development is appropriate here.

*3. A designer has specified an on-line transaction that will do 500 I/Os. A member of the data base administration staff comments that that type of processing should not be done on-line. The designer points out that the manual states that that sort of processing can be done.

      A. Just because something *can* be done does not mean that it *should* be done.

      B. The on-line process probably will be done better off-line.

      C. The user needs to know the impact of his requirements, which will be a negative one.

      D. Not only will the transaction run slowly, it will cause other transactions to run slowly.

      E. There are many ways in which the same data can be processed without affecting the on-line system. The designer should look not at changing the business function, but implementing that function differently.

XIII

Growing Out of a Machine

□□□

13.1 GROWTH

Data processing managers who desire to remain in an action rather than a reaction mode must know something about hardware selection and the limitations of hardware and software. The cost of large mainframe computers is not cheap and the corresponding cost of software is not small either. The optimal position a manager can be in is to be able to select from many options come the day that hardware or major pieces of software must be acquired. The worst position is to have only a single choice, or nothing but a selection of bad choices. In the latter case the manager must "react" to the forces of the environment rather than control those forces.

The growth of computer utilization has been explosive over the past two decades. User demands and new ways to use the computer have fueled this growth, which probably is still in its infancy. The growth can be measured in many ways, but its explosive force is clear just from the standpoint of the raw utilization of processing power. The utilization is even more startling in light of the increases in hardware speed, capacity, and architecture.

For the manager at a given installation, it is not enough to focus on the mere growth of processing power in his or her shop without having an in-depth understanding of why this growth is occurring. Limiting ones focus is myopic and can lead to some very awkward and incorrect conclusions. If the manager of hardware acquisition and planning is isolated (by choice or otherwise) from the forces that drive the growth, it is likely that the problems endemic to growth will manifest themselves in the worst possible form. On the other hand, if there is a clear communication and understanding between the parties in charge of managing growth at the hardware level and those closest to the forces causing the growth (such as users, application development, etc.), growth is not likely to cause undue difficulties.

178

13.2 ROOTS OF GROWTH

Where are the roots of growth? Where does this constant need for computing power come from? The answer is, new applications. The way in which applications are built is directly related to managing growth at the point when an installation moves to a larger processor or processors. There is a great temptation for those in capacity planning and hardware procurement to spend a minimum amount of time understanding or influencing applications, laboring under the false sense that all computer problems have a technical solution.

This practice is very dangerous in that the architecting of any application can and will *greatly* influence the ways in which an organization can grow, although it is not immediately apparent. In fact, the relationship between the architecting of the application and the management of growth is not obvious until growth actually occurs. By then a rearchitecting of the application is not feasible. Thus it is much to the hardware planner's advantage to be concerned with the architecture of the applications being built in his or her shop.

There is a temptation to look at the increases in speed and capacity of processing power and draw the conclusion that growth of computer utilization will be satisfied by technological advances. If the growth of computer utilization were linear, this might be the case, but the technological advances have done nothing more than stem the tide of demand for processing power.

13.3 PROCESSOR UPGRADE

The simplest choice the hardware planner has when computer utilization begins to exceed available capacity is to acquire (usually purchase or lease) a machine with more capacity. This upgrade is depicted by Figure 13.1.

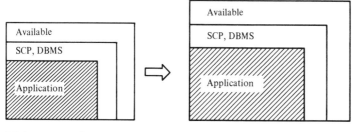

Figure 13.1 Upgrade of machines.

This type of upgrade is the cleanest because there is *no* impact on existing software; that is software that runs on a smaller machine needs no changes (or an absolute minimum amount of change) to run on a larger machine.*

*For some environments where this is not true, the forces of growth loom even more ominously.

If this were the only type of upgrade ever done by an installation, there would be little need for communication between the hardware processor and the application developer.

There is a problem with this approach as the only approach to managing growth of computer utilization, and that is that there is a finite amount of processing that can be purchased (i.e., where does a shop go when it grows out of the largest and fastest processor?). This question is considered in depth later in the chapter.

13.4 UPGRADED RECONFIGURATION

Another option the hardware planner has is to upgrade processing capacity — not by going to a larger machine, but to a duplexed configuration of machines such as an MP–AP (multiprocessor–attached processor) configuration. In this configuration one processor runs subordinate to the other, sharing the workload. This configuration is illustrated in Figure 13.2. When two machines are configured together as shown, the total achievable throughput is less than the achievable processing power of each machine running separately and added together. Typically, a maximum ratio of 1.7 performance enhancement of throughput is possible in a coupling of two machines.

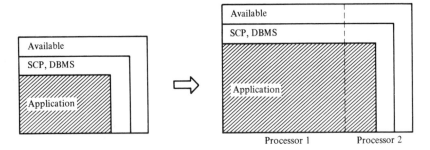

Figure 13.2 Upgrade to duplexed configuration of machines.

It is possible that the enhancement of performance (i.e., achievable throughput) in certain environments could be significantly less in the light of certain software. In this case the software becomes as much of or more of a bottleneck than the hardware. An enhancement ratio that is typical in environments where software degradation occurs is something on the order of 1.4 for a coupling of two machines. It behooves the planner to be very careful of the environment in which he or she operates, because such a low ratio of throughput enhancement is very expensive.

There is one advantage to an upgraded reconfiguration such as an upgrade to a larger machine,— there is *no* impact on existing software. If the only two options to be considered by the hardware planner were single-machine upgrades or reconfiguring processors, there would be little need to understand what is transpiring at the application level. The hardware planner should recognize the expense and limitations of reconfiguring as the different options are considered.

13.5   SPLITTING WORKLOADS

Another possibility to achieving more system throughput is the splitting of workloads across machines. This option is shown in Figure 13.3, where the workload has been split over two machines. The planner may have chosen more than two machines; for the sake of discussion we will settle on two. The machines are of approximately equal size and capacity, so that software running on the original machine runs on either of the new machines (of course, one of the "new" machines is probably the original overloaded machine). This workload splitting from the overloaded machine can be

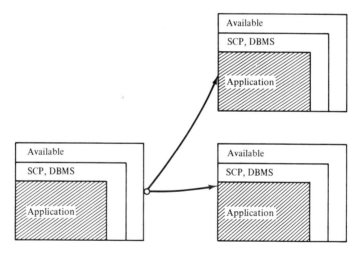

Figure 13.3 Splitting of work loads across machines.

done over as many machines as necessary, *if in fact the split can be done at all.* There are few technological limits on the number of machines that can participate in workload splitting, thus removing the constraint of a "finite limit" of processing power. The problem is: *Can* the split be made at all?

There really are two types of workload splits: the major software division of work (such as removing TSO from an IMS machine) and the splitting of a workload within a major software domain (such as moving part of IMS on-line processing to another machine). The first type of split is very easy to do (relative to the second type of split). Because the first kind of split is obvious and easy, it presents few headaches for the manager.

The headaches come when the second kind of processing must be split over a number of machines. The manager with one major piece of software on a machine whose capacity is being exceeded and who does not (or cannot) upgrade has a very difficult set of choices unless his or her applications have been developed very carefully.

There are two things that need to be split: data and transactions (processing). Using such facilities as IMS MSC (Information Management System Multiple System Coupling) or CICS/DLI ISC (Customer Information Control System/Data Language One   Intersystem Coupling), the splitting of transactions across machines is a fairly straightforward process because the software has been architected to handle such a split. However, the splitting of data is an entirely different matter. Data is easily split *only* if the application designer has planned for it from the outset. If the designer has built small, disjoint data bases (i.e., data bases with few or no interconnections and interdependencies), and specified transactions that access an absolute minimum number of data bases, there is a good possibility that the workload can be divided across a number of machines with little or no problem. It is unlikely that a designer would have adopted those philosophies by chance because (1) the advantages are not obvious, (2) they contradict much traditional wisdom, and (3) they are 180° opposite of batch philosophies. Only if the designer had been aware that growth was to be a major concern would those philosophies normally have been adopted.

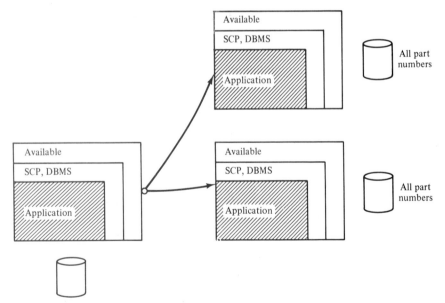

Figure 13.4 Duplication of data across a number of machines. If all part numbers are to be spread from one machine to a number of machines, some major considerations are (1) redundancy, (2) synchronization of values, and (3) update of data.

Figure 13.4 depicts one option the hardware planner has—simply duplicate data across a number of machines. This is not a feasible option unless the application was prepared for this eventuality long ago. Retrofitting this solution is *very* difficult and potentially very awkward. The data must exist redundantly in two environments, and that is a waste of space. Furthermore, there is a major problem with the synchronization of data values when one piece of data on one machine disagrees with the counterpart on the other machine. The third problem is that of update. When an update occurs on one machine, it must also be transacted against the other machine to keep the values in synch. It is obvious that this configuration is a very poor choice unless some ground rules can be established, such as updating only on machine A, and nightly refreshing data on machine B. This means that during the day data on machine B will not be current.

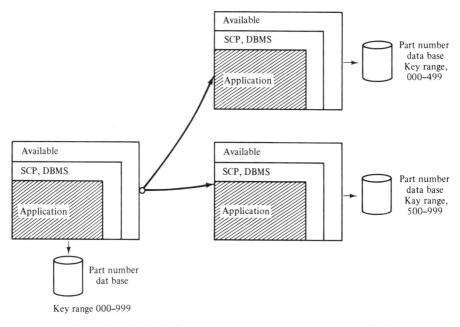

Figure 13.5 Distribution of data across machines using a splitting algorithm.

Figure 13.5 shows that the hardware planner can avoid the problems of data redundancy by distributing the data across machines using some appropriate splitting algorithm. This approach works quite well as long as the application has been designed along these lines from the beginning. The difference between this configuration and the previous configuration is that redundancy of data and all the associated problems—synchronization of values, wasted space, and so on—are not a factor. The definition of the data—the semantics—is redundant, but the actual values are not. In the case presented, any query or update for a given part number will go to a single machine, based on the particular part number that is desired. Retrofitting splits by key range of data is not a trivial task. A retrofit involves program logic and the very way that processing is accomplished.

13.6 OTHER PROBLEMS

The splitting of data is an important consideration, but it is not the only one. Another option the hardware planner has is splitting the workload along a subdivision of applications; instead of spreading the transactions of a single application across a number of machines, the planner can move entire applications onto separate machines. This works well as long as there are no commonly shared data bases, such as those shown in Figure 13.6. In this figure all is well until the planner decides where to put the terminal and table data bases. At that point the considerations are the same as discussed in splitting a single data base across several systems. There are no easy answers.

If the hardware planner *ever* wants to consider splitting the workload across a number of machines, he or she must communicate with and influence the application designer *early* in the life cycle of the design of the application system. Application divisibility is not a normal option.

13.7 WORKLOAD DISTRIBUTION

Another option the hardware planner has is to distribute the workload to smaller machines. This option is very similar to the option previously discussed, with the exception that the workload is to be distributed not to machines of equal or similar processing capabilities, but to machines of very different capacities. This split is shown by Figure 13.7, where several smaller machines assume some of the burden of processing previously done in the main processor. Typical of the workload being spread are editing, interactive user communication, and gathering of work to be processed on the larger machine. This option is appealing in that there is virtually no limit to the processing capacity; whenever more processing power is needed, the hardware planner acquires more small processors. There is the same problem with data as discussed in the previous option—that of splitting processing among a number of machines. There is, however, a very different complication as well.

When machines are of a different size, there may be a compatibility problem in moving software from one machine to the other. Software is normally upwardly compatible but is not always downwardly compatible. This presents a barrier to the hardware planner unless the system has been

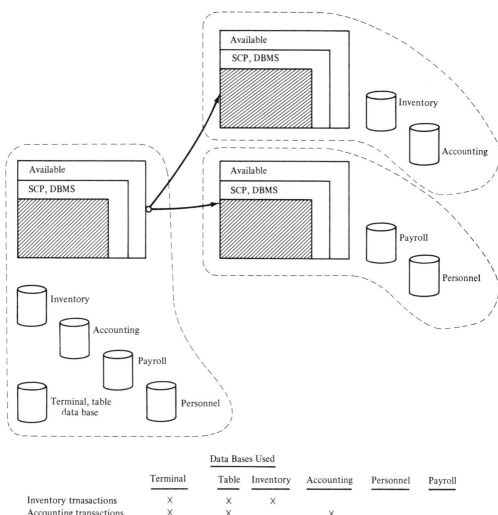

		Data Bases Used				
	Terminal	Table	Inventory	Accounting	Personnel	Payroll
Inventory trnasactions	X	X	X			
Accounting transactions	X	X		X		
Payroll transactions	X	X				X
Personnel transactions	X	X			X	

Figure 13.6 Splitting of work loads along a subdivision of applications.

designed from the beginning for this distribution of the workload. As in other options, retrofitting major architectural application considerations is not feasible.

13.8 PLANNING ALTERNATIVES

It should now be obvious why the hardware planner should communicate with the applications designer. If the hardware planner *ever* wants to have

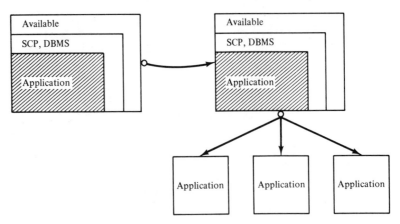

Figure 13.7 Distribution of work load to smaller machines.

options other than single-system upgrade or reconfiguration, the planner must make his or her plans known very early in the design process. To reiterate, the options available to the planner should a workload have to be moved onto a number of machines are:

1. Split a single system across a number of machines.
2. Split subsystems across a number of machines.
3. Simply not do certain functions.
4. Rewrite code and redesign data.

The first two options require long-range planning; the last two options require no great planning effort but are hardly palatable.

13.9 CORPORATE DATA BASES: SPLITTING DATA OVER A NUMBER OF MACHINES

One of the side issues of managing growth out of a machine is that of splitting data over a number of machines. Data bases that tie several applications together (or even entire large applications together) are not desirable from the standpoint that it makes splitting work loads difficult if not impossible. Usually, these data bases are utilitarian in nature, such as terminal, control, table, or audit data bases. One technique in handling data spread across a number of machines is to split the data bases so that they exist in several places but with a different content of data (i.e., split by key range).

There is redundancy in this approach because the same data base is defined in a number of places. This conflicts in general with the notion of corporate data bases. However, as mentioned in Chapter 12, the reduction of redundancy should be addressed from a logical perspective: from the

186

definition of the data base and the programs that use the data and not in the physical implementation. The answer lies in controlling the definition of the data base (i.e., semantic control).

Redundancy of data is a bad design practice in general (there are some notable exceptions, however), but has certain useful forms which *if controlled* can be very beneficial. One of the major drawbacks of redundancy is the need to redefine the same data structures in more than one place and to write a number of programs that will perform the necessary functions of update, deletion, and insertion.

The designer and/or data administrator does *not* have to give up control (and thus suffer the problems of semantic redundancy) if he or she controls the definition of the data at the source code level. Figure 13.8 demonstrates this control.

Were the designer to build separate support code for each data base, *then* the problems of redundancy would arise and become a major problem. The necessary control of the data is taken to mean control at the source level, not a lower level. Data administration can exercise control and still have a great deal of structurally redundant data.

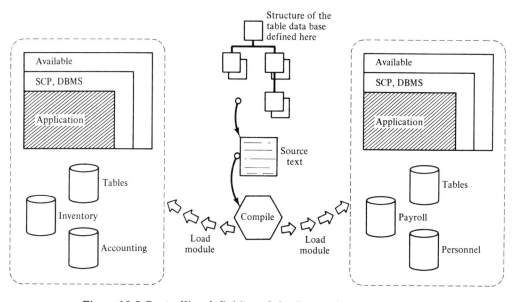

Figure 13.8 Controlling definition of the data at the source code level. The contents of the table's data base differ from system to system, but the definition of the data and the source code that updates, inserts, and deletes the data come from a single source.

13.10 SUMMARY

The long-range hardware planner pays close attention to the applications being built that will create the growth that will cause utilization of a machine to be greater than the machine's capacity. Failure to communicate and plan with applications may lead to serious consequences. By communicating closely with applications the hardware planner can provide many more options in preparation for the time when hardware must be acquired. The planner will be in an action mode. Not communicating with the applications designer leaves the hardware planner open to making decisions in a reaction mode.

If growth were the only measurement of success, the designer would build systems that are:

1. Broken into small, disjunctive units of processing
2. Broken into small, disjunctive units of data

Spreading data bases over a number of systems does not introduce the problems of redundancy if control of the definition of the data is maintained at the source level.

REFERENCES

Lecht, Charles, *Waves of Change*, Advanced Computer Techniques Corporation, New York, 1977.

White, W. W., *Attached Processing (AP) System Performance Characteristics and Considerations*, Daps Code 0910.0911, GG22-9004-00, May 1977, IBM Corp.

CASE STUDY

The Alaska Oil and Pipe Company has experienced an unusual growth pattern. Six years ago there was no corporation. Four major oil companies in the lower 48 states bonded together and formed Alaska O and P and the result was an instantaneous company. One of the first acts of the chief executive officer was to organize the company around automated processing. For the last 4 years, the systems being run have occupied a large mainframe computer.

The systems that have been developed are heavily integrated. This means that data and files that exist are used in many applications and across functional boundaries. This philosophy was developed in the name of integrated systems and data bases. Most processing takes place in the on-line environment, although there is a hefty nighttime batch process that must be run. The same vendor that supplies the software also supplies the mainframe computer and certain other peripherals. The level of support by the vendor is considered to be good.

The vendor supplies all sorts of expertise that is otherwise difficult to come by. This expertise is free, for the most part. The existing workload is just about to overflow the current piece of hardware, which is one step down from the largest machine that is available. In addition, management is facing a new problem. A new oil field is being developed and will be brought into the pipeline in another six months. When this time comes, the projected workload will approximately double—grossly overflowing the existing capacity. Management is aware of this coming event and is busily contacting hardware manufacturers. The choices have boiled down to three basic options.

1. Continue with the current vendor. All the software that runs on the machine now will run on the new configuration. The problem is that the current vendor can supply only an MP configuration, which means that the enhancement achievable by combining the two machines will be at most 1.7 times the capacity of a single machine. Furthermore, management has heard that in the on-line environment the enhancement ratio may be as low as 1.2. The vendor assures management that this is not the case. Even though this option is expensive, management is leaning toward it because of the support the vendor gives. The vendor is viewed as a full-service vendor.

2. Switch to a vendor that supplies a UP that is less expensive than the MP and achieves approximately the same amount of throughput. This option is less expensive, but is questionable because the second vendor has no software of its own. Instead, it runs the software of the existing vendor. Thus long-term support is questionable because the second vendor clearly does not have nearly the organization behind it that the current vendor has.

In either option (one or two) there is a fear—it is possible that the workload will exceed either configuration. Since the configurations represent the maximum that can be purchased, Alaska O and P may be stuck. The third option considered allows Alaska O and P to expand the workload infinitely if, in fact, it can be expanded at all.

3. The third option is to split the workload across a number of machines rather than upgrading to a larger machine. This works well if (a) the transaction workload can be split and (b) data can be split. Given the architecture of the software, it turns out that splitting the transactions is no problem. The real problem comes with the data. Unfortunately, the data is "integrated," which makes the workload very difficult to split. Several design suggestions are made, but it turns out that retrofitting a split of data is very difficult. A designer points out that at the point of system design, a split of data would be simple if only it had been planned from the start.

While management is mulling over its options, a new development effort is begun. The designer wants to put up a new application while using existing data and facilities. The new application will be nicely integrated into Alaska O and P's systems.   ■

Comment on the Following

1. Buying the MP configuration has many advantages that are intangible, but is more expensive per se, for the purchase of the machine.
2. Buying the UP is less expensive, but risks losing vendor software support.
3. In either the UP or MP, there is going to be a major problem when the workload exceeds the capacity of the processor(s).
4. Building integrated systems has forced management into an unwanted predicament.
5. New hardware technology can be relied on to produce machines that have capacities that will meet the growing demands for processing.
6. One of the points at which management could have avoided its current predicament was at the moment of system design.

MULTIPLE-CHOICE QUESTIONS

1. A manager desires to split the workload of one processor, not to two processors (of approximately the same size as the first), but to an environment where there is a mainframe processor and a number of smaller machines that are attached to that processor.
   A. Software is normally upwardly compatible, but not downwardly compatible.
   B. The time to plan for this type of workload split is at the moment of system design.
   C. Attempting to retrofit this type of workload split where it has not been planned is either very difficult or impossible.
   D. This strategy for hardware utilization is appealing because there is the possibility of splitting the work load to *many* smaller machines.
   E. Line transmission of data becomes a factor in this environment.
2. A manager has a machine from vendor A. Vendor B sells a machine to the manager that replaces the machine from vendor B. However, vendor B's machine runs on software from vendor A.
   A. Vendor A has an obligation to see that its software runs properly whether or not the shop has hardware from vendor A.
   B. Vendor B's machine may not run the software as efficiently as vendor A's.

    C. The general support from vendor A may be expected to diminish or disappear altogether.

    D. With the savings made from purchasing vendor B's machine, the shop can afford to buy what expertise it needs when it loses support from vendor A.

    E. Vendor B promises a high level of support. The precise meaning of support should be defined in writing before the purchase is finalized.

*3. A designer decides to build a system whose workload can be split. He determines that the problem is not in splitting the transactions and processes that must be run, but in splitting the data across a number of machines.

    A. The designer can write, acquire, or wait for software or technology that will allow him to share data across systems.

    B. A number of copies of data can be created for a number of machines.

    C. A machine can have its processing and data segregated by function; that is, only certain kinds of data and certain kinds of processes can be run on a given machine.

    D. Data can be split by function or key range across a number of machines.

    E. Data can be stored on a single machine and transported for processing where desired.

EXERCISES AND ESSAYS

*1. Why is data tied more closely to a machine than transactions or other processes?

2. What is the cost (in terms of financing, etc.) of waiting until the last minute to make hardware acquisition decisions? What by-products result from this kind of philosophy?

3. What is a machine worth after two years of use (i.e., what is its residual value)? Should residual value be a factor in determining whether to lease or buy a machine?

*4. What are critical components of a machine? How has technology improved their performance and capacity in the last 10 years? In the last two years? What improvements can be anticipated in the near future?

5. What types of processing can be done today that could not be done five years ago? What is the cost of processing? Has it increased or decreased (per unit of processing)? Has the total amount spent on processing increased or decreased? Why?

6. What role should the user play in determining hardware acquisitions?

XIV

Perspectives
on Data Dictionaries

□□□

14.1 WHAT IS A DATA DICTIONARY?

Few facilities in data processing have as much promise and have been marketed as aggressively as data dictionaries. Few have achieved as miserable a track record. This is not to say that some installations do not successfully use a data dictionary. However, many installations have implemented a data dictionary, spent a great amount of money on software, computer resources, and personnel only to abandon the project later. Implementing a data dictionary can be a very costly exercise with little or no benefits unless management is very sure of (1) why the data dictionary is being implemented and supported, (2) what the real (as opposed to theoretical) benefits are, and (3) what the pitfalls are. Misusing a data dictionary or misunderstanding it can cost a company a great deal of money.

A data dictionary is a combination of software and procedures that aid an installation in "controlling" its data. The controlling of data generally amounts to an inventory of the data that is being processed within the system of a shop: the location of the data, a description of the meaning of the data, the relation of data to other data, how the data is used, where the data is used, who is responsible for the data, the source of the data—in short, a store of all the appropriate information about the data.

The documentation of a shop's data should take place at many levels. Some typical levels of documentation are: data elements, program layouts, system flow, control blocks, physical views of data, logical views of data, and many other perspectives of data. Once data has been captured either manually or automatically, a data dictionary generally makes the data available in an automated form to enhance and control such efforts as system generation, system documentation, or system change.

14.2 HOW IS A DATA DICTIONARY IMPLEMENTED?

A data dictionary is implemented in either or both of two ways: formally or informally. When a data dictionary is formally implemented it is accomplished specifically through the use of software in support of the data dictionary. This implementation can be referred to as the "formal" data dictionary. There also exists an "informal" data dictionary. In many shops, there is *no* formal data dictionary, *only* the informal one.

The informal data dictionary typically is realized by means of program listings, program specifications, procedure listings, cross-reference listing, control block libraries, system documentation, and other vehicles. In some installations, the level of administrative control is such that there is no great need for a formal data dictionary. In other shops, the existence of a formal data dictionary in the absence of administrative control by no means implies the shop is running under the dictionary concept or is deriving any major benefits from a data dictionary. The mere existence of a formal data dictionary in the absence of administrative support and control is an exercise in futility. The dividing line between control of data and lack of control of data lies in organizational discipline and control, not in the formal or informal embodiment of a data dictionary.

The software under which a data dictionary is realized (in the formal sense) is usually the domain of the data base administrator or data administrator. The responsibility for an informal data dictionary rests on the different parts of the data processing organization—programmers, operators, designers, users, technical support, management, and development personnel.

14.3 DATA DICTIONARY APPROACH—AN INVENTORY CONTROL OF DATA

The data dictionary concept can conveniently be described as an "inventory control" of data. The data processing organization needs control of its data in much the same way that a manufacturing company needs to control the parts it uses and builds. As applications become more complex and numerous, control of data becomes much more important. Some of the typical advantages of an "inventory control" of data are the ability to answer the following questions:

* What data exists in systems today? If the data is not documented, the shop is dependent entirely on the informal collection of documentation which is probably uncentralized, unorganized, inaccurate, and highly dependent on personnel.
* Of the data that exists and is documented, what does the documentation mean? Is it up-to-date? Is documentation complete? Is it accessible?

- What means exist to keep track of data? Data changes over time just as do other aspects of systems. The data dictionary is a vehicle that can meet the need to keep track of changes.

- What mechanism is there to minimize future duplication of development effort? Without a data dictionary, the designer is almost totally dependent on human interaction to prevent redundancy. Furthermore, the redundancy that occurs here is at a *very* high level: the duplication of entire systems and subsystems.

- Where should changes be made? When system modification is to occur, where are the appropriate places to make changes? What is the difference in making changes to one place in the system rather than another?

A fully implemented data dictionary is designed to answer these questions and provide other services, such as automatic generation of code. In a large, growing shop, a properly implemented data dictionary unquestionably is a valuable asset. New growth can be coordinated with existing systems. Existing systems can be modified in a state of awareness rather than ignorance. Searches of archived data become a rather simple task. For these reasons and quite a few others, a data dictionary's potential may well be worth the investment.

This entire discussion of a data dictionary does not assume any specific software. The conclusions are based on many observations of installations in various industries. It is interesting to note that an identical piece of software can be used very unsuccessfully in one environment and used very successfully in another, which leads to the conclusion that success with the data dictionary concept lies in the way the organization implements and uses the software, not particularly on the merits of the software itself. This fact is *very* important for the manager to understand because it is *easy* to make the software a scapegoat when problems arise.

14.4 ACHIEVING A DATA DICTIONARY'S POTENTIAL

The potential advantages of a data dictionary are many. Savings of development time, maintenance time, and control of the data of the organization are some of the advantages. The ability to integrate systems is another advantage. With these major advantages, it would appear that every shop would enthusiastically support a data dictionary, but that is not the case at all. The problem is that the potential of a data dictionary is not easily achieved.

14.5 90 PERCENT-10 PERCENT SYNDROME

Based on observations of *many* shops using many forms of formal data dictionary, the following (very nonscientific) statement can be made: 90% of the shops that have or have had a data dictionary installed have not found that it has lived up to its potential, whereas 10% of the shops that have a data dictionary support it enthusiastically and derive from it very real benefits. Very few shops that have installed a data dictionary for any length of time are neutral. For all the potential advantages of a data dictionary, why is there this disparity between its potential and the realization of that potential? What are the problems that an installation faces in unlocking the potential of a data dictionary?

14.6 PROBLEMS WITH A DATA DICTIONARY

The major issue with the use of a data dictionary is that a data dictionary implies a degree of organizational discipline. If that discipline is not *already* a fact within the organization, then a data dictionary (the software) is not going to somehow impose that discipline on the organization. Without organizational discipline, the software *will not produce meaningful results.* This is the reason why the same piece of software is very successful in one shop and very unsuccessful in another. The success lies in organizational discipline (or lack thereof), not in the elegance or sophistication of the software.

To achieve the necessary organizational discipline that is at the heart of a successful data dictionary, the manager must understand exactly what a data dictionary is, what it can accomplish, the role of each part of the organization in making a data dictionary work, and the ultimate cooperation and commitment by the various organizations involved and their management. Without that discipline, a data dictionary can achieve only a fraction of its potential. Once again, it is not particularly the merits of the software that make a data dictionary a success or a failure, it is the organization that uses the dictionary that makes the difference.

14.7 RESISTANCE TO A DATA DICTIONARY

Where does the resistance to data dictionaries come from, and why does it come? Programmers throw up the most immediate and deep-seated resistance. They often view a data dictionary as just one more level of red tape— one more obstacle—to be overcome in getting to the work at hand. If the concept of the data dictionary and its ensuing implementation is not presented to programmers very carefully, their concerns may be very real and justified. A data dictionary, handled improperly, *can* present a barrier to progress, and the programmer can be entirely correct.

The next wave of resistance usually comes from system designers. Just as the programmer views a data dictionary as an obstacle, so may the designer. Just like the programmer, the designer may be correct in assuming that a data dictionary is a hurdle to be overcome. Unless the data dictionary is being handled very carefully, the designer may be correct. The use of a data dictionary requires discipline and implies a certain amount of control. That discipline and control imply time and effort, both of which are chronically in short supply from the viewpoint of the designer. Thus it is easy to see the rationale of the designer in resisting a data dictionary.

The third wave of resistance comes from management—both management of applications and, surprisingly, data administration. The concern of management is that the advantages of a data dictionary are a long time in coming and, in the meantime, active and expensive resources are being consumed. At a moment of crisis, it is very tempting to take personnel working on a data dictionary and apply them to the crisis at hand. A data dictionary requires a long-term commitment by management. Interruption of that commitment usually wastes efforts toward a data dictionary carried out prior to that time because, quite often, the people pulled off a data dictionary never return to the project. Also, whenever the momentum of the data dictionary project is lost, it is very difficult if not impossible to regain, because of morale problems, lack of commitment, and a certain amount of justifiable cynicism.

The fourth wave of resistance to a data dictionary comes, usually very slowly, but fairly predictably, from data administration itself. A data dictionary requires personnel that could be employed elsewhere, as has been mentioned. But the very nature of the type of personnel required produces resistance. Building a data dictionary is both a clerical *and* a technical task. Assigning the task to a purely clerical person creates a potential problem in that major parts of the dictionary project may not be done correctly because of the technical inexperience or background of the clerical personnel implementing the dictionary. On the other hand, assigning experienced technical personnel to a data dictionary is expensive and subjects the technical personnel to a data-entry task that is often tedious. Thus there is a built-in element of resistance from the very people who are responsible for the success of the data dictionary.

14.8 CIRCUMVENTING A DATA DICTIONARY

Another reason a data dictionary often is not as successful as it can be is that there are usually many ways to circumvent the control and discipline imposed by a data dictionary. On the one hand, if the data administration constructs a data dictionary so that the dictionary is integrated and *forces* all parties to use its facilities, there is a very good chance that programmer resistance will be high, possibly justifiably so. Programmers feel that they have lost an essential part of their job—defining and maintaining the form of the data they work with. If the controls of a data dictionary are relaxed, programmer resistance may not be high but the benefits of control are then in jeopardy. So data administration is damned-if-they-do and damned-if-they don't.

If the data dictionary is not integrated into applications so that data definitions *must* be done through the dictionary, there will be even more opportunities to bypass the data dictionary. Even with a fully integrated data dictionary, a programmer can always create "work" areas in a program or redefine certain areas and format them as desired. Without a corresponding administrative review and restraint, control is not enforced by the data dictionary. There are many other ways in which the automatic controls of a data dictionary can be bypassed if it is to be implemented solely as a software package. Because a data dictionary can be bypassed as desired by programmers, and because there usually is resistance, the possibility of circumvention of a data dictionary is one of the main reasons for its failure to achieve its full potential.

14.9 INITIAL IMPLEMENTATION OF A DATA DICTIONARY

Another major barrier to success is the difficulty of initial implementation of a data dictionary. Usually, a data dictionary is brought into an installation after many systems are up and running. Data administration is faced with two choices: retrofit a data dictionary on old systems, or use a data dictionary only for new systems. If a data dictionary is to be retrofitted, a very large, labor-intensive effort is usually necessary, even with automated packages supplied by many vendors of data dictionaries. If a data dictionary is *not* to be retrofitted, data administration runs the very real risk of not having the tools to control system redundancy for existing systems. Again data administration is given some very hard choices.

Even if a data dictionary is brought up as an installation first goes into producing systems, there are still some difficult choices to be made. A data dictionary can address data at many levels—the data element level, data layout level, system level, and so on. If data administration chooses to use a data dictionary at its lowest level—that of data elements—there will be much work necessary before the data dictionary can bear fruit. The effort of a data dictionary may, in fact, significantly *delay* the development effort, thus fulfilling the fears of the designer. Most installations elect to implement a data dictionary at this level and quite a few failures have been the result. A data dictionary can be used successfully at other than the data element level and can produce benefits rather rapidly at those levels.

Retrofitting a data dictionary on existing systems is usually done in one of several ways:

1. *Manually*. Data elements, layouts, and so on, are transcribed manually from programs, reports, procedures, and so on, onto a data dictionary.
2. *Automatically*. Programs scan other programs or procedures and information about data is extracted.
3. *Combination of manual and automatic transcription*. Information about data is captured and transcribed onto a data dictionary in a number of ways. Retrofitting is usually done in phases rather than all at once. Quite a few attempts to retrofit a data dictionary all at once have resulted in a massive waste effort.

Some of the problems of retrofitting a data dictionary onto existing systems lie in the logical equation of data. When are two elements that have the same name really different? When are several elements that have different names really the same? How should names be resolved? What about data that exists in different source languages? How should an alias be handled? Synonyms? What naming conventions are to be followed? What changes should be made?

All these questions represent the mere *beginning* of considerations involved in the administration of a data dictionary.

14.10 OTHER PROBLEMS

Other reasons why a data dictionary often fails to live up to its potential are failure of data administration to concentrate on the most important issues, and lack of understanding of the importance and techniques of abstracting data correctly and to the right level.

A typical example of concentrating on the wrong issues is in placing a heavy emphasis on naming conventions, at the expense of such critical issues as management education. Naming conventions are important and play a part in the success of the implementation of a data dictionary, but the best naming conventions in the world are superfluous if management does not understand the importance of the data dictionary concept and the long-term commitment necessary to the success of a data dictionary.

Another reason for lack of success with a data dictionary is the improper abstraction of data. Data should be abstracted, understood, and controlled at its most fundamental level. For example, a designer specifies two data elements: an active policy and an inactive policy. Should the data elements be defined separately? From the data administration standpoint, absolutely not! A policy is a policy, whether it is active or inactive. By allowing separate definitions of data, data administration is allowing the designer to represent status or relationships of data at a level of definition that can easily lead to redundancy. Redundancy carried far enough can lead to unintegrated systems. Data should be understood and controlled at its most fundamental level of meaning, and that level is appropriate in the dictionary—not just any definition that someone somewhere happened to come up with.

14.11 MAKING A DATA DICTIONARY WORK

From all the preceding discussion of the problems of making a data dictionary work, it is a wonder that a data dictionary project is ever successful. It is interesting to note that nearly all of the problems of data dictionaries stem from the use, control, and understanding of the data dictionary, not from the software itself. That is why some installations are successful and others are not, given apparently identical environmental circumstances.

There are some practices or considerations that, if heeded, will afford an organization the best chance for success in data dictionary implementation. Some of them are:

1. Determine if there is a *real* need for a data dictionary. A data dictionary is conducive to large, complex, growing environments. It is expensive to implement and will be implemented informally. A data dictionary solely for the sake of a data dictionary is not a worthwhile activity.

2. Determine if the organization has the discipline to support a data dictionary. If the organization does not have this discipline, there is a very good chance of failure. If different parts of the organization are not willing to change their mode of operation for a common advantage, a data dictionary has little chance of success.

3. "Sell" the users on a data dictionary; do not implement it by edict. Only when all parts of the organization see the immediate and long-term benefits of a data dictionary will implementation be successful. Implementation by edict causes negative reactions, not just to the data dictionary but even to the way it is being implemented.

4. Identify resistance and make compromises to reduce resistance. Taking the attitude that resistance will not arise or will be negligible is not realistic. Understanding that resistance will occur, understanding the reasons for resistance, then compromising or otherwise reducing resistance is a realistic and effective posture for the data administrator.

5. Make sure that adequate resources exist and that there is adequate commitment to fulfill a data dictionary project. If there are not enough adequate resources or commitment for those resources, a data dictionary is doomed before it begins, regardless of any other justification.

6. Install a data dictionary where the most good will happen the soonest. This may mean that data element definition will be the *last* part of the dictionary implemented. Implementing a data dictionary at the level of interfering with the programmer will meet with a minimum of success. Using

a data dictionary as a controlling device to determine where systems should be integrated is an effective use of the tool. A data dictionary at this level of system development is probably transparent to the programmer and, furthermore addresses the large issue of system integration in a very appropriate place.

7. Integrate a data dictionary as much as possible. The less integrated a data dictionary is, the more redundancy of data and work there is. Furthermore, there is a greater opportunity for confusion and lack of control when definitions are strung out over many places.

8. If the dictionary software is purchased, buy it to fit the business need; do not try to make the business need fit the software.

REFERENCE

DB/DC Data Dictionary: General Information Manual, IBM Manual GH20-9104-0.

CASE STUDY

The New Orleans Jumbalay and Gumbo Manufacturing Company has had data processing for about 15 years. The systems encompass most aspects of the company that can be automated, and in general the data processing department and its management are well thought of and have earned a good reputation over the years.

Last year data processing members of management attended a convention and a well-known consultant spoke about the advantages of a data dictionary. For years New Orleans J and G has been operating with an "informal" data dictionary. After listening to the consultant, management decides that it is worthwhile implementing a formal data dictionary. After evaluating several pieces of sofware, one dictionary is selected and implemented.

Management has high hopes that the dictionary will serve as a vehicle for better documentation, faster systems development, and easier maintenance, and would act as an aid during system analysis. Also, management expects that a data dictionary is necessary for the construction of integrated systems.

The data base administrator (DBA) is charged with implementing and executing the data dictionary. The actual implementation and installation of the software is accomplished easily and quickly. However, the DBA runs into problems in the actual use of the dictionary. The first step is to convert existing systems. There are about 250 systems of various sizes and about 12 programs per system. The vendor has supplied software that is supposed to make this initial conversion easy, but the experience is that the conversion is a labor-intensive and arduous task. The effort is taking much more time than anticipated.

The DBA has assigned some very good technical people with the initial conversion. The enthusiasm is high for the first few months, but when the technicians begin to grasp the enormity of the project, their enthusiasm wanes. Morale sinks lower each day the job drags on.

On another front, the enthusiasm for the data dictionary project is lagging. Applications personnel resist the dictionary effort because they view the dictionary as another roadblock to progress. The benefits of a data dictionary are anything but obvious, but the overhead and red tape inherent in a data dictionary are very obvious. In short, the applications people view the data dictionary as an interference. Even though resistance is not open, it is still there and progress is very slow.

After six months of effort, management begins to question the worth of the data dictionary. The investment that has been made is considerable and the return on the investment is certainly not obvious.

In the meantime, there has been a new acquisition. New Orleans J and G has acquired Pontchartrain Crawdad Company. Even though the lines of business are very similar, there are some fundamental differences. To make Pontchartrain Crawdad fit into New Orleans J and G systems, some modification of systems is necessary. Unfortunately, there is a backlog of work already for the systems development staff, so management looks about for available staff. The only available personnel are those assigned to the data dictionary. Because of the pressing need for system change, the personnel on the dictionary project are temporarily reassigned.

The Crawdad project lasts longer than anyone expects and immediately following it comes an even more pressing project, so the personnel from the dictionary project are reassigned on more than a temporary basis.

Two years after the data dictionary staff have been reassigned, a manager notes that rental fees are being paid on dictionary software. The computer room has allocated two disk packs for the data dictionary and there has not been a single use of either resource for over 12 months. The manager questions whether the data dictionary is a wise allocation of New Orleans J and G resources.   ∎

Comment on the Following

1. The major problem is in the implementation of the data dictionary.
2. The major problem is in management commitment to the data dictionary.
3. The applications people are to blame for the data dictionary's failure.
4. If the DBA had had a more conscientious staff, the data dictionary would have been a success.
5. The DBA should have concentrated on shorter-term benefits.

6. To overcome resistance, the DBA should have emphasized the benefits of a data dictionary.

7. A data dictionary is actually a bad idea and is never a success. The benefits of a data dictionary are grossly overrated.

8. Better software should have been chosen.

MULTIPLE-CHOICE QUESTIONS

1. Management has read about the pitfalls of the data dictionary. They have confirmed how much money other companies have spent and the usefulness of their data dictionary efforts. They are properly skeptical. On the other hand, a bright, young consultant advises that if management wants to reduce maintenance costs, some form of integrated systems will be required and that will necessarily entail the use of a data dictionary.

   A. A data dictionary can be used in only one way. Since other companies have failed, it is a good bet that a data dictionary used as a tool for system integration will be a failure.

   B. The advantages of a successful data dictionary effort are such that the cost and probability of failure are justified.

   C. There is no necessary connection between system maintenance and integrated systems. Even if there is, a data dictionary plays a minor role.

   D. It is difficult to impossible to achieve short-term results in a data dictionary effort aimed at integrating systems.

   E. A data dictionary is a one-time effort that requires little follow-up effort or commitment.

2. Management has decreed that a data dictionary is a shop standard and will be used for all forthcoming projects. The DBA is in charge of the data dictionary and requires that all activity that ends up on the dictionary be done by his group or at least be approved by his group. In the past when applications have attempted to put something on the data dictionary that they felt they needed, there has been a delay of up to 6 weeks, and in some cases, the changes have never gotten on the dictionary. The DBA is reluctant to give the applications people any feedback whatsoever. Currently, the application's group is devising ways to avoid use of the data dictionary.

   A. A data dictionary cannot be circumvented effectively. It provides a means of control to the DBA.

   B. The DBA group is justified in using the data dictionary as a means of controlling the applications personnel.

   C. The applications people are justified in devising ways to get around the data dictionary.

   D. The major issue here is the data dictionary and its proper use.

   E. A better implementation of the data dictionary or better data dictionary software would solve the problem.

EXERCISES AND ESSAYS

1. What are the steps that should be taken to make a data dictionary a success?

2. Should management expect short-term results from a data dictionary project?

3. Is the preparation of a data dictionary a clerical or a technical task? What can be done to ease the tedium of the technician? What can be done to upgrade the clerical staff? Where can a balance be struck?

4. How important is the software that supports a data dictionary? In relation to other factors, such as management understanding and commitment? Application acceptance? DBA understanding and support?

5. What are the problems in converting existing systems to a data dictionary? Should existing systems be converted to a data dictionary? What is the exposure in not converting existing systems?

6. Describe the media on which informal data dictionaries exist. Will informal data dictionaries disappear when formal data dictionaries are implemented? What role do informal data dictionaries play when there is no formal data dictionary? In light of a formal data dictionary?

7. What is more important—naming conventions for data elements, or management understanding of proper dictionary usage? Prioritize a list of data dictionary benefits.

XV

Software Architecture Limitations

□□□

It is normal for large, complex application systems to have a few problems once the systems are put into production. The new system goes through a certain amount of normal "settling" and the constantly changing user's environment causes changes to be made to the new system. The newly appointed manager usually has some difficulty in distinguishing the scope of changes and problems that will arise as the project is implemented. Are some changes much more (or less) cumbersome than they appear? Are some problems so bad that the system should be redone?

The manager needs to be able to distinguish when he or she is facing a surmountable problem and when he or she is facing an unyielding constraint. To do this, the manager needs to be aware of some of the nonnegotiable constraints of software. A constraint is nonnegotiable and represents a problem or shortcoming of a system that necessitates redesign and rewrite of the system and/or moving the system to some other environment. In short, when a manager is facing a true hardware, software, or otherwise-constraint, by definition, there is *nothing* that can be done to salvage the existing system in its existing form.

15.1 TYPICAL SOFTWARE CONSTRAINTS

The following are some of the more common software constraints.

1. *Arrival-rate limitations.* In some cases the arrival rate of on-line activity (transactions) is so high that even in the face of a well-designed, well-written, well-tuned system with ample resources, response time is not adequate, nor will it be in the future. For example, suppose that a system can adequately handle a maximum arrival rate of 10 transactions per second. When the arrival rate rises above that, queue times will build. As an exam-

ple, if total response time is 120 seconds for a given transaction, 118 of those seconds will typically have been spent in queues once the arrival rate goes beyond the amount the system can handle.

2. *Total transaction throughput.* This constraint is very similar to limitations of on-line arrival rates, with one large difference. Arrival-rate limitations apply to a short or finite amount of time, whereas transaction throughput applies across all the time the system is up and functioning. As an example, suppose that a bank only runs 20,000 transactions a day and that software will support that amount of throughput if the transactions are reasonably spread out throughout the day. However, if all of those transactions are entered between 11:00 A.M. and 1:00 P.M., the arrival rate of the transactions will be such that response will not be adequate. On the other hand, if 200,000 transactions a day are to be run through a system that can handle a maximum 100,000 (however they are distributed), the arrival-rate measurement is meaningless.

3. *Processing limitations.* Some types of processing simply cannot be done given the current hardware and software environment. For example, suppose that a designer has specified a program that will scan an entire data base on-line and at the same time the programmer wishes to produce a 3- to 5-second response time. With today's hardware and software that kind of processing cannot be done if the data base is of any size at all, and all the system tuning that can be done will do nothing to alleviate the problem. The point is that if a certain kind of processing is required, it should be accomplished within the framework of what can be handled by the hardware and software, not at cross purposes to it. In the example above, it may be possible to scan the entire on-line data base, but not in 3 to 5 seconds. Or it may be possible to redesign the data base so that an entire scan is not necessary.

4. *Maintenance bind.* Some software is in such a state that *no* changes to it can be made. This may be because (a) the system is old, (b) the system is very large and complex, (c) the system is not documented (either at all or adequately), (d) the system has been maintained to the point where nothing else can be changed without fear of disturbing something, or (e) a combination of these factors. On occasion, systems reach a state of unmaintainability such that the very next change to the system, however small, will cause a rewrite.

5. *Data base size limitations.* Some applications and some data base management systems have a limitation on the amount of data that can be handled. Usually, this limitation is a pragmatic one rather than a technical one. When the designer has specified more data to be handled than can be handled, something must give.

6. *Application architecture limitations.* When application software is developed, the designer has in mind some framework around which the sys-

tem will be built. When that framework is not fundamentally solid or when use of the system varies greatly from that that has been anticipated by the developer, the system may have to be scrapped. For example, suppose that a designer wants to build an on-line system without adhering to the standard work unit. Once the system is constructed, the designer throws hardware at the system and directs competent tuners to "give him performance," all to little or no long-term avail. The fact is that if the designer wants on-line performance, he *must* build it in at the point of design, and the best way to do that is through the standard work unit. Performance cannot be retrofitted without rearchitecting the application.

In the case where a system is used beyond the boundaries anticipated by the designer, there is little to do except rearchitect the system. For example, suppose that an inventory system is built to keep track of office supplies. Once the system is functional, a manager sees how useful it is and decides to apply it to all the manufacturing inventory of the company, and then the system falls on its face because of transaction arrival rate, total amount of data handled, or for some other reason. If an inventory system for manufacturing goods is to be applied to a system designed to handle an order of magnitude or less of material, it is not surprising that a system rewrite is called for.

15.2 FACING CONSTRAINTS

What can the manager do when he or she is bumping up against a constraint? The *only real, long-term solution* is to *redesign* and *rewrite* the *application*. This may mean going to different hardware and/or software. This step is almost *always* unpopular because (1) it requires much personnel and other resources, (2) the lead time is probably not desirable, and (3) most important, it is an open admission of a mistake in design, judgment, and/or planning. Thus it is not surprising that rewriting systems is an unpopular thing to do. In some shops it is political suicide, despite the fact that it is the *only real, long-term solution*.

There are some popular ways to avoid "having to bite the bullet." They are:

1. System tuning
2. Hardware acquisition
3. Technical "quick fix" or gimmick
4. Making the best of things until the system causes an even larger crisis

The best these solutions do is to postpone and thus create a false sense of happiness; ultimately, these "pacifiers" will cost more than plunging into the long-term solution.

The cost of not recognizing a constraint (or recognizing the constraint but not accepting the fact that it is a constraint) is high. The cost is measured in terms of user morale and dissatisfaction with the system, programmer and designer frustration in having to put energy into a hopeless cause, and hardware and software costs. Ultimately, the cost of not "biting the bullet" is much higher than the cost of recognizing and facing the problem. Managers who look only at short-term costs face a temptation not to accept constraints when they occur. The long-term costs are significantly raised by nothing but a short-term attitude.

CASE STUDY

The Calgary Collateral Company runs loan, savings, and checking operations throughout Alberta and Manitoba, Canada. They have 60 or so branch offices connected by a network. The processing is done on a centralized computer in Calgary.

The teller has one basic transaction that is entered each time a customer presents himself or herself at a window. That transaction tells such things as a customer's address, home loan information, savings information, checking balance, last five checks received, electronic transfer of funds information, and any additional charges or interest. It takes about eight data base calls to achieve this function.

The system is running on the biggest, fastest computer that can be bought. It is fully configured with memory, channels, and so on. The data base software under which the system runs is the industry standard for fully functional data base management systems.

From 10 A.M. to 1:30 P.M. every day, but especially on the first of the month, the last day of the month, and Fridays, the bank begins to fill with customers. During the nonpeak hours, the system response time is normally about 1 second. However, during peak-period processing the response time gets progressively worse.

The system technician estimates that the transaction arrival rate is about eight per second during the peak period. She notices that queues begin to form inside the computer when the arrival rate goes to approximately five per second. When queues begin to form, the response time begins to soar. It is not uncommon on a bad day to see response times of 5 to 6 minutes. Of that 5 to 6 minutes, only 1 second is spent in execution; the remainder is spent in the queue waiting for execution. The expected transaction arrival rate is projected to go as high as 30 to 40 transactions per second as business expands in the next two years.

A consultant outlines management's options:

1. Convert the system to different software that can sustain a higher transaction rate.
2. Redesign the system so that only a single piece of information is returned per transaction.
3. Do both option 1 and option 2.

It is clear that the existing system must be changed. Management does not like it, but it is simply a fact of life. To convert the existing software to other software that can sustain a higher transaction rate is distasteful because the conversion promises to be less than easy. To redesign the system so that only a single piece of information is retrieved at a time makes sense from a business standpoint because very few customers want all the information returned. However, the consultant points out that doing just one data base call per transaction means that the software can handle only about 15 transactions per second.

The third alternative is to do nothing and let the customer suffer.   ∎

Comment on the Following

1. Management is butting up against a software constraint. How could it have avoided this problem? What can management do about it now?
2. Will purchasing a faster computer help? Why not?
3. When was this problem foreseeable? What would have been the cost of dealing with the problem when it was first predictable? What is the cost of dealing with the problem now?
4. Who should be responsible for the mistake that was made? Who should be responsible for correcting the mistake?

MULTIPLE-CHOICE QUESTIONS

1. A shop has a system that is so old that certain key programs cannot be maintained because they have been altered so many times that program logic is very, very difficult to follow. Management crosses its fingers in the hopes that the user does not want changes or that the programs do not experience errors.
   A. An immediate rewrite is in order.
   B. Every program has a natural life span. Scrapping old programs is no crime.
   C. The effort that it takes to make a small change would probably be better directed at rewriting part or all of the system.

     D. When the system is rewritten, care should be taken to make the code as reusable and modifiable as possible.

     E. Management will have a real problem come the day that big changes need to be made, especially if those changes are critical.

2. Management has a problem system that should have been rewritten long ago. Instead, a series of short-term "fixes" have been applied, leaving management with a long-term problem that arises over and over.

     A. Biting the bullet long ago would probably have been the cheapest solution in the long run.

     B. Political expediency is probably a significant reason why the long-term solution has not been implemented.

     C. There is no guarantee new problems will not crop up in the event of a rewrite.

     D. The longer the systems exist under a series of short-term quick fixes, the less chance the long-term solution has of being implemented.

     E. Quantifying long-term costs and short-term costs is difficult.

EXERCISES AND ESSAYS

1. What short-term solutions exist when data base size poses a problem? Is data base size a predictable factor? In every case? Usually?

2. What can be done when a system becomes unmaintainable?

*3. A salesman for a data base management system claims that there are no technical limitations to the amount of data that can be handled. However, necessary utilities, such as reorganization and recovery, take progressively longer to run as the amount of data grows. Can this DBMS really make the claim that there is no limit to the amount of data that can be handled? Is the limitation a pragmatic one rather than a technical one?

4. What options does management have when the transaction arrival rate is faster than can be handled?

XVI

Approaches to System Design

As the role of application design becomes increasingly important, so does the general approach of management of the design process. Indeed, the direction given by management determines *much* about the cost and effectiveness of data processing. Several common approaches have been selected and "profiled," and the characteristics of each approach are discussed. The point of interest is the relative costs associated with each approach—what the differences between approaches are and where the dangers lie.

The approaches presented are a composite representation and do not reflect a particular installation. Indeed, in a large shop several approaches may exist side by side or in combination. The profiles have been drawn from observations of many data processing installations across many industries.

16.1 ROLE OF THE DESIGNER

As an installation grows in maturity, the role of the designer changes from a moderately important role to one of the most important roles in the organization. This is especially true as on-line systems begin to be built. Even in the absence of on-line systems, the importance of the designer grows as the number of applications grow. The reason for the shift in the importance of the designer stems directly from the fact that the design of applications ultimately is the single largest factor responsible for the long-term success of on-line systems. Applications design also has a great influence on an organization's ability to integrate systems and the future options available to the hardware planner.

When systems were small, isolated, and relatively simple, the role of the system designer was important, but only in a limited sense. The success or failure of the system designer was rarely noticed outside the designer's immediate domain. However, the success or failure of the designer in larger, more sophisticated, more powerful, and more complex computer applications greatly magnifies the role of the designer. Whether management or the designer likes it or not, the spotlight is on the designer.

16.2 APPROACHES TO DESIGN

Because of the shifting importance of the role of the designer, it is worthwhile to examine some of the more common approaches to design. These are by no means the only approaches, and even within these approaches there are elements and combinations of other approaches. The most common approaches are:

1. Standard approach
2. Hyperproductivity approach
3. Technological approach
4. Theoretical approach
5. Errorless approach

16.3 THE STANDARD APPROACH

The standard approach to system design is found, in whole or in part, in almost every installation. The approach is typified by the developer who perceives his or her function as primarily to satisfy the user (and user requirements), to build systems within the confines of available (or soon to be available) equipment, to use technology (or slight upgrades) that is familiar, to attempt to develop projects within schedule and budget, and to use established design techniques and methodologies (structured techniques, review methodologies, etc.).

The primary motivating force of the designer's life is the user, although management, technical support, and other organizations have influence. As long as the system is constructed on time, within budget, and is functional, the designer has done his or her job. Upgrades in hardware and software technology are generally done gradually.

Some of the earmarks of the installation operating under the standard approach is the common ratio of one designer to every four to six programmers. The size of the installation operating under this approach is variable; the standard approach can be found in an installation of any size. Typically, programmers spend 50 to 70% of their time on maintenance, most of which is system modification or extension. Only a small amount of the maintenance effort is problematical rectification (i.e., "fixit" maintenance). Education comes in two forms: formal and informal. Formal education is done in one- and two-week classes that address a specific subject, and is taught by a vendor, outside agency, or, in the case of some large shops, by an internal education department. The formal education comes from contact with peers, management, and exposure to day-to-day problems. Most of the formal education addresses the mechanics of system development, not design philosophies or approaches.

Schedule and budget overruns are the rule. Overruns of up to 200% are common. The success of meeting deadlines and budgets usually lies more with the background and philosophies of the manager setting the schedule than with the diligence or intelligence of the designer.

The designer is usually one or more human links removed from the user. In many cases the user communicates with the user analyst, who then communicates to the designer. Occasionally, there is direct communication between user and designer, but not frequently.

The pattern of the life cycle of system development is: a feasibility study, system requirements, design, programming, testing, implementation, and finally post-implementation cleanup. This is shown in Figure 16.1.

Feasibility ⇨ Requirements ⇨ Design ⇨ Programming ⇨ Testing ⇨ Implementation ⇨ Post-implementation

Figure 16.1 Standard phases of system development.

When a user analyst is involved, the designer's involvement in feasibility is minimal or nonexistent. Involvement in requirements definition and analysis is also minimal. Data and program design consume the most attention of the designer, quite naturally. Programming and testing require some of the designer's attention. Implementation requires even less of the designer's attention until the moment of truth comes—that first moment when the system is finally installed and it is determined whether it will or will not work and will or will not satisfy the user's requirements. At that point, if the answer is negative, the designer becomes dedicated to the system in post-implementation design.

16.4 PROBLEMS OF THE STANDARD APPROACH TO SYSTEMS DEVELOPMENT

The problems that are encountered during the development of systems using the standard approach to design are common and are found in one form or the other in almost every installation. Some typical problems are:

1. Projects are never allocated enough development time and there is always an ever-increasing backlog of applications to be built or modified and extended.
2. Machine resources are hard-pressed to keep up with the demand for more and more resources.
3. The first time a new technology is utilized or a new type of applica-

tion is built, the result is less than entirely satisfactory. In cases where the first effort should be a learning experience, management becomes overambitious and makes the mistake of making the first experience a very critical one.

4. Educating users and management to the reality of system development is a tedious and risky task. Users and management learn best by experience. All the wisdom in the world from conversation is not worth one good experience. Unfortunately, those learning experiences are usually costly.

As a standard for comparison to other approaches to development, a baseline cost model will be developed. It is depicted by Figure 16.2. The costs selected for analysis are:

1. *Development costs.* This figure covers system costs from feasibility study to first iteration of implementation and includes both human and machine costs.
2. *Post-development costs.* This figure includes the cost of system redesign from first iteration of implementation to user acceptance. This includes the same costs as development.
3. *Operational costs.* These costs include the human (computer) operational costs that occur after the system goes into production as well as the hardware and software costs.

The different approaches to design will have various impacts on these costs; that is why they were chosen for scrutiny.

Development   Post-development   Hardware/
costs   costs   software/
                                                    operations   Figure 16.2 Baseline cost model.

16.5 A SECOND APPROACH TO DESIGN: OPTIMIZATION OF DEVELOPMENT TIME

With the backlog of data processing requests that exist, there is no argument that system development time should be an important consideration in the building of systems. As long as system development time is conscientiously and carefully balanced against other trade-offs, such as performance, availability, and flexibility, there is no problem. It is when system development time becomes the *major* and *only* objective of an organization that problems arise. Such attitudes are common among batch-oriented shops since the major criteria for success in those installations is speed of development and correctness of code.

When the emphasis is *only* on speed of development or the emphasis in that area is overdone, some interesting phenomena result. Often, installations that emphasize speed of development are fairly advanced in design and programming methodologies such as structured design. It is also typical to find productivity aids such as TSO or VM/CMS at these installations.

16.6 PROBLEMS

Systems are usually produced more quickly at shops that emphasize development, but the quality of the systems produced is often inferior. The components of quality that are sacrificed are future system flexibility, system performance, and/or overall system availability. There is rarely a firm conceptualization or understanding of the data at the user level because systems are heavily shaped around processing requirements, not around the "natural" shaping of the data. Systems are nearly always designed around direct translation of output specifications or requirements and, as such, are very fragile in the face of changing user requirements. One of the hallmarks of these installations is the post-implementation correction of large and small design errors *after* deadlines have been met and code has been written. It is not unusual to find post-implementation design taking up several times as much effort as that required in the original development phase.

Because of the large propensity toward post-implementation design, the levels of productivity so vocally advocated by the "hyperdevelopers" is very suspect. Perhaps with slower, more careful design, less post-implementation design would be necessary, thus producing a real gain in productivity.

16.7 ADVANTAGES

When done by very knowledgeable system designers, the hyperproductive approach to system design can produce good results quickly. When done with less than sophisticated designers, this approach produces quick results nearly all of which are unacceptable and most of which have to be modified immediately or redone to be workable. Management adopting the hyperproductive approach should be *very* careful to determine whether this approach is valid.

16.8 DANGERS

The more complex the environment, the greater the risk there is in adopting the hyperproductive approach to development. In a simple, highly disciplined environment, there is less chance of major error and more opportunity for graceful recovery from errors than in a complex, undisciplined environment. Complex environments give the designer greater opportunity to err, and those errors ultimately translate into work being redone. The opportunity for error arises in the complexity of the data, in the relationships of data, and in the amount and complexity of processing of the data.

Another tangential problem of hyperproductivity is inefficient code. Often, organizations that purport to build code quickly virtually ignore the actual optimization of the code. A final preproduction pass of the code through a compiler optimizer may be the extent to which that performance is addressed. This usually leads to the classical case where poor performance is not recognized until it is very expensive to correct (i.e., after the system is up and running). On a larger scale, this leads to greater machine costs than are necessary and general user dissatisfaction with the system.

16.9 COMPARISON WITH BASELINE COSTS

The comparison with baseline costs is seen in Figure 16.3, which shows that initial development costs are indeed lower than the baseline costs that represent the standard approach. However, post-development costs more than offset the savings in initial development costs, and ultimately operational costs are significantly higher.

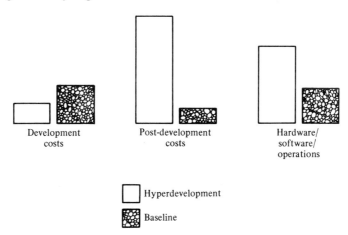

Figure 16.3 Comparison of hyperproductivity approach to baseline costs.

16.10 A THIRD APPROACH TO DESIGN: THE TECHNOLOGICAL APPROACH

The technological approach to controlling systems involves either or all of the following: (1) significant dependence on nonstandard technology; (2) use of standard technology in a nonstandard way; or (3) massive immersion into the technical details of standard technology.

An example of dependence on nonstandard technology is the use of equipment or software not found or supported elsewhere. When an installation opts to modify standard operating systems or software, or chooses to use regular software exits in an unconventional fashion, it is using standard technology in an unconventional manner. The third option—delving deeply into the detailed technological aspects of standard software or hardware—is most common. In this situation almost all of the options available in the software are tried and utilized, many for their own sake. It requires comprehensive and in-depth understanding (and ultimate mastery) of the technology on which an installation's systems operate.

The technological approach to the control of system design works well where there is *some* discipline imposed on the application designer and some coordination between the designer and the technician. If there is *no* imposition of discipline on the application designer, even the best tuned system is likely to be a failure in view of the uncontrolled design practices. One of the hallmarks of the technological approach to the control of system design is the use of technological features for their own sake. Often, there is no business justification for the implementation of sophisticated features, only the curiosity of the technician.

The long-term result of this approach is a motley collection of software and hardware. Despite this assorted collection, the technician can hardly be blamed for this condition because the emphasis of their job is on their expertise in using and understanding a wide variety of devices and techniques, not necessarily on their wisdom in the choice of those devices and techniques. The responsibility falls on management that fosters such an attitude. There is usually a widespread emphasis on "will it work" before implementation and "how well will it work" after implementation. The approach to performance is purely technical, one of struggling with the final output of the system developers, with only a minimal attempt to influence the designer earlier in the development cycle. In essence, the technologists must live at the point of the whip being cracked, not the handle doing the cracking.

16.11 DANGERS

One of the primary dangers of the technological approach to controlling system development is that technology is often viewed as an end in itself, not as a means to an end. Many technicians view their role as the *only* role, thus missing some of the major points of sound organization of computer development and operation.

Another drawback to the technological approach of controlling the development and operation of systems is that there are only a few qualified technicians and there is always a heavy demand for their services. If management elects to hire technical expertise from outside the company, it will have to offer high salaries. If management elects to "grow its own" expertise, the demand for that expertise will be such that a high turnover rate may develop. Furthermore, when technical experts leave an installation, it is often difficult to replace them or even to continue their work, because it is typical for technical "gurus" to leave scant documentation.

Another major problem with adopting the technological approach is that, after long development, whole systems may not work, especially where an entirely new technology is being tried. When this happens, major rewrite and redesign may be necessary before a system gets into production. Another problem is that a "technological masterpiece" may not be extendable to future requirements. Technology may have been stretched to the point where the system works "as is" and no further. This situation may be only slightly more acceptable than systems that refuse to function in the first place. The problem occurs because technology may have been extended to the point where it cannot be stretched any further. Technology then acts as a constraint, not as a vehicle for advancement.

16.12 COMPARISON WITH BASELINE COSTS

The costs of the technological approach to controlling system development fall into two categories: the cost of successful projects and the cost of unsuccessful projects. When a project is successful, the costs may well be below the baseline costs. When a project is not successful, if the project is ever able to be implemented, the costs may run well above the baseline costs. Figure 16.4, which shows this disparity in costs, illustrates the fact that when a technological failure occurs, it is expensive. However, technological successes may gain savings in the areas of post-development design, and operational costs.

16.13 A FOURTH APPROACH TO DESIGN:
THE THEORETICAL APPROACH

The theoretical approach to systems development places a great deal of emphasis on theory and certain academic aspects of development and design. Typically, data analysis and modeling are done almost to the exclusion of other necessary aspects of system design. Quite often, one or two points of systems development are done so finely and to such a level of detail that other points that should be refined are sketchy. Very often, pragmatic issues such as performance and implementation may not be considered at all. This may stem from the fact that the theoretician building the system has not faced systems that require a large volume of data or transactions. Nevertheless, a certain degree of pragmatism is necessary. The theoretical approach is by no means to be found exclusively in academia, and within academia there are plenty of examples of nontheoretical systems. The tag "theoretical" refers to an attitude, not a class of designers.

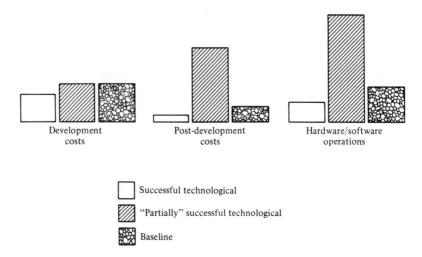

Figure 16.4 Comparison of technological approach to baseline costs.

One trademark of this approach is construction of elaborate data models based on fundamental user data relationships. This can lead to a high degree of flexibility, but if the logically constructed models are directly translated to a physical model (as sometimes happens), the result can be a poorly performing implementation.

One of the problems of the theoretical approach to systems development (wherever it is practiced) is that systems development often takes an inordinate amount of time. Not only does this increase development costs, but there is the very real danger that the system requirements will change so much from the initial set of requirements to the way they will look once the system is built that satisfying the initial set of requirements will no longer be acceptable.

Another danger of the theoretical approach is that design trade-offs are usually not done properly. It often happens that one set of parameters of design optimization comes into focus to the exclusion of other parameters. This, of course, leads to problems once the deficiencies inherent to the imbalance come to light.

16.14 COMPARISON WITH BASELINE COSTS

Figure 16.5 illustrates the theoretical approach to the comparison to the baseline costs. Although the operational costs are not significantly different from baseline costs, the development and post-development costs are significantly higher for the theoretical approach.

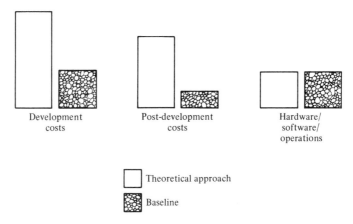

Figure 16.5 Comparison of theoretical approach to baseline costs.

16.15 A FIFTH APPROACH TO DESIGN: THE ERRORLESS APPROACH

A less common approach to system design can be termed the "errorless" approach. The errorless approach is one in which only a minimum amount of error is tolerated prior to the striking of code. Every minute detail of data and processing must be reviewed. This is difficult, if not impossible, to do in any environment where there are many and complex requirements. Furthermore, some requirements may conflict with others. And, given time, *all* requirements change—to some degree. It is not surprising then that the errorless approach is not popular because it is simply not pragmatic. Given an environment where requirements are limited and static, the errorless approach may make sense.

In any case, when the errorless approach is used for data base and system development, the result is a *very* large initial development period, so large in fact that it is not uncommon to have the project canceled.

The costs related to the errorless approach are depicted by Figure 16.6. An analysis of the costs shows that system development time is *much* greater than the baseline figures. Once the system is built, operational costs tend to be minimal (that is, after all, one of the vagaries taken into account by the error-free designer). The danger is that the system will never be built and that the tremendous initial development effort will be wasted.

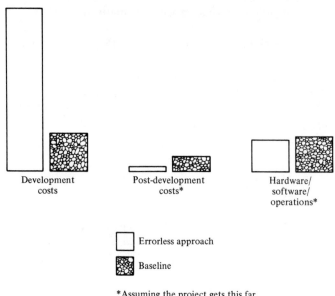

Development
costs

Post-development
costs*

Hardware/
software/
operations*

☐ Errorless approach

▨ Baseline

*Assuming the project gets this far.

Figure 16.6 Comparison of errorless approach to baseline costs.

REFERENCE

Dorn, Philip, "1979 DP Budget Survey," *Datamation*, Vol. 25, No. 1 (1980).

CASE STUDY

The Dallas Doomsday Company, an insurance company specializing in disaster insurance, prides itself on the state-of-the-art level of its computer systems. Over the years, Doomsday technicians have done some things that have been first in the industry and management feels very proud of the high level of technicians that they have been able to attract and keep employed. At every level there is a stress on technical expertise. In part, this may be a fallout from the influence of the vice-president of automated processing, who worked his way up from his start as a wire-board operator in the 1950s.

Dallas Doomsday buys standard software—operating systems and data base management systems—and modifies them in many places. The modifications are done through both nonstandard and standard software exits. Psychologically, when Doomsday does a modification, there is a feeling of technical superiority over the authors of the operating system and data base software. Indeed, the better the improvement and the more complex the change, the greater the feeling of superiority and the more acknowledgments that are received from peers at Doomsday.

It is true that on occasion Doomsday enjoys an advantage in automation over other competitors. Doomsday can sometimes get more out of its environment than other shops can achieve. This shows up in a slightly enhanced performance profile and in features that other environments do not have.

There are, however, some drawbacks to modifications of standard software. One drawback comes when the software vendor releases a new version of the operating system or data base management system. Hand in hand with the release usually goes a date when the current release will no longer be supported. In general, each new release offers enhancements, improvements, and features not attainable with the current release. Over time, most shops move from release to release and thus enjoy an environment in which the software vendor does a great deal of the work of evolving the software.

In the Doomsday environment there is a problem. As each new release comes out, careful analysis must be made of the differences between one release and the next, because the technicians have to be prepared to apply the current modifications to the new system; otherwise, systems that run in the current environment may not run at all in the new environment. Where modifications are not done, it is standard that whatever runs in the current environment will run in the new environment (i.e., under the new release). As long as there are no major differences from one release to the next, Doomsday has no problem. However, when there are significant changes from one release to the other, Doomsday has a problem. One small slip in a modification can lead to unknown results later.

Another insidious problem faced by Doomsday is that it is rather easy to attract technicians (because of Doomsday's orientations), but once hired, they usually leave because there is a large market for their skills.

One day the operating system comes to a halt because of a very strange problem. The operator resets the machine and processing continues. It is later discovered that data has been improperly written to a particular disk pack.

About a week later the same problem occurs, but this time the data mishandling occurs on a data base, which later brings down the on-line DBMS. The business of Doomsday comes to a halt.

The technicians begin to scramble for a solution. At times like this under normal circumstances, the software vendor is usually available for consultation. However, when modifications are made to standard software, the software vendor assumes no responsibility and only brings his experts in for a fee—a large fee.

It takes the technicians 36 hours to discover the problem. In the meantime, the on-line system has been unavailable to users. ∎

Comment on the Following

1. If the technicians had been smarter or more careful, they would not have had the problem.
2. If the system software had never been modified, (a) the chances of such an error are minimized and (b) the software vendor would lend assistance.
3. The business of the company may have been jeopardized in the name of higher technology.
4. Is there a danger that a software release will become so modified that it will not be possible to go to another release?
5. If the problem is really in the standard software and not the local modifications, it will be very difficult to prove.

MULTIPLE-CHOICE QUESTIONS

1. A designer has chosen to build a system so that, once final code is produced, there will never be a need to go back and change the code. His interest is to produce a perfect design. He spends a great many resources refining and reviewing his design, down to the finest level of detail imaginable.

   A. If the user's environment is a static one, he *may* succeed. In the case of a changing user's environment, he has no real chance at success.
   B. The approach risks losing much design and analysis effort because the system may never be built—so much time was taken in design and analysis that the user's needs have changed and the design is now obsolete.
   C. It is typical to have reams of documentation in the analysis and design phase.
   D. Analysis to too low a level of detail may not be the correct thing to do.
   E. The intent of producing a sound design is probably a good idea; producing a perfect design may be impossible.

2. A designer claims that the key to success is the building of the logical structures of data. He spends a great deal of time making different user views of the data. The data is then modeled. Then it is analyzed through a process known as normalization. Of the six months allocated

for data base design, the designer spends five of them getting to the normalized form of the data.

   A. His project is probably going to be late.

   B. The design of the data from the logical model to the physical model is as important as synthesizing the user's environment to produce the logical model.

   C. The approach is more likely to produce a sound design than is simply building a system around a set of user requirements.

   D. Whatever the user requirements are, they represent a snapshot of the user's world that will change over time.

   E. The designer may be overlooking other systems that will need to use the data at a later time.

EXERCISES AND ESSAYS

1. Why does the importance of the role of the designer increase as a shop matures? Does a growth in shop size mean that a shop is maturing?

2. How can the user be educated to the appropriate expectations of data processing?

3. What are the advantages/disadvantages of the hyperproductive approach to design? The technological approach? The theoretical approach? The errorless approach?

4. How can the costs of a system be measured? Development costs? Implementation costs? Operational costs? User costs? How can the savings be measured?

XVII

User Requirements

□□

Universally, data processing exists as a service organization within the company. The service is for the user, and the satisfaction of the user ultimately determines the success or failure of data processing. Another major factor in the success or failure of data processing is in the budget allocated for data processing. At the highest levels, user satisfaction and budgets are the two most important and visible factors of data processing. What is interesting is the relationships between the two—budgets and user satisfaction. A large budget does not necessarily equate to large amounts of user satisfaction; indeed, the reverse is often the case.

It is much to the benefit of managers to pay careful attention to the issue of specification of user requirements. Managers can make entirely correct decisions in other areas of responsibility in data processing, but if they fail to understand the importance of managing user requirements properly, they have exposed themselves to all sorts of evils. When user requirements are not set down properly, the door is open to user dissatisfaction and budgetary increases in the short run and the long run. It is thus appropriate that managers understand the issues of user requirements.

User requirements represent one of the foundations on which system development is built. When user requirements are analyzed and documented properly, system development can proceed in an orderly and straightforward fashion. On the other hand, when user requirements are analyzed and documented improperly, development efforts are based on a very shaky foundation at best and, in some cases, system development should not proceed. The danger in doing system development when requirements are not settled is that entire major parts (or all!) of the design must be redone, thus wasting precious effort. Solid system requirements thus are at the very basis of productivity.

224

17.1 USER'S ENVIRONMENT

It is assumed that the user's environment will change. The needs of users, the way data is viewed, the environment in which the user operates, user management, the corporate organization—all of these factors will change in time. The only difference from user to user is the rate of change. In light of this constantly changing users environment, it is not unreasonable that user requirements will change, and this is what gives the system designer problems. The system designer needs a set of requirements with which to work that is as static as possible. Most designers can absorb some degree of change of requirements during the development phase (usually depending on how flexibly they design their systems), but an inordinate amount of change or a constant change in requirements cannot be tolerated. What can be done in those environments where the user *is* rapidly changing requirements?

Some of the instances where the user may have a legitimate need for requirement changes at the outset of the project are:

1. In the specification of a new system
2. In the specification of a system in an environment not encountered previously
3. In an unstable (political) user environment
4. In the face of data that is inherently unstable

Just because there are legitimate cases for instability of user requirements does not mean that the designer should throw up his or her hands and accept the consequences of a design based on a very insecure foundation. Some of the approaches to helping the user stabilize requirements are:

- System prototyping: building a system quickly and allowing the user to experience it firsthand. The danger is that the interim or prototype may become the final solution, which is seldom a sound choice in the long run.
- Quick construction of a subset or a phase of the system as specified by the user: this allows the user the opportunity to inspect the system firsthand. Sweeping changes can then be made without affecting a large amount of existing code and data.
- In any case, build the user's system with as much elasticity as possible in the data structures and transactions.
- Make the user aware of the fact that changes in requirements cost time and money. The user is free to make whatever changes he or she wants as long as he or she is willing to pay for them. (For this purpose it is mandatory that requirements be drawn up formally.)
- Allow the user to inspect similar systems elsewhere and to exchange ideas with active users of the existing system. This will help the user to envision

the system and may point out pitfalls to the user and the designer at an early stage.

17.2 ONCE REQUIREMENTS ARE STABLE

At some point, requirements *must* become stable (or system development will never begin). When this point is reached, the requirements will be drawn up formally and agreed on by the designer and the user. The resultant document will be a "covenant" or "contract" that forms the basis of the relationship responsibilities, and the obligations of the user and the designer, and becomes the foundation on which further design efforts will proceed. The document formally specifying the requirements should be signed and dated. It should be concise, clear, complete, and formally agreed upon by both parties.

A cost analysis should accompany the features requested. The cost analysis should include both development costs and production costs. Omitting either one can lead to faulty conclusions. The types of costs covered should be personnel, computer use, overhead, and support costs. In addition to the costs of the project, the benefits should also be analyzed. What exactly will be saved by the system? What is the worth of the system to the company? It may be useful to cite the origin of the request should any feature be peculiar, unreasonable, or otherwise out of character.

17.3 MISUSE OF REQUIREMENTS

The need for the high degree of formalization of user/designer understanding of requirements stems from the fact that the definition of requirements has such a profound influence on the system *and* the fact that the requirements are easy to misinterpret. As an example of problems that can arise when requirements are not drawn up properly, consider the following cases.

1. *Requirements not defined.* If they are ambiguous or unstated, they are open to different interpretations. For example, suppose that the user requests "adequate response time for on-line transactions." Does this mean that an average of 5 seconds will do? Can the user complain if he or she gets a 15-second response time? Can the designer feel slighted when the user complains about a 2-second response time? If the requirement were to read "an average of 10-second response time with 90% of transactions responding in 12 seconds," there is an objective basis for discussion once the system becomes operational; otherwise, there is *never* likely to be harmony, because of the ambiguity of the original requirement.

2. *Overspecification by user.* Either the user specifies unreasonable parameters for satisfaction or goes so far as to specify physical implementa-

tion criteria for the design. The user should touch on physical implementation only in the broadest terms. The designer should have the freedom to choose whatever technical solutions are appropriate for the problem at hand. When the user specifies physical implementation, he or she limits the designer in a very fundamental way.

3. *Requirements used as a tool to justify poor design.* In this case the designer justifies every decision he or she makes under the guise of "user requirements." It is common to hear this tactic in design reviews, and for that reason it is useful to have the user attend the review. Since the user *cannot* specify requirements that will affect physical implementation, the designer *cannot* use "user requirements" as a justification for poor design choices.

4. *Designer "add on" of design features that are unnecessary.* There is a fine line between system enhancement and unnecessary overspecification of a system. Often the user lays out a requirement, the designer adds an auxiliary requirement, the next designer adds some more, so that, by the time the system is implemented, the requirements are much more than the user specified originally. If the designer is going to add or modify requirements, he or she should notify the user and have the user formally sign off on the addition or modification, because the addition or modification costs precious development time and may produce results that are actually undesirable or superfluous.

All of these problems arise when requirements are not specified formally and openly. Without a clearly written "contract," a shop is susceptible to one or more of these problems. With that document, these problems either disappear or become resolvable.

17.4 WHO SPECIFIES REQUIREMENTS

The user is responsible for specifying user requirements, not the analyst representing the user. On occasion, systems are put up without a user. These systems are built primarily to sell a user on new software, hardware, and so on. When this occurs, the analyst must act on the user's behalf. Requirements must be drawn up and firmly defined before the onset of design. The same previously stated ground rules apply—new changes or additions to requirements cost time and money. The analyst acting in behalf of a user cannot arbitrarily change requirements once design has begun without taking responsibility for the impact of the change.

In any case, systems with no user involvement at the point of design are fairly rare. In all other cases it should be a standard that the user doing the requirement definition is *not* a part of the data processing department (unless, of course, the system is being written for data processing).

17.5 CONTENTS OF USER REQUIREMENTS

Operating under the philosophy that the user may not specify requirements that will force a particular physical implementation, what exactly *should* the user specify? The most important criteria are:

1. System objectives
2. Scope of the system
3. Raw data requirements
4. Inputs and outputs of system (which may include screen layouts, re-ports, etc.)

Specifically, raw data requirements should include:

- Identification of major data elements (includes any relevant data charac-teristics, ranges of values, and relationships to other elements)
- Relation of input to output for identified processes
- Environment for which the system is to be built (the user, where the user is, etc.)
- Raw source of the input data
- Periodicity of the data or processes (on demand, scheduled, etc.)
- Approximate volume of the data
- Security requirements
- Timeliness of the data

The raw processing requirements at this time are in terms of "black boxes." The user does not specify processing, merely what input must be trans-formed to what output.

Overall system requirements should include:

- Backup/recovery needs
- Availability requirements (downtime—planned, unplanned)
- On-line response expectation (clearly defined)

In short, the user can specify what he or she needs, so that the designer understands how the user envisions the system, but the user cannot specify requirements that force a particular physical implementation. Using this guideline the relationship of the user and the designer is clearly delineated. This gives the designer the freedom to fulfill system requirements with the best technical solution. It also means that the designer cannot use "user requirements" as an excuse for poor design choices at the moment of review.

17.6 RESPONSIBILITY OF THE USER

Before the user signs the document stating requirements, he or she should have done the following:

- *Ensure the completeness of the document.* Anything missing from the document that should be there will cause delay of the system development and increase development time and costs. Make sure all assumptions are *clearly* spelled out.
- *Ensure the clarity of the document.* The designer is in a position to interpret any ambiguity as the *designer* wishes. The user must clearly and specifically represent his or her own interests.
- *Ensure the timeliness of the document.* Design cannot begin until the document is finalized.

17.7 RESPONSIBILITY OF THE DESIGNER

Before the designer commits himself or herself to the document, he or she should have done the following:

- Edit the document and point out as many ambiguities as can be found to the user and allow the user the opportunity to clarify them. The designer should bring up any necessary specification that is not included. If the designer adds any new specifications, the document should state that it was in fact the designer who included the specification, not the user.
- Edit the document for reasonableness. When unreasonable terms or expectations are specified, the designer must make sure that they are resolved before the document is finalized. Once the document is finalized, it is the designer's responsibility to fulfill the requirements.

The finalization procedure includes proper levels of signatures of both the user and designer departments. The document should be dated. It represents both a commitment by development and a limitation on development. Cost estimates should be a major part of the commitment.

17.8 APPROACHES TO USER REQUIREMENTS

There are fundamentally two ways in which users approach the definition of system requirements. They are: requirements based on the immediate needs of the system to be constructed, and requirements based on the fundamental modeling of the data at the user level. These two approaches are illustrated in Figure 17.1, which shows that system requirements can closely describe

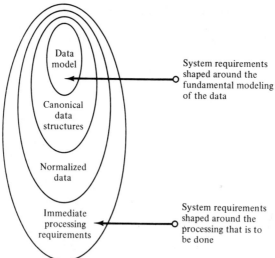

Figure 17.1 Two approaches to the definition of system requirements.

immediate processing requirements or can be shaped around the fundamental data model. In actuality, most requirements have some characteristics of both extremes; usually, requirements specifications lie somewhere between the two poles. Figure 17.1 shows a progression where user requirements are synthesized into "normalized" data (i.e., a basic form of data). The normalized data is then related to other data by means of a "canonical" form.* Then the fundamental data model is created by considering alternative views of the data and future views of the data. The final form is one that "makes sense" (in terms of the data identified and the relationship of the data to other data) with *all* user views: past, present, and projected (on the foreseeable horizon).

It is natural for the designer to follow the lead of the user, and many design decisions can be traced back to the philosophies of how the user wrote the requirements (not the actual requirements themselves). What, then, are the design tendencies when the user has specified requirements in one extreme format or the other?

17.9 USER REQUIREMENTS BUILT FROM PROCESSING NEEDS

When the user views requirements primarily from the perspective of satisfying only the processing requirements, the result tends to be a design that performs well but is inflexible. Typical of designs that come from this

*Refer to James Martin, *Computer Data Base Organization*, 2nd ed. (Englewood Cliffs, N.J.: Prentice-Hall, Inc., 1977), Chaps. 13–15, for an in-depth discussion.

approach are much data redundancy at the element and structure level, data structuring to meet the processing needs, and an emphasis on the format of screens and reports. In this environment it is common to have structuring of the data based on such things as the form of the data on input forms, and data elements conglomerated together physically so that different elements that represent very different parts of the user's environment are physically adjacent in their storage and transportation through the system.

Typical of systems designed from user specification of requirements are systems that are put up quickly and perform well as long as processing specifications do not change or the contents of the data or data relationships do not change. Of course, in a world that is constantly undergoing change, it is a matter of time before change occurs. When it does, the resultant system changes (at the implementation level) are likely to be very costly. In general, the approach of designing systems from requirements based on processing alone has very little to recommend it other than the expediency of development and performance of the first iteration of design of the system.

17.10 USER REQUIREMENTS FROM THE FUNDAMENTAL DATA MODEL

User requirements built from the fundamental data model tend to produce systems that have a long life. In general, these systems exhibit a high degree of data elasticity. This means that changes in the user environment have only a minimal impact. It often means that performance may not be quite as good as the first iteration of a system designed around processing needs, but the nth iteration of changes will affect performance of the system built from the fundamental data model *much* less severely than systems constructed otherwise. Furthermore, systems are free in form, and can easily change over time (insofar as any system can reasonably change).

Characteristics of systems built around the fundamental data model are systems with little or no data redundancy, with data that is physically separated into small units corresponding to how they are actually related in the user's environment, with data that extend to other interpretations (beyond the needs of the immediate processing requirements), and with basic units of physical organization (such as segments, records, etc.) corresponding to the logical grouping of data.

Systems designed in this fashion do not necessarily exhibit poor performance, although they are not optimized for performance. They are optimized for change, which means that there is elasticity at the data and process levels. They are integrated or can be integrated across different user areas because their foundation is based on fundamental data modeling.

CASE STUDY

The Boston Bean Company has been in data processing for many years. The computer has been used for applications such as payroll and accounting. It was suggested by a management consultant that better use could be made of the computer by building computer systems that are closer to the actual business of the company. To this end a large effort has been made to develop inventory and shop floor control systems for the manufacturing activities. This is the first attempt made at automation for this particular user area.

Because it is the first attempt, the user has been given carte blanche by data processing management. DP management has told the system designers and user liaison personnel that it is their job to make the user content.

The requirements for the inventory and shop floor control systems have been developed as a joint project between data processing system designers and liaison and manufacturing representatives. Some of the requirements are written in a book. Other requirements exist as an agreement between the two parties. In this case, the data processing personnel translate the requirements into design specifications. In the case where requirements exist as a written document, the document is really no more than unrefined notes made of the meetings between the two parties, with some supporting materials. On occasion, it is possible to find something concrete, such as a sample report layout, but for the most part, the document is cryptic, unorganized, and full of notes and markings intelligible only to the writer.

After six months of effort in analyzing the user's environment, DP management meets with the responsible user liaison and design personnel and they determine that they are ready to begin specifying design criteria. Thus begins the design phase of the system.

About two months into the design phase, the user points out to a design technician that the part number key that has been specified is not sufficient because an entire product line was not discussed. A meeting is held and the designers change the places where the part number is used (quite a few places). It takes about a month to correct this design oversight.

Six months into the project the user states that there is a need to see major parts of the data in a sequence not previously specified. This means a redesign of about 50% of the data in the system. Data processing management becomes aware of the problem and investigates. It turns out that there indeed is a need to have data accessed in an order other than what has been specified. The responsible data processing personnel remembered the discussion but thought the data was to be ordered otherwise. The entire discussion was never recorded or formalized, so it is difficult to say whether data processing misunderstood what was going on or whether the user changed his mind. In any case, the user says the data must be reordered.

This change sets the project back at least three months because files and data bases must be redesigned and some programs must even be rewritten.

At last the project goes into implementation. The first results are beginning to come out when user management declares that the system must be modified to prepare for a material requirements planning system. This means that certain basic information must be added to the existing system. This change results in a change of definition of almost every file and data base, which in turn affects many programs (70% of the existing programs). At this point data processing management is very upset. The user assures DP management that the changes are essential. DP management asks why they have been told so late in the game. The written document is brought up and on one page there is a reference to MRP information, but nowhere else is there any further reference.

The user claims that it is DP's responsibility to understand the inference. DP claims that the user never made clear what the problems were and at this point the user should live without the MRP interface. At this point the frustration is felt at the user level, the designer level, the programmer level—in short, throughout the organization. The problem escalates to upper management.   ▪

Comment on the Following

1. The user's needs should be the foremost concern of data processing.
2. Data processing should design its systems better and with more forethought.
3. Repeating work and rewriting systems is acceptable as long as the user's requirements are met.
4. The MRP changes should be made because they are the last changes the user will need.
5. Because the user has written his requirements—however cryptically and disorganized—he is justified in being upset with data processing.

MULTIPLE-CHOICE QUESTIONS

1. A set of requirements has been drawn up between user and data processing. It is comprehensive, well organized, and straightforward.
    A. Future requirements that cannot be anticipated should not be a concern of the designer.
    B. The quality of the document releases the user from the responsibility for further system design.
    C. Where requirements are unclear, the data processing designer may make interpretations.

    D. The length of time taken to draw up this formal document is probably unjustified.

    E. Data processing management is responsible for the completeness of the document.

2. A document has been drawn up specifying user requirements. The system has been built, but the user is not satisfied. The resulting system is not at all what the user had envisioned.

    A. It is possible that data processing has added new requirements that the user had not specified.

    B. Data processing may have interpreted the user's requirements incorrectly.

    C. The user may not have understood the ramifications of her own specifications.

    D. The user may not have understood what was possible and workable within computer technology.

    E. Since the user had formally drawn up specifications, data processing management feels that it is not responsible for the ultimate success of the system as long as the requirements have been met.

EXERCISES AND ESSAYS

1. Can data processing refuse to accept a set of requirements? Under what circumstances? Can data processing change the requirements? Under what circumstances?

2. Even in the face of formalized requirements, is system prototyping desirable? If the first system for a user is to be a learning experience, does it make sense to make that system crucial to the business of the user even in the face of extensive, formalized user requirements?

3. What is the impact of a simple requirement change in the early stages of a project? In the later stages? What is the impact of a complex change?

4. Draw up the minimum specifications for data, data relationships, and processing of data that would suffice for user requirements.

5. Given that every user's environment will change with time, what is the relationship between user requirements and the changing user environment?

6. Given the fact that a user is responsible for his or her requirements, draw up plans for estimating the impact of changes to requirements on the project so that the user can quantifiably determine whether requirement changes should be fulfilled.

XVIII

Design Review Methodology

Throughout this book the importance of proper design is stressed, especially as installations mature. One of the greatest dangers managers face is in allowing application systems of poor quality to be constructed. When poorly designed systems are built, the result is a long-term drain on personnel, computer resources, and morale. And ironically, it is cheaper in the long run (but more expensive in the short term) to junk a poor design and rebuild the system properly, even though it is the usual practice *not* to rebuild systems. Instead, the poor design is nurtured and limps along because of management's political and short-term attitudes.

How can this cycle of poor design and long-term maintenance of that design be broken? One major step toward breaking the cycle is to build systems of quality, and that can be accomplished through design review methodology (DRM). DRM is a tool for quality assurance of system design before the design is built. If there are problems with the design, the manager has a chance to learn about them before application code is written. This can mean *great* long-term savings to an installation.

This chapter is not meant to be a recap of a subject already adequately documented. There are three works in particular that directly address design review methodology: *IMS/VS Data Base Application Design Review* by Dechow and Lundberg; Chapter 9 of *Effective Data Base Design* by Inmon; and *Design Review Methodology for a Data Base Environment* by Inmon and Friedman. Instead, this chapter is meant to discuss DRM from a management perspective, touching on those issues relating indirectly to DRM but still important to the organization. The three works mentioned above should provide the reader with more than enough information as to *how* and *when* to do reviews. The focus here is on *why* design reviews should be done and their potential impact on the organization.

18.1 USEFULNESS OF DRM

DRM is most effective when used on large, complex on-line systems. It is not particularly profound in the review of small and/or well-designed systems, especially batch systems. The strength of DRM is in balancing the many variables of success that face the software developer. One difficulty the designer faces in building complex systems is the challenge of satisfying a number of criteria for success, many of which are at odds with each other, and many of which manifest themselves in unanticipated ways. Typically, since there are so many areas that concern a designer, he or she recognizes *some* of the problems but not *all* the problems. The resultant design, therefore, is deficient in one or more aspects, which ultimately translates into user dissatisfaction with the system. It is not enough for the user to have *most* expectations fulfilled; to be content the user must have *all* expectations fulfilled. Thus the need arises to account for *all* of the system variables. DRM provides a convenient vehicle for an exhaustive analysis of the design.

DRM can be used to profile a system before it is ever struck into application code. This means that the designer can project and analyze a system as it will operate without having to construct it. The most effective time for review is before programming is begun, since changes become very expensive to make once the design is cast into the concrete of application code. Discovering a basic system design flaw through the actual building and running of the system is a very painful way to uncover design errors or omissions. Unfortunately, this method of discovering errors occurs in many environments with great regularity. The whole purpose of DRM is to uncover system bottlenecks before they are actually built into the system. The earlier in the life cycle of development the flaws are discovered, the better.

18.2 MOTIVATION FOR DRM

DRM is normally used for three types of design:

1. New systems, where management senses a considerable exposure should the system be less than satisfactory
2. Existing systems that are not functionally satisfactory and that have been deemed to need all or part of the system rewritten
3. Systems in development where there is evidence that something is "not right"

The primary difference between the first and third cases, where DRM is typically used, is that in the first case, DRM is used as preventive maintenance even though the system design may be perfectly adequate, and in the third case, the project management has discovered evidence of problems.

DRM is nothing more than a vehicle for quality control of application design. The difference between DRM and most quality control methods is the complexity of the entity being controlled, and the cost and exposure of not controlling quality. DRM addresses the core of the success or failure of systems—the application design. In doing so, DRM indirectly addresses the issue of productivity, in that the post-implementation phase of a project is drastically reduced or even eliminated, thus freeing precious human resources.

Furthermore, DRM serves as a control point for the concerns of the data base administrator (DBA) and the data administrator (DA). The communications and the differences of opinion of the various groups are openly aired and documented. The first iteration through this review process is usually painful, but the pain is a healthy and maturing thing and the next iteration of review will be much less painful. An air of cooperation and understanding is fostered by DRM in that design is no longer a private matter but a public one. In this respect DRM has a maturing effect on an organization.

18.3 BASICS OF DRM

Some of the primary concerns addressed by DRM are:

1. *Performance.* How quickly does the system respond from the time the user enters data and starts the transaction until the user receives the first output of the reply?

2. *Flexibility.* How easily can the data and the processes that manipulate the data be changed?

3. *Availability.* What percent of the time is the application up and useful compared to the amount of time the user expects the application to be up and useful?

4. *User effectiveness.* Does the application satisfy user requirements in a cost-effective and meaningful fashion?

There are other, less important topics addressed by DRM, such as security, reliability, and system development time. A much more detailed description of these issues is found in the references cited earlier in this chapter.

The point of DRM is *not* to show *how* to do design. The designer is free to structure data and transactions as he or she wishes. However the design is done, DRM will project the resultant system so that shortcomings can be uncovered before the design is transformed into an actual system. DRM projects the outcome of a design quite accurately. Even though DRM is not to be used as a tool for dictating *how* design is to be done, it gives the designer a very clear set of criteria on which the quality of the design will be judged. In that sense it may be said that DRM indirectly affects the design process.

18.4 EFFECTIVE USE OF DRM

To be effective, DRM must be used on a design that is in a state of flux. If, after several reviews, it is seen that no changes are resulting from the reviews, one of two things is happening. Either the systems being reviewed are flaw-less or DRM is being used as a "rubber-stamping" process. An organization can delude itself into a false sense of security by going through the motions of DRM without really getting anything meaningful out of the process. If a system design is truly cast in concrete, it makes no sense to perform a review. That is an exercise in futility.

18.5 INITIAL RESISTANCE TO DRM

When DRM is first introduced to an organization, there is usually a fair amount of resistance, especially from the application area, since DRM represents a formal acknowledgment of the need for design control outside the application. It is normal for any change in this direction—especially DRM—to be resisted. DRM represents a loss of influence to applications and also presents an opportunity for the public exposure of design flaws. Interestingly, both reasons for resistance are ultimately in the company's long-range best interest, even though applications may not view it that way.

Other resistance may come from management. Their concern is that DRM will slow down project development time. Also DRM represents a vehicle by which control may be lost. The concerns about project development time being extended are false in that DRM ensures quality control at a critical time, thus enhancing development time by reducing the need for post-implementation design and development. The control of design heretofore has been the private domain of applications management and they quite naturally resist sharing that control.

18.6 OVERCOMING RESISTANCE

Several approaches can be taken to overcome resistance. A direct approach is to present the merits of DRM to applications and/or management and invite candidates to participate. Another argument for DRM is to say that if a project is really well designed, DRM will cost only a minimal amount of effort. This argument is for those who insist that there is no need for a review of their project. If the project really is flawless, there should be no fear in having a review. Once the review is done, if there are real problems, those problems will have been openly discussed and formally documented. At that point it will be difficult for the designers to ignore the problems, since doing so would be foolhardy once the problems begin to manifest themselves. The designer cannot use as the excuse for his or her failure at a later time that he was not warned about the pitfalls of the design.

The real secret to overcoming resistance to DRM is to sell management on the benefits of DRM. Fortunately, there are many real short-term and long-term benefits to DRM. It requires a bare minimum of foresight to see the benefits of DRM. Only management that truly does not care about the success of the development effort in their installation ignores the benefits of DRM.

18.7 CONDUCTING THE REVIEW

DRM is most effective when conducted by an impartial, technically competent outsider. An outsider can make critical statements about the project which, if made by someone associated with the project, could be construed as personal criticism. When an outsider makes the same statements, the criticism can be taken in a truly constructive fashion, pointing at no one individual. Also, it helps to have a new perspective on the design. DRM must be as objective as possible to be successful. The greater the degree of subjectivity of the review process, the less effective the review.

DRM is a fact-finding process that attempts to bring to light all relevant facts to determine the strengths and weaknesses of the project. DRM does not pass judgment on a design—it merely analyzes the design and lets project management make what judgments it will.

Unfortunately, it is expensive to hire an outsider to conduct all the reviews a corporation needs. If it is not feasible to bring in an outsider, the review should be conducted by an employee of the corporation, but one who is outside the project—the further outside the project, the better. DRM should *never* be conducted by a participant in the project.

18.8 ADAPTABILITY OF DRM

Some review methodologies are more adaptable than others. Even a methodology such as the one described in *Design Review Methodology for a Data Base Environment*, which is purposely designed to be adaptable, will require some effort to fit into corporate procedures. Other methodologies may require more of an effort to be adapted. The need for adaptability is brought about by differences in the development cycles in different corporations, in their technical environments, in their backlog of experience of development, and other areas. Furthermore, the technical world regularly undergoes changes that must be taken into account by DRM. Just as the user's environment changes over time, so should DRM.

To be effective, DRM should include as participants anyone affected by the development, operation, or use of the system. This obviously means the applications designers. It should also include data base administration, data administration, and technical support. It may include operations and systems programming. Experience has shown that if at all possible it should include the user, even though a certain amount of technical discussion will not particularly concern the user. Management may or may not participate in the review, but will certainly hear the findings of the review committee once the review is complete.

18.9 OTHER ISSUES

Despite the thoroughness of DRM (and to be effective it must be thorough), there are several important aspects that are addressed at best tangentially or not at all. Some of these considerations are:

- System integration
- Media on which system will be realized
- Very long range system planning

These issues have to be addressed, but are usually so broad and so fundamental that they are taken for granted. If any great degree of design has progressed and these issues have not been settled, it makes no sense to continue design until there is resolution.

In addition, there may be levels of review required other than the traditional levels of architecture, physical data, and program review. At the early project phase it may be necessary to have a requirements review or a logical system design review. Toward the end of the project it may be advantageous to have a pre-implementation review and even a post-mortem review to extract the full amount of learning out of what has transpired.

18.10 DRM AND MANAGEMENT

DRM is a tool for management of the development process, not a replacement for management. DRM is nothing more than a sophisticated method of quality control of development. It *does not* replace management decisions.

There is *no replacement* for rational thinking or good judgment; DRM merely brings facts to the surface so that rationality and good judgment will prevail. DRM is an excellent fact-finding tool. It analyzes a system completely and impartially when executed properly. Because of its potential benefits and the openness of the process it is difficult to ignore the results of a review. If DRM does nothing else it enhances the openness of design decisions, and that is a very healthy process in itself. DRM makes communication failures easy to spot in that it provides an open forum—a microcosm of the project—in which all interested parties are publicly solicited for input.

The marginal utility of DRM over time probably decreases in that the first few systems will be greatly enhanced; that is, the systems will be put on a solid footing by the active use of DRM. However, after several iterations the fundamentals of design stressed by DRM will become so ingrained in the designers that DRM will not be as effective actively but will be passively effective.

REFERENCES

Dechow, Esther, and Don Lundberg, *IMS/VS Data Base Application Design Review*, IBM Manual G320-6009, 1977.

Inmon, W. H., *Effective Data Base Design*, Prentice-Hall, Inc., Englewood Cliffs, N.J., 1980.

Inmon, W. H., and L. J. Friedman, *Design Review Methodology for a Data Base Environment*, Prentice-Hall, Inc., Englewood Cliffs, N.J., 1981.

Perry, William, *Effective Methods of EDP Quality Assurance*, QED Information Sciences, Wellesley, Mass, 1980.

CASE STUDY

The Chicago Wind Tunnel Company has had data processing systems for many years. The company has gone through the normal cycle of sequential systems to batch data base systems to on-line data base systems. Management is a strong supporter of quality control of system design. The Chicago Wind Tunnel Company was one of the first advocates of structured walkthroughs of code reviews. When design review methodologies became popular, they investigated and adopted what they considered to be the best methodology.

Their keen interest in quality control of system design arose because they have wasted money and resources on systems in the past and do not want to repeat unnecessary waste, especially waste from which there is little or nothing that is salvageable. Going to the on-line environment has been its own education. They have learned the hard lessons of on-line performance and availability from experience. When an expert speaks on these subjects, they pay close attention.

They feel their selection of a design review methodology has been done carefully, thoughtfully, and with intelligence. The first review methodology they investigated centered attention on the final products of development—the data bases and programs. It was more of a tuning exercise than a review of a system. Even if the methodology helped Chicago Wind Tunnel determine that there was a problem, it was too late in the development cycle to do anything meaningful about the problem.

The next review methodology looked much more appealing. A consulting firm sent in experts to review the system at various points in the life of the project. The expertise provided was very competent but, when the review was over, the experts left and it was an expensive proposition to bring them in every time a review was needed.

Finally, a decision was made for a methodology that was applicable to a project throughout the project life cycle and that could be repeated without depending on outside expertise. Chicago Wind Tunnel adapted the methodology to their environment.

The DBA was charged with the responsibility of conducting reviews, although the DBA did not have final project rights of approval or disapproval. Initially, there was much enthusiasm for design review by all parties—management, user, DBA, and applications.

In the last six months, there have been six reviews conducted by the DBA. Management is quite comfortable in the belief that they have adapted the best procedures possible for system quality. The greatest change that has resulted from a review is the removal of a data element from one segment to another segment.

One of the systems that has been reviewed is ready to go into full production. A few days prior to cutover to the production system, a data base tuner notes that a transaction is executing occasionally for 2 minutes in the test system. The DBA is alerted and begins an investigation of the reasons for the poor performance of the transaction.   ∎

Comment on the Following

1. There is really nothing to worry about. Freak occurrences happen all the time on the test system.
2. Design review methodology is a failure. It has allowed performance problems to go unnoticed.
3. If the DBA had the rights of project approval or disapproval, the reviewers would take him more seriously and the review process would be more powerful.

4. If the DBA has rights of approval or disapproval, there is no need for management; in essence, the DBA has replaced management.

5. It is a sign of organizational maturity to allow the DBA to have rights of project approval or disapproval.

6. If the review process is a rubber-stamping process, it is a waste of time.

7. Any review methodology is healthy merely from the standpoint that the appropriate parties meet and openly analyze the system. There is a beneficial exchange of information even if nothing else transpires.

8. Over time, the results of design review will be diminished because system designers learn what to expect and consequently build desirable attributes into the system without having the review process point out the needs for those attributes.

9. Even for the best designed system, the review recommendations will appear to be critical. This is a naturally occurring phenomenon.

MULTIPLE-CHOICE QUESTIONS

1. Management has decided to purchase an application package from an outside firm. There is concern over the quality of the application package. The DBA has suggested that design review methodology be applied to determine system characteristics prior to the purchase of the package.
   A. Design review methodology should be useful in evaluating the software.
   B. If design review is not directly applicable, it should be readily adapted to purchased software analysis.
   C. Assumptions made in design review which dictate that a design can be changed if necessary may have to be modified when reviewing purchased software.
   D. It may be cheaper to benchmark purchased software than to review it.
   E. The manager must be concerned with the same fundamentals of purchased software as if the same software were being developed in-house.

2. Management has decided that system prototyping provides a much cleaner and convincing picture than design review. All application decisions will be prototyped as a basis for making a decision as to correct design options.
   A. Prototyping is expensive.
   B. Prototyping can be done only very late in the game. Prototyping is not applicable in the early days of analysis.

      C. Prototyping addresses only certain obvious issues, such as performance.

      D. Prototyping requires much technical expertise to execute.

      E. Prototyping is generally more accurate than a design review when done properly. Perhaps they should be used together.

3. Management has decided to implement a design review and has determined that it is primarily a function of data processing. For this reason, the user is permanently excluded from attending or participating in design review.

      A. The user is not interested in all the technical details that occur in a design review.

      B. It serves no useful purpose for the user to hear and comment on what the designer perceives to be user requirements.

      C. It is not particularly important for the user to understand what the consequences of his or her decisions are on data processing.

      D. The user is usually not interested in communicating with anyone other than the analyst assigned to the project. There really is no benefit in having open communication between the designer and the user.

      E. Since the user ultimately pays data processing's bills, anything the user wants that can be afforded is acceptable.

EXERCISES AND ESSAYS

1. What are the fundamentals of design review?

2. When is design review appropriate in a project?

3. Should the intensity of design review vary with the size and criticality of the project?

4. How can the effectiveness of design review be measured?

5. What other quality control tools can be implemented? In the place of design review? In conjunction with design review?

6. Part of the success of design review depends on the objectivity of the reviewers. How can a review be made as objective as possible within the organization? Why is a review objective when conducted by an outsider?

7. What level of management should hear the results of the review?

8. When a reviewer feels particularly strong about the findings of the review, how can the reviewer make those feelings known?

9. What should be included in the design review recommendations? Should management be held accountable for its actions in the face of those recommendations at a later time?

MANAGEMENT
TOPICS

XIX

Discipline

□□

Discipline in the data processing environment refers to the control by management of the computer environment as opposed to having the environment unduly influencing management. An environment in which management normally acts in a planned (or action) mode is a disciplined environment. An environment in which management reacts to the environment— where it is on a treadmill and cannot get off— is an undisciplined environment. To achieve discipline management must effectively control its resources at the point of the user interface, system development, system maintenance, system operations, and technical support. In addition, the usage, acquisition, and disposal of such major resources as hardware and software must be controlled. In an environment where so many complex variables are constantly changing and are truly important to the success of the company, it is no wonder that discipline of the data processing environment, in its many forms, is a real issue.

In a disciplined environment work is done in a controlled, orderly, planned mode. The converse is an environment where work is done in a reaction mode. Once an installation reaches a point of operating primarily in a reaction mode, it is very difficult to move to a disciplined environment. Furthermore, even in the most disciplined data processing environment, a certain amount of the work that is done *must be* done in a reaction mode. The difference between the disciplined environment and the undisciplined environment is the relative amount of reaction-mode work that is done.

19.1 DIRECT CAUSES OF AN UNDISCIPLINED ENVIRONMENT

There are many reasons and combinations of reasons why a data processing organization gets into a reaction mode. When an installation is primarily without discipline, it is probably for a number of reasons rather than a single reason.

One of the initial roots of the undisciplined environment is the desire to please the user or, to be more specific, to sell the data processing department. In many cases it is in a company's best long-term interest to automate systems. This means replacing existing manual systems, which usually implies resistance from the user because the established flow of work must be changed. To placate this resistance, the data processing department becomes extremely accommodating to the user. This may initially overcome some resistance, but in the long run an attitude is fostered such that the user views data processing personnel and resources as being "free." In essence, the data processing department will do practically anything to keep the user happy.

A certain degree of diplomacy is required, of course, but if the user learns to expect unreasonable results, data processing is initially and automatically put into a reaction mode. The result of this relationship between departments is overly ambitious systems that attempt to do more than is possible or desirable, and this further stretches the precious resources of the data processing department. In the early stages of the maturity of the company, this type of environment and these attitudes are almost mandated if the data processing department is to get off the ground.

Another related cause of lack of discipline is the attitude that by far the best measure of success of the developer is the speed with which systems are constructed. Certainly, system development time is *one* of the measures of success of the developer, but ignoring other parameters of success leads to systems that will operate and be maintained eternally in a reaction mode. As long as systems are developed quickly under the foundations of good systems design, the organization can be considered to be disciplined. What are the fundamentals of system success other than speed of development? They are:

- *Flexibility*. Can the data be semantically modified gracefully? Can the programs and transactions be changed with a minimum of disruption? Can a number of people work on the system without getting in the other people's way? Are interfaces well-defined? Is the system extendable?
- *Performance*. Can the user get adequate throughput or response? Can the issue of performance be addressed across all systems? At the single-system level? In light of systems to come?
- *Availability*. Are systems available to the user a high percentage of the time? What is the cost of an outage? What outages have been experienced? Can they be predicted?
- *User function*. Does the system fulfill user requirements? In a cost-effective fashion? From a development standpoint? From an operational standpoint? Can the users' future needs be satisfied?

Systems that are developed very quickly may please the user with the responsiveness of the developer, but if the system is not properly designed around the aforementioned fundamentals, it is a matter of time (usually short) before the user becomes unhappy. Speedy development for development's sake usually produces results that force the data processing department into a reaction mode of operation.

19.2 OTHER DIRECT CAUSES OF AN UNDISCIPLINED ENVIRONMENT

Another reason why a data processing organization can get into a reaction mode is that management does not view problems in the proper perspective. In this case data processing management takes a myopic view of organizational problems. It is typical to find management viewing the world as if the only solution to any given problem were technical (for example). The answer to some problems *will* be a very technical solution, but it is folly to assume that the answer to *every* problem is technical. It is in this environment that *only* technical people are promoted to positions of responsibility, thus propagating the narrow viewpoints of management. The problem is that technical competency does not necessarily equate to managerial ability. Furthermore, in this environment there is an orientation to do things technically that might best be handled otherwise.

The point here is not to illustrate the inadequacies of the purely technical approach to solving the problems of discipline of the data processing department, but to make the statement that *any* imbalance of approaches to organizing and managing a shop will result in undesirable consequences which will ultimately lead to a lack of discipline. It is interesting to note that there *is* a tendency toward overplaying the technical aspects of data processing. And it is often easier to spend more money acquiring technical resources and people than it is to analyze and address the roots of the problem.

Some other orientations that, if overplayed, will lead to a different set of problems are: a purely applications orientation, a user-friendly orientation, an overemphasis on budgeting, or an overemphasis on the theory behind systems. In short, if upper management does not have a clear picture and perspective of all aspects of the data processing environment, the tendency will be to overemphasize some aspect at the expense of others.

19.3 INDIRECT CAUSES OF LACK OF DISCIPLINE

One of the indirect causes of lack of discipline is the inability of an installation to learn from past mistakes. If a manager suspects that an installation is operating in a reaction mode, he or she should keep a log of errors that he or she suspects are causing most of the problems. These may be program errors, operational errors, design errors, and so on. The manager is free to focus on *any* errors he or she deems to be important. The errors should be collected and analyzed. The item of interest is not the solution to the problem but how the problem could have been prevented in the first place. This exercise should be continued until patterns appear.

Once the pattern can be identified, the origin of the problem can be identified so that (1) the problems can be corrected at their source or (2) at least the problems will not be repeated in future systems. Never analyzing problems from this synthesized level may allow certain basic problems to recur because the symptom is being discovered and treated, not the disease itself.

Another form of this inability to learn from past mistakes that leads to a lack of discipline is highlighted by the "delayed feedback syndrome." Consider the development cycle of on-line systems. The system is analyzed, designed, programmed, tested, implemented, and put into production. In many environments the designer actively participates up to the point of programming, then moves on to another project. This approach works well in the batch environment. But in on-line systems the designer does not know whether he or she is successful until his or her design efforts have gone into the full production mode. This may be *months* or *years* after the system designer has left the project.

By the time the system has shown its true profile and operating characteristics, the designer is no longer available to learn from his or her mistakes. To complicate matters further, the design flaws may be categorized as tuning problems or maintenance problems, not as fundamental design errors. In fact, the designer by this time is probably proliferating the same mistakes in other systems. Feedback as to whether or not he or she has been successful has been delayed so long that the designer *never* learns from mistakes, and this level of learning is usually the most powerful and beneficial. The designer benefits from mistakes made earlier, and this means that usually he or she does not recognize the levels of control and discipline that are necessary in large and sophisticated systems.

19.4 LEVELS OF DISCIPLINE ACROSS INDUSTRIES

There is an interesting correlation between the level of discipline found in the data processing department and the industry of the parent company. In general, the more critical the systems are to the operation and profit picture of the parent company, the higher the level of discipline. This is somewhat generalized but is not surprising. Some of the more interesting experiences that relate to organizational discipline come from companies where data processing systems relate closely to the companies' profit picture, but their data processing departments *are not* disciplined. These companies soon learn the value of discipline, usually through a painful episode or two. Figure 19.1 illustrates some typical high- and low-discipline industries; of course in any industry there are exceptions.

Although the major factor in determining the level of discipline found in a shop relates primarily to how systems correlate with the profit picture of the company, there are other factors. One of these factors is the size of the company and another is the profitability of the company. The larger the company and the more profitable it is, the less the amount of discipline in the company's data processing organizations. This combines with the nature of the system to produce a matrix, shown by Figure 19.2.

Criticality of systems

		High	Low
Profit margin	High	Higher discipline	Lowest discipline
	Low	Highest discipline	Lower discipline

High-discipline industries	Low-discipline industries
Airlines	Insurance
Banks	Utilities
	Oil companies
	Nonprofit organizations

Figure 19.1 Typical high- and low-discipline industries.

Figure 19.2 Discipline level related to size and profitability of company.

19.5 ACHIEVING DISCIPLINE

If discipline is desirable and it is not necessarily a natural thing that just "happens," what can management do to achieve discipline? Before any further comments, it must be stated that it would be impossible to change an undisciplined installation into a disciplined one overnight. Achieving discipline is a lengthy, step-by-step process that requires change and involves overcoming resistance and inertia.

The first step toward instilling discipline in the organization is to understand what the various components of the data processing environment are and how they fit into the long-term direction of the parent company. Without this very basic understanding, it is unlikely that management can control the environment. Once the components of the organization are identified, management must identify the problems associated with the components and effect a resolution of the problems. If problems are ignored or allowed to be solved by default, the resolution of problems will be by the relative strength of the position of the individuals involved in the organization and/ or the personalities involved. Such a resolution probably will not be in the best interest of the company.

Furthermore, the very nature of discipline changes over time. What can be construed as a high degree of control at one point may in fact be poor control when the environment changes. The environment will change as the relationship of the data processing organization to the user matures, as the types of processing that are being done change, as the scope of automation within the company changes, and as the parent company itself changes. Some of the components of the organization and major issues that must be actively managed are:

- *Hardware/software.* The issues include: limitations, capabilities, costs, long-term extendability and compatibility, and implementation considerations.
- *User organizations.* The issues the manager must understand include: the user's perspective of existing and future systems; interfaces with data processing; the backlog of successes and failures; the resources user will commit; the resources the user expects data processing to commit; and the long-term direction of the user.
- *Technical staff/operations.* The issues here include: the handling of day-to-day responsibilities; critical points to the running of systems; the expectations of management involvement; support and direction; in-depth understanding of critical technical and operational details; and limitations—practical, actual, and rational.
- *Development staff.* The issues here include: definition of responsibilities; the amount of backlog of work; the past record of successes and failures; the bias toward or against certain techniques, methodologies, approaches, or software; the limitations of the development staff; and the long-term goals and directions.

A major issue that affects hardware, software, and the entire data processing organization is that of growth. The manager wanting to control his or her environment must be aware of how the following issues relate to growth. Where does it come from? How much is coming? Why is it coming? In what form will it manifest itself? What are the limitations of the installation? What technical vehicles are there for managing growth? Other vehicles?

If a manager is well versed in these topics with regard to his or her own installation, he or she has a firm foundation from which to address the issue of organizational discipline. Without that foundation, the manager may be equipped to control one or more aspects of the installation but not all aspects.

19.6 DEFINITION OF DOMAIN

The next step is creating an environment that can be controlled is to define clearly the boundaries of the domain of each organizational unit and ensure that each organization understands its role in relation to the entire data processing organization. This means that the rights, responsibilities, obligations, and interfaces—in short, the domain—between groups will be clearly, explicitly, and formally defined and that each group will be notified of this definition. The manager should be aware that these domains are not static. They change over time, so this is an ongoing issue.

This is the time for the manager to introduce the proper perspective of each group into the organization. Failure to do so can lead to an organizational imbalance later that will result in less than optimal results. The larger the data processing organization, the greater the need for formal clarification of duties and rights. If previous systems have suffered because of organizational imbalance, now is the time to rectify the roots of the imbalance. Instituting procedures such as a review methodology as a facilitator for open forums ensures that decisions that affect a number of organizational units will be openly discussed, not privately enacted.

The alert manager should anticipate problems, not discover them by waiting for them to occur. This can be done by exchanging ideas with other installations, getting outside advice, and keeping current in the literature.

19.7 ORGANIZATIONAL CONTROLS

There are certain issues that are so important that the manager should address them by instituting organizational controls. One issue is that of performance and availability of the on-line system. This issue can be addressed by creating the data base administration (DBA) function and vesting within it the power to ensure online performance and availability. This will undoubtedly mean changing the organizational balance of control but will be a healthy and mature direction in anticipation of future needs. The second organizational unit that can be created is that of data administration (DA). The DA is charged with creating an environment in which systems can be integrated. As with the DBA, this means rearranging the structure of responsibility within the organization, but in the long run it is much to the organization's benefit to do so.

The third organizational unit that may be created as a data processing shop grows large is that of direct user interface. This function can serve several vital purposes. The most immediate is that of an initial point of contact for user inquiries, problems, and day-to-day concerns. However, the most useful function this organization can play is that of monitoring user requests for new systems or modifications to old systems. When the user asks for features that should not be implemented, the user should be put through a polite and firm education process that will allow the user to know what is reasonable *before* he or she asks for it the next time.

19.8 ACCOUNTABILITY

The third step management can take to create an environment of organizational discipline is to build vehicles for accountability wherever possible. A simple mechanism would be to "charge" users for development and operational services. This would reinforce the idea that data processing services *are not* free. A side benefit of "charging" is that the user will be the driving force behind the standard work unit. This means ultimately that systems (or parts of systems) that do not belong on-line will not be put there. The user must be made to realize that there is a limitation to what can be requested.

Another variation of this technique is to allocate a certain number of worker-days to a user, then let him or her decide how they should be spent. On a larger basis, a manager may want all users to meet and decide how personnel should be allocated. This removes some of the control from the data processing manager but frees the manager from the burden of having to explain why one user cannot have a new system at the expense of other users.

Another extension of the concept of accountability is to base the system of organizational rewards on results achieved. This means basing the fruits of success on the *full* cycle of system development, not on the limited cycle as is the practice in the batch environment. One of the major problems with the "delayed development feedback" syndrome is that rewards for success are passed out long before it is known whether the system being developed is really successful.

19.9 FAILURES

One of the major problems with discipline and accountability is the recognition of what is and what is not a failure. Failures are very useful in that *nothing* serves as a better vehicle for learning. When an organization does not learn from its failures, it wastes an extremely valuable opportunity. The problem is in recognizing a failure when it occurs. Some of the problems in failure recognitions are:

- There is nothing to measure the failure against. The failed system stands alone in the installation and there often is no comparable system or set of experiences by which to judge the failure. The only basis for comparison lies outside the company and the last thing management wants is to expose internal problems to outsiders. Even comparing results with other installations is risky because there can be many relevant factors which may not be at all equivalent.
- Certain aspects of a failure may be perfectly adequate. There are so many facets to a system that certain parts may be quite adequate, whereas other

parts render the system useless. Can a system be called a failure when it succeeds in certain aspects?

- Documentation of responsibility for decisions may be lacking. Because of the size and complexity of large systems, when a system is a failure it is often hard to determine exactly *why* and even harder to determine *who* made the improper decision. Thus the feedback loop for rewards is made even more unclear.
- Failure is subjective. What is the dividing line between a long term failure and an immediate set of problems?
- Failure can occur in so many different ways for so many different reasons.
- Failure may be a long time in coming. A system at first may seem to be successful but may take years to show its true colors.

Because of the following reasons, basing rewards on job performance is at best a risky thing. There is no doubt that the roots of failure are very difficult to ascertain when failure occurs.

REFERENCES

Bernard, Dan, James C. Emery, Richard L. Nolan, and Robert H. Scott, *Charging for Computer Services, Principles and Guidelines*, PBI, a Petrocelli Book, Princeton, N.J., 1977.

Brooks, Frederick P., Jr., *The Mythical Man-Month and Other Essays on Software Engineering*, Addison-Wesley Publishing Company, Inc., Reading, Mass., 1974.

Nolan, Richard L., "Managing the Crises in Data Processing," *Harvard Business Review*, March–April 1979.

Sanders, D. H., and S. J. Birkin, *Computers and Management in a Changing Society*, McGraw-Hill Book Company, New York, 1980.

CASE STUDY

The Albuquerque Aerodrome Company manufactures airplane parts that allow a plane to get much more mileage. The company also builds specialty parts for space aircraft. In the past few years, the business has really blossomed and the company's profitability picture is very high. Part of the competitive edge has come because the company computerized its systems when it was just beginning to grow.

Three years ago, the backlog of requests for services from the users began to pile up much faster than data processing could service the requests. The users had grown used to very fast response to their requests. Upper management's attitude is that the users are to be given a blank check when it comes to having data processing deliver services. To enhance the service level provided, a new manager of data processing development is hired.

The manager of development is an expert in programmer productivity. It is felt that she can greatly speed up the development process and thus provide the users with more satisfaction. At about the same time the manager is hired, Albuquerque Aerodrome commits to the on-line environment. To demonstrate the speed of development, an on-line manufacturing application is chosen as the first on-line system.

The application will collect information about the various manufacturing steps. The work flow of the shop will be run by the system. It is estimated that inventory can be reduced by 25% with this system. Because of the efforts of the development manager, the system is put up in a record six months. The users are quite pleased with this service from data processing. The development manager begins to line up her next project.

For the first nine months of operation, the on-line system runs adequately. On two occasions there are malfunctions that bring the system down and cause the manufacturing work flow to be stopped. On those occasions the problems with the system were dismissed as "startup" problems.

However, over the past few months the on-line system has been delivering very spotty response time. Some days the system will respond in 1 to 2 seconds. The next day response time will be on the order of 40 to 50 seconds. When response time is bad, manufacturing processes are significantly slowed down.

To make matters worse, there have been three system failures that have brought the system down from 2 hours up to 10 hours. In those cases, the work flow of manufacturing was severely interrupted and the cost was a waste of inventory that had not been experienced at Albuquerque Aerodrome before. To make matters worse, the manufacturing operation depends entirely on the on-line system for control, having given up manual and batch facilities with the advent of the on-line system. Operations personnel are becoming very frustrated with the system because it is they who are under immediate pressure when the system has problems, and they feel helpless because each problem is a new one, not one that has happened in the past. The programming staff is beginning to suffer a morale problem because they are constantly being pulled off current assignments to address problems in the on-line system. The problem is that the fixes and the corrections put in do not seem to really help. It is like trying to plug a dike with many leaks in it.

The morale is really lowest at the user level. Their initial satisfaction with having the system put up in a short time is dwindling in light of the fact that availability and performance of the system are so poor.

In the meantime, the development manager is just about to finish with her next effort, which has taken only nine months to produce. The application user is very pleased with the new system.   ∎

Comment on the Following

1. The manufacturing on-line system will probably get better over time.
2. The application development manager probably will have produced the same errors in the second system as she did in the first.
3. The new on-line system will simply make matters worse for the existing applications that have to share common resources.
4. Because of poor decisions made earlier, the manufacturing on-line system will create a reaction mode environment for its lifetime.
5. Because of the profitability of Albuquerque Aerodrome, a mistake such as the manufacturing on-line system can be tolerated.
6. Who should be held accountable for the mistakes? What is the cost of *not* holding the proper parties accountable?
7. It is a temptation to say that a high degree of technical expertise, a competent tuning professional, and an upgraded operations staff could solve the problems here. Is this just passing the buck? Is this just a form of treating the symptoms and not the disease? What is the disease? How should it be treated?

MULTIPLE-CHOICE QUESTIONS

1. Data processing has been working on an accounting system for a long time. The system is near completion. The total budget overrun was about 250%. The system was originally scheduled to be completed in 14 months. It looks as if it will finally be finished in 36 months. For the longest time the users complained furiously. At this point, they are happy to get anything at all. The system being delivered bears a resemblance to what was promised. In the meantime, the data processing managers are congratulating themselves on the completion of the system.

    A. The early estimates were unrealistic. The users should not have based any expectations on them.

    B. Quality systems take a long time to build.

    C. The system is not a failure; it is being delivered.

    D. Management should view data processing in a favorable light—it has delivered what was specified.

    E. Because the project required more personnel than was originally estimated, the original designers of the system have several people working for them now and should be promoted.

2. Data processing universally is a service organization to the user. Ultimately, the user pays the bills. For this reason data processing must satisfy all user requests.

A. Some requests are unreasonable and should not be satisfied.

B. In some cases the cost of the request is such that it should not be honored. It is data processing's role to direct the users in these matters.

C. Users must be held accountable for their decisions just as are other parts of the organization.

D. The relationship between user and data processing is a two-way street with rights and responsibilities on each side.

E. When data processing is establishing automation in a company, the users are treated with an extra level of tenderness.

*3. Operations has experienced a problem with an application. As a standard practice, the application is stopped. In the morning, systems programming becomes upset because the problem with the application was that a library belonging to systems was accessed. Systems claims that operations should have never allowed this to happen and, in any case, should have notified them when the error occurred. In the meantime, applications has been notified and they are busy explaining to the user why the problem will not happen again. They became upset with systems because proper protection was to be done on their library. They are upset with operations because the actions by operations shut down their processing, even though the action was a standard one.

A. Planning could have reduced the friction between departments.

B. Clear responsibility should be laid out for procedures in times of error or recovery. Not defining them opens the door for misinterpretations.

C. Even though operations was the first to discover the problem, they are not really responsible for the problem.

D. It is not reasonable to blame operations for problems when they react in a predictable way.

E. Systems programming should have protected their library better.

EXERCISES AND ESSAYS

1. Where in the organization is it most important to have accountability? How can an atmosphere of accountability be created where there is none? The ultimate in penalties is termination. What lesser degree of penalties can be instigated?

2. In the case of a budget overrun, either the project leader or the budgeter has made an error. What is the consequences of the error? What type of penalty should be delivered by management?

3. Describe parameters that can be used to determine whether a project is a failure or a success. Are there degrees of success? Of failure? What kinds of rewards or penalties should be supported by management? In reality, what kinds of rewards or penalties are supported? What is the long-term consequence of not supporting penalties and rewards?

4. An old maxim in data processing goes like this: "It is less expensive to spend more money now to correct a problem at its roots than it is to spend less money now and treat the symptoms of a problem." What are the issues here?

5. Why do large size and high profitability of a company contribute greatly to a lack of discipline. What is the real cost of a lack of discipline?

6. Why is a lack of definition of domain a contributory factor to a lack of discipline? What happens when domains are firmly defined? What happens when a firmly defined domain needs to be changed? What happens when there needs to be a firm definition, but there is none?

7. If management insists on calling a failure a success, what can be done?

XX

Managing Growth

□□

However managers address their responsibilities and whatever shape their installations are in, there is one common factor that challenges data processing managers everywhere—and that is growth. The never-ending demand for more and new processing means that there are *never* enough resources to go around—human, computer, or otherwise. By the time new resources are acquired, the demand for more resources has already consumed the new acquisition. It is this explosive growth that constantly challenges managers. In a less demanding environment, many of the problems so painful in data processing may not be nearly as critical.

20.1 WHERE IS GROWTH COMING FROM?

Growth in the data processing environment can be measured in two forms that are separate and yet interrelated. On one hand, growth can be measured in the number of systems and subsystems that are operational in the installation and in the number that are currently being constructed. On the other hand, growth can be measured by the total amount of processing activity, from whatever source, that is being run in an installation. To use an analogy, consider measuring the use of the automobile. One measure would be the number of vehicles currently owned by the public and vehicles being built; another measure would be the total number of miles driven over a period of time, regardless of which or how many vehicles drove them. This chapter is concerned primarily with the measurement of growth in the data processing environment in the first sense—that of analyzing the growth of existing and developing applications—although it is recognized that the other measure of growth is also valid.

Where, then, does growth of applications come from? There are primarily three sources of growth: (1) the development of new applications, (2) opportunities to build old applications in new and better ways, and (3) the growth of existing applications.

20.2 NONLINEAR GROWTH

In today's data processing world, the growth of applications is nonlinear. Once the first application gets built, it is normal to follow it with more and larger applications. Usually, the first few applications only whet the appetite of management and the users. This growth pattern is apparent even in installations that build purely sequential systems, but is all the more obvious in installations that operate within a more sophisticated environment such as the on-line environment. The notion exists that if one system produces desirable results and success, five new systems will produce five times as much success. In addition, when an installation changes environments (to a bigger machine, to a more sophisticated machine, to a different mode of operation, etc.), there is an urge to exploit to the fullest the new potential, thus bringing into the picture new demand for more applications and new types of applications. The spiral of growth seems to feed on itself.

Even the existing applications developed in a disciplined environment grow. Many times the user finds ways to use the system that were not intended originally and requires that the application code be extended. In other cases, there is a growth of business functions brought on by a change in the business environment or by an expansion of business functions made possible by the advent of an automated system. Growth by no means applies only to new applications.

20.3 IMPACT OF GROWTH

Where has this growth of applications been felt? Hardware is a most obvious answer, and it is a correct one. The advances in technology and production of machines hardly keeps pace with the demand for new computing power. But hardware is not the only area that growth of applications has affected. Software has also been shaped by the explosive processing needs that are occurring. Not only does the software architect have to worry about the utility and long-term viability of his or her product, he or she must also contend with the fact that application needs and performance requirements will stretch the product to the limit.

However, the biggest impact of growth of applications has probably not been at the hardware or software level but at the development level—designers, programmers, technicians, operators—all are stretched to keep pace. Their efforts are required for systems that often are queued up waiting to be built, maintained, or significantly modified. Few installations are without a significant backlog of work for their development staffs and indications are that the backlog is increasing. It has been suggested that, over time, hardware and software costs will pale in comparison to human costs. This fact is underscored when analyzing the percentages of the data processing budget spent on human costs versus hardware and software budgets over the past five years. It is worthwhile to analyze this typical backlog of applications waiting to be constructed in light of this future trend of costs.

20.4 APPLICATION BACKLOG

What are the major factors that contribute to this backlog of applications development? The obvious factors are lack of qualified personnel to address the backlog, lack of budget to hire qualified personnel, and a seemingly never-ending increase in demand for services. But behind these obvious factors are quite a few underlying reasons for the growth of the backlog. Some of them are:

1. *Complexity of applications/technical complexities.* The task of the designer and developer is not an easy one—the applications being built are often very complex. The algorithms, the structure of the data, the multiple uses of the systems, the speed of change in the user's environment, the capabilities of the system—all contribute to the complexity of the application. Technical complexities arise in the translation of the design to the computerized environment. The successful designer must be able to bring together a wide diversity of considerations that must all fit in a technological framework. With the many design variables that must be managed, it is understandable that systems take a long time to develop because of the great care that must be taken in their development.

2. *Criticality of applications.* Once the user finds that automation can become a significant aid in the running of a business, more critical applications are scheduled for automation. The company can make or save money by automation as well as lose it on a large data processing budget. Because of the potential gains or losses, a great deal of care should be taken in the construction of the system, and the time and effort necessary to ensure that proper degree of care add to the backlog of applications.

3. *Volume of work to be done.* Even if applications were not complex and critical, the designer would still be faced with the problem of the sheer volume of applications waiting to be developed.

4. *Post-implementation development.* In the haste to meet deadlines, developers have created a new phase of development—the post-implementation development cycle. The initial development deadline is met and literally any system design or code is constructed and is held up as fulfillment of the deadline. Once implementation begins and it is discovered that the hastily designed system has many shortcomings, a post-implementation effort is set in motion. Politically, this post-implementation development is tenable because the original "deadline" has been met. However, post-implementation design can take many times as long as the original design effort, with a cor-

responding drain on human resources. Doing the design correctly from the start would reduce the need for most or all post-implementation design effort and thus free precious human resources to address other systems in the development backlog.

5. *Unintegrated systems.* When systems are unintegrated, it is common to see different development groups working on similar or identical projects, thus needlessly "reinventing the wheel." Coordinating the efforts of the developers, so that when a problem occurs it occurs in a single place, would free more talent to work on other projects in the backlog.

20.5 IMPACT OF GROWTH WITHIN THE BACKLOG

One of the first and most immediate effects of growth of the backlog of applications to be built is seen in the increase of data processing staff. This expansion of staff should not be measured by numbers alone. Figure 20.1 shows that as the numbers of people increase, the degree of specialization of those people grows.

The more systems that are being constructed, the more difficult management of facilities, projects, and personnel becomes, and individual job skill specialization is one of the ordinary approaches to achieving an orderly growth process.

In addition to growth of applications leading to job specialization, this growth also leads to a need to formalize communications among organizations. Figure 20.2 shows a typical flow of communications among the different organizations of the data processing environment. From the diagram it is clear that flow of communications is quite a bit more complex, as well as formal, in a large environment that would be true in a smaller organization. This means that there are more opportunities for misunderstanding, delays due to coordination mishaps, a greater need for prioritization of projects, and in general, more chances for communication misfires to occur. Another problem is the clear definition of the ending of responsibilities of one group and the beginning of responsibilities of another.

A by-product of the need for more formal communications as the organization grows larger is a greater need for project control because work is being done on the project in different parts of the organization. Figure 20.3 shows the flow of project control from one organization to the next. In this kind of environment it is normal for organizational substructures to begin to appear. The substructure is typified by an informal coalition of workers who have a high degree of communication and cooperation. The substructure appears because some groups work better with certain other groups. Substructures also appear because alignment with other groups forms the basis for political solidarity within the organization. In some cases certain individuals use substructuring of the organization to build an

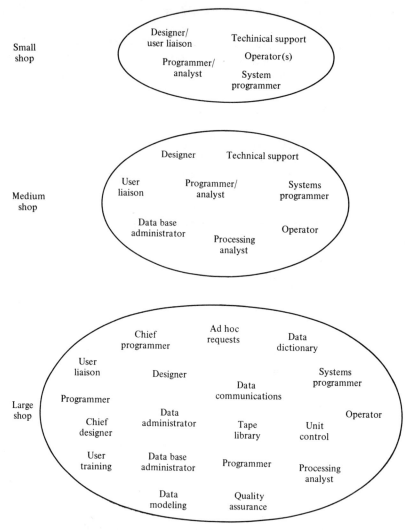

Figure 20.1 Expansion of staff related to job specialization.

"empire" within the organization. The growth of substructures in the organization nearly always begins informally and usually is formally recognized after a period of time.

The growth of substructures is not surprising in light of the basic need to understand and control the data processing environment in order to do productive work. When a project becomes so large that the key architects of the project are unable to control all necessary aspects, it is a normal reaction to reduce the project boundaries to a controllable, manageable size. However, in doing so, the organizational roots of unintegrated systems and substructures are laid.

264

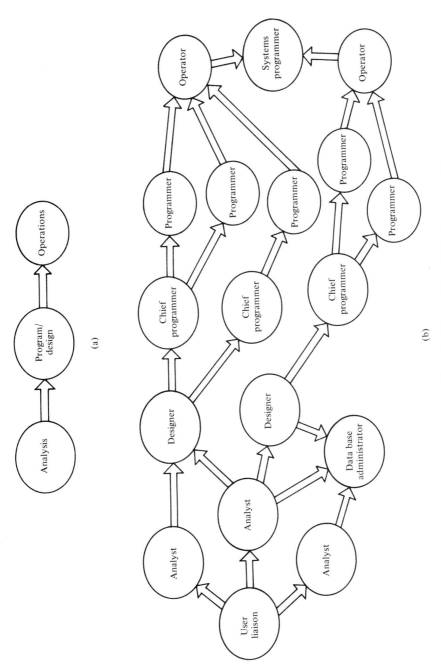

Figure 20.2 Communication flow in (a) a small and (b) a large operation.

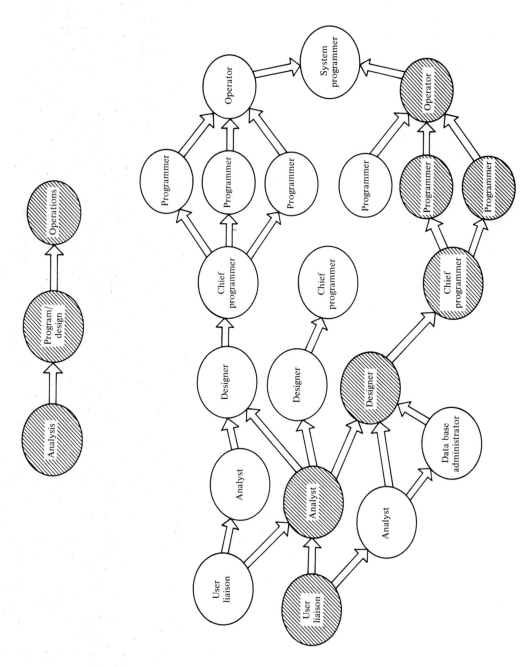

Figure 20.3 Project flow control in a small and a large operation.

20.6 DANGERS OF GROWTH TO THE ORGANIZATION

One of the by-products of the organization's rapid growth is the high degree of specialization (especially technical) and the need for highly skilled individuals. There are some drawbacks to specialization, however. At any moment in time there may be little or no work to be done for a given specialization. This is so because specialization causes the project to flow in a very disjoint fashion. Because the flow is disjoint, certain specialties may be flooded with work, while other specialties are idle, waiting on the finished product of the group that flows work to it. Salaries and overhead must still be paid regardless of the vagaries of the scheduling of work. Furthermore, in a highly specialized environment—because of the formal communications required between organizations, the learning curve necessary to understand what work needs to be done for a given project, the coordination of time-phased activities, and the possibility of overloading a specialized organization at a given moment in time—the flow of work through the organization tends to be slow. For these reasons, specialization is not without its drawbacks.

Another drawback of large organizations is that substructures within the organization may not view their role as a means to an end, but as an end in itself. This is particularly true for functional components of the organization such as data base administration, program development, and operations. What happens is that the organization that oversteps its bounds loses sight of the fact that data processing, as a whole, is a service organization, and that each component of the data processing organization also exists for service—to each of the organizations with which it interfaces and ultimately to the user. When components of an organization lose sight of that perspective, other lesser goals take on a degree of importance out of proportion to that which is beneficial. The resulting substructures within the organization become more of a detriment to service than a facilitator.

Once organizations grow large and the organizational structures and substructures (formal and informal) stabilize, organizational changes become a very difficult thing to accomplish. Organizations develop an inertia and are resistant to change, much as individuals within the organization are resistant to change. This inertia can be an impediment to progress in the face of a need for change, but the inertia is perhaps more insidious in a passive way. The passive drawbacks of this organizational inertia involve compartmentalization and stagnation of personnel within the organization. Because of skill specialization and the slowness of change, individuals become labeled and marked by their specialty and their role within the organization. As long as individuals are growing within their environment and are happy with their roles there is little problem. However, once individuals attempt to move into other areas of interest, they encounter great difficulty.

The other problem with specialization and departmental inertia to change is that individuals can become satisfied with the mastery of a set of skills and become complacent. With technology changing at a high rate of speed, it is only a matter of time before an employee's skills are dated and thus his or her usefulness to the company. Specialization creates an environment in which individuals must constantly struggle to broaden their skill base.

As noted before, the sheer size of large data processing organizations produces a tendency toward many smaller, interrelated, unintegrated application subsystems. This lack of integration of systems at a corporate level produces an environment in which the same work is done over and over for each subsystem. This is unquestionably a waste of effort.

20.7 OTHER APPROACHES TO ORGANIZING WORK

The problems of skill specialization and organizational compartmentalization are not new phenomena. In response to the problems created by these phenomena, other ways to organize work in the data processing environment have been implemented. As an example of such an approach, consider the organization that addresses the problems of specialization by creating a development group that can handle *all* the development needs of a given user area. These needs include analysis, design, programming, implementation, and certain technical services. This type of organization differs from the organization previously discussed in that all specialist skills are bound into one group, that is, the organization is not divided along lines of organizational function.

The user area being serviced normally represents much more than a single application. The user area is probably an operational arm of the company. By adopting this approach, workers within the development group have a freer, less formal communication line in accessing other people working on the same project, and have the potential for mastering more than one skill. Figure 20.4 illustrates an example of this type of organization. Project control flows entirely inside the confines of the development group. Since lines of communication are informal and project management flows along the same lines as departmental management, the flow of work of a given project can proceed with a fair degree of speed. A project does not need to be waiting due to the lack of a particular skill, since the project is self-contained as far as necessary skills are concerned.

There are some major drawbacks to this particular organization in the data processing environment, however. Certain disciplines need to be uniformly practiced over an entire organization, not just within a development group. These disciplines include data administration, operations, and systems programming, among others. Given the "development group" organiza-

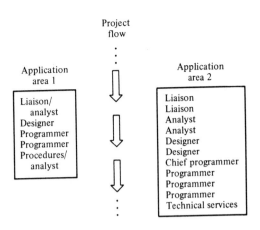

Project
flow

Application
area 1

| Liaison/ |
| analyst |
| Designer |
| Programmer |
| Programmer |
| Procedures/ |
| analyst |

Application
area 2

| Liaison |
| Liaison |
| Analyst |
| Analyst |
| Designer |
| Designer |
| Chief programmer |
| Programmer |
| Programmer |
| Programmer |
| Technical services |

Figure 20.4 Development group
organization. Instead of making
each specialized job function
independent of an application,
the development group organization
aligns people of different backgrounds
with a specific application area.

tion, it is difficult, if not impossible, to achieve a unified effort in these areas, and in the long run this can be very expensive.

From a different perspective, the development group approach to data processing organization fosters an environment of separatism within the entire organization. Each development group views its needs and plans as the most important in the entire company. In an on-line environment, (especially one that is experiencing great growth) this attitude is very expensive and short-sighted, because there are only a limited number of on-line computer resources to be shared among all application groups, whatever the attitude of the development group.

Another problem with the development group approach lies in the inability of the organization to integrate data and systems across group boundaries. In the long run this can be very expensive because of the duplication of similar and/or identical work that results.

20.8 RESOLVING PROBLEMS OF GROWTH

The problems of growth can be addressed at several levels. At the level of the organization chart, it is seen that whatever choice is made for the organization, there are still problems; there appears to be no "ideal" organization of people and resources.

Another level at which the problems of growth can be addressed is that of the manager—however the organization is laid out. There are several practices and attitudes that managers can adopt. Some of them are:

1. *Problem recognition.* Recognize problems as they are occurring, not after the fact. Managers who bury their heads in the sand will lose whatever control they have and the ability to influence the destiny of their managerial domains.

2. *Problem anticipation.* Anticipating problems and creating an environment in which the manifestations of the problem will not become acute saves money and morale.

3. *Understanding trade-offs.* Every problem has at its core at least two sides, and most complex problems are multifaceted. Focusing on a single set of parameters as a measurement of success can cause inordinate expenses elsewhere.

4. *Varied sources of input.* Whenever managers listen to the same sources of input over time, they adapt the perspectives of those with whom they are communicating. In a world as complex and changing as data processing management, it is very healthy to get new viewpoints and weigh the differences in opinions.

5. *Share experiences with other companies.* Other companies are at different stages of organizational maturity. Much insight can be gained by exchanging experiences.

6. *Create a "planned" environment.* Some problems will always occur that are of the reaction variety. However, when all or most of an organization's problems are of this type, deeper problems are indicated. *All reaction-mode activity should be recorded and later analyzed to learn how the organization fell into that mode and how to stay out of that mode in the future.*

REFERENCES

DoLotta, T. A., M. I. Bernstein, R. S. Dickson, Jr., N. A. France, B. A. Rosenblatt, D. M. Smith, and T. B. Steel, Jr., *Data Processing in 1980–1985*, Wiley–Interscience, New York, 1976.

Dorn, Philip, "1979 DP Budget Survey," *Datamation*, Vol. 25, No. 1 (1980).

Lecht, Charles, *Waves of Change*, Advanced Computer Techniques Corporation, New York, 1977.

Lientz, Bennett, and Burton Swanson, *Software Maintenance Management*, Addison-Wesley Publishing Company, Inc., Reading, Mass., 1980.

CASE STUDY

The El Paso Tortilla and Chile Company began in 1934 as a co-op for farmers in the El Paso area to sell their produce. The emphasis was on Mexican foods. Over the years, the business has changed; now the Tortilla and Chile Company is a nationally recognized supplier of high-quality Mexican foods. The real growth in business has been in the past 20 years as the fundamental orientation of the business changed from a local farmers' exchange to a national food distributor.

The owner of T and C has long been a believer in automation. One of the first automatic data processing pieces of equipment was installed in his shop. Since the business has grown as it has in the past 10 years, T and C has kept pace with upgrades in computers, software, and new applications. For the past two years, T and C has operated an on-line order system that is connected to wholesale food brokers around the United States.

For the past three years, the backlog of requests for new systems and additions to existing systems have outstripped the ability of the development staff to produce those systems. In the same vein, the amount of processing being done has pushed T and C into four computer upgrades and acquisitions in the last five years. Every time a computer is ordered, it appears it will supply power for the next year or two. By the time the computer arrives and is installed, it is virtually consumed within a few months.

The computer operations and development staff has grown each year, but the demands for their services have grown even faster. At first, generalists were hired, but as the hardware and software became more sophisticated, the job classifications became more specialized. Management is in a quandry as to what to do about acquiring computer expertise. One approach is to hire junior staff and upgrade them technically. This means that staff can be hired at a reasonable salary, and while they are in the learning curve (six months to two years), they are fairly content. Yet over and over as the personnel mature professionally, they go to other companies at much higher salaries.

The other approach is to hire seasoned professionals. The problem here is that they command a steep salary, and on occasion an incompetent is hired and management is stuck with the messy proposition of disposing of the worker. Neither approach is foolproof. Another problem relating to people is that in the growth of the department, as work becomes more specialized it seems to take longer and longer to get projects done. Some people seem to be constantly overworked, whereas other people do not seem to have enough to do.

The growth of hardware has been as amazing as the growth of department sizes. Even though the unit cost of processing keeps going down, the total units used are going up even faster. T and C continues upgrading to larger processors. Management wonders if that is the proper long-term strategy. One fear is that processing may exceed the biggest machine or configuration of machines available. The other concern is that splitting workloads onto a number of machines may be a sound long-term strategy financially, but T and C does not really know where to start.

T and C has chosen to stay with mainstream software. Their operating system and data base management system are the de facto industry standards. Over time, T and C has seen the software change to be able to handle growth, new capabilities, and new technologies. The software—although not perfect—has been serviceable and has not presented a barrier to T and C's growth. Management is secretly comforted whenever they hear stories of shops that have not chosen mainstream software and have run up against a constraint of the software for which there was only a set of poor options. Over the years, T and C has adopted the attitude that if a user is large enough and powerful enough, the user can and should call the shots as to the systems developed. This has resulted in quite a bit of data and system redundancy over time as users are not happy about sharing the control of their system with another department that they do not have control over.

Five years ago, T and C data processing management estimated that 15% of their staff effort was directed to maintenance. Today they estimate that 45% of their effort is for maintenance.   ∎

Comment on the Following

1. Selecting mainstream software is probably a good long-term strategy for handling a growing workload.
2. Selecting hardware that is upwardly compatible is a sound strategy for handling a growing workload.
3. Maintenance is a big factor in handling a growing workload. Underestimating the resources spent in maintenance can be a serious mistake.
4. Building unintegrated systems is contrary to good management of growth because (a) the development process takes much longer because the same systems must be developed over and over, and (b) maintenance of a number of redundant systems is *much greater* than is necessary when systems are integrated.
5. Managing growth is a long-term proposition.
6. New technologies such as usable systems present novel ways of addressing part of the problems posed by the backlog of user requests.

MULTIPLE-CHOICE QUESTIONS

1. Now that a user's first system has gone up, he is excited and wants enhancements made to it and a new system constructed for other parts of his business.
   A. It is normal for a user to want enhancements to a new system because the user probably had a hard time envisioning just how it would operate until he actually saw it run.
   B. Perhaps a prototype system put up quickly would have allowed the user to see what he was getting and would have prevented the

need for an immediate request for enhancements once the system was put up.

C. If a prototype system had been put up, the user may have wanted to use the prototype as is.

D. The second, third, fourth, and so on, systems put up by the user normally are *more* important to a business than the first.

E. If the first system was to interface heavily with the following system, the time to prepare for the interface is at the design of the first.

2. A company has organized its data processing staff around a "pool" concept. In this environment, programmers are put into one pool, designers into another, and so forth. As design requirements come down, personnel are selected from the pool based on availability. This organization has resulted in a slowing down of the development process. A reorganization is held where programmers, analysts, designers, and others are grouped together by user function (i.e., one user group has its own set of development personnel, another user has its own set, and so forth).

A. The development process may be shortened because, over time, development personnel get to know the user quite well.

B. This organization of people may be one of the reasons why unintegrated systems will be built.

C. Informal communication occurs much more easily in the new organization of personnel.

D. In the new organization, there is still a great need for a formal set of user requirements.

E. In the pool organization, a programmer was given a chance to get a broad exposure to lots of systems.

3. The systems being developed in a shop are very unintegrated.

A. Maintenance will be a long-term problem, much more so than it would be if systems were integrated.

B. Development time is longer because more people are involved in this duplication of effort.

C. If a workload must be split onto another processor at a later time, unintegrated systems may be a very good idea.

D. There is more processing to be done when systems are unintegrated.

E. Since the roots of unintegrated systems often lie with the user, the problem should be attacked high in the corporate management structure rather than technically.

EXERCISES AND ESSAYS

1. Based on the idea that one system spawns several more, is it possible that hiring more people implicitly results in the need to hire even more?
2. Is there a limit (practical, technical, or otherwise) to how much processing can be/should be done for a user, even if he or she can afford it?

XXI

Management Styles

□□

In data processing certain management styles and approaches are very noticeable. In some installations these styles are very obvious when they are carried to the extreme; in other, more moderate environments, the styles are not as pronounced. Most installations have some of the characteristics, in one form or the other, of all of the styles to be discussed. It is of interest to note the advantages and disadvantages of each style and how they originated. To make the examples more discernible, the management styles will be presented in their extreme form, almost as in a caricature, so that the differences will become more obvious. Very few, if any, installations actually are at the extremes depicted.

The four styles of data processing management to be discussed are:

- *The traditional approach.* Things are to be done the way we have always done them.
- *The infinite budget approach.* Address problems with more hardware, software, and/or people.
- *The cost-conscious approach.* Get the most out of all resources (even beyond normal constraints).
- *The technologist approach.* The answer to *all* problems is through technology.

21.1 FACTORS INFLUENCING APPROACHES TO MANAGEMENT

The approaches presented here have been shaped by many factors. They are, in fact, a result of the many environmental forces that are relevant to the running of the data processing installation. Some of the major influential factors are:

- *Budget.* Must there be a fairly large budget to support any data processing activity? What happens when there are *more* than ample resources? Less than ample resources? In fact, what *are* ample resources?

- *The user.* Ultimately, the user pays the bill for data processing services, so it is data processing's business to satisfy the user. What is reasonable? Unreasonable? How far should data processing go in satisfying the user?

- *Profit.* Usually, a company's profit is a big motivator and data processing plays an increasingly large role in that picture—both from a profit and an expense perspective. In other cases profit is not a factor; in fact, some companies consider it an advantage to *raise* operating expenses.

- *Growth.* The capabilities of computers are expanding in an exponential fashion. New features and new capacities make *feasible* today what was not *possible* yesterday.

- *Growth.* Corresponding to the increase in capacity is the increase in demand for services. The demand for services outstrips even the explosive growth of capabilities. Many times this growth causes decisions to be made because they *can* be done, not because they *should* be done. This subtle shift in emphasis leads to many difficulties.

- *Parameters of success.* Because of the rapidity of change in the technological world, what was a successful practice yesterday is not a successful practice today, yet the organization is not geared to change with technology. An installation often becomes set in patterns that were learned earlier but are not effective in a changing world.

- *Relation of the systems of data processing to the business of the company.* Some companies rely on data processing systems almost entirely, whereas other companies use the services of data processing tangentially. Generally speaking, the closer the systems are to the business of the company, the more critical the systems become. The size of the company also bears a relationship to the criticality of data processing systems.

Each of these factors (and others) influences the ways in which management cope with the problems facing them. Some factors are felt as a pressure, pushing management in a given direction. Other factors are viewed as a drawing force, pulling management instead of pushing. Still other factors are viewed as constraints—either psychological, political, financial, or technological.

21.2 TRADITIONALIST APPROACH TO MANAGEMENT

Certain aspects of the traditionalist approach to management are found, to some degree, in *every* environment. This approach is usually characterized by conservative, orderly management. Change comes slowly (relative to other installations). The traditionalist is *never* the leading edge. The preference is to let other installations try ideas, software, and hardware and let them work out the problems. Once the shakedown period is over and a track record has been established, the traditionalist then acquires the product or approach. For the most part, ideas, practices, and procedures are homegrown and in-grown. Ideas that come from outside the organization are suspect and slow to catch on. Most of the staff has been grown internally, quite a few from the entry level.

Voluminous standards manuals are part of the traditionalist data proc-essing department. The standards manual typically is very large, docu-menting even the obscure, and is seldom referred to in actuality. Because of its size and the difficulty in updating a manual, in many cases the manual is out of date. Management puts much faith in the manual because it exists and is large; but in reality, it is not useful. Management feels that the organi-zation is disciplined because of the manual, even though the manual plays *no* real part in the shaping of the data processing environment.

There usually are many formalized procedures in the traditional organization. Requirements, program specifications, operation procedures— are all documented in a rigorous fashion. A data dictionary holds some of the installation's data elements, but is incomplete and is not actively being pursued. The environment has long testing procedures and an intricate imple-mentation process. Despite the formalized procedures, most of the day-to-day work of the installation proceeds along informal lines—lines that have been established in past projects. The turnover rate tends to be lower than the industry average, and each project has its own set of pioneers who can be relied upon to solve problems when they arise. Many people stay in the same type of job a long time, rarely switching to a different category of job. They feel a sense of security and stability. This attitude further reinforces the traditionalist approach to management.

Crises are handled by a reliance on past proven performers or by follow-ing patterns of resolution previously established.

An advantage of the traditionalist approach is that people know where they stand within the organization. There are a minimum number of prob-lems caused by new equipment or software, lines of work flow are well established, and the domain of each part of the organization is established, either by default or by plan. Some of the disadvantages are that changes come slowly and this may mean missing opportunities, that changes in re-sponsibility cause hard feelings, that personnel tend to get pigeonholed as to their capabilities, and that streamlining processes such as development time is very difficult.

21.3 INFINITE BUDGET APPROACH TO MANAGEMENT

The infinite budget approach is typical of installations whose parent com-pany is large and/or very profitable, of some governmental agencies, and of regulated industries. In some cases, the amount of profit a company makes is so high that it behooves the company to raise its expenses, and data processing is very good for this. In other cases, a regulated industry is allowed to make a certain percent of profit based on expenses. In this case, it means that a company can make more absolute profit by raising expenses. In cases where profit is not the primary force behind the raison d'etre of the company, the data processing department is given a virtually unlimited budget.

Some of the characteristics of this approach are seen in the ways in which problems are solved. One technique is to buy hardware—the biggest, fastest, and most expensive. Compared to other organizations, the infinitely budgeted management get much less out of its hardware than do comparable shops. Another technique for solving problems is to buy much software. Every time a new problem comes up (or an old problem arises in a new form), the solution is to buy a new piece of software. It is typical of this approach to have *many* varieties of software in-house, all purchased or currently leased, very few of which are actually being utilized.

Another characteristic of this approach is the attitude toward human resources. The "Mongolian horde" theory is the result. Using this theory, it is held that a one person-year effort can be done in one day by 365 people (which, of course, is not true). People tend to have *very* narrow job responsibilities, thus accounting for the fact that there is a high degree of specialization in these environments and also extensive periods of time when individuals remain idle because there is no immediate need for their services.

Management operating under the infinite budget approach tends to "buy" solutions rather than coming to grips with the problems facing the data processing organization. Because of this, there is no real recognition of the problems, and there are very few merits (or demerits) based on individual performance in the organization. Instead, job advancement is almost haphazard, based much more on company politics than on competency of effort. Because of the resources available to management, there is no need to find out what the problems are or who can come to grips with those problems. There is very seldom any tracking, analysis, or pattern recognition of past errors.

There is usually a lengthy development cycle with no feedback loop for the designers. In the cases where the infinite budget installation does have quick development, there is usually a very lengthy post-implementation development cycle.

Whenever a crisis occurs, this type of organization responds by looking for a new resource to solve the problem—either a new piece of equipment, an upgrade to existing equipment, a new piece of software, or the hiring of more personnel. There is virtually no organizational discipline of any kind in this environment.

One of the advantages of this kind of installation is that resource allocation is never a problem. It is an excellent place to work from the viewpoint that virtually any piece of software or hardware can be found and used for a learning experience. Many times new types of systems come out of this environment by virtue of the fact that no other type of installation has the resources to develop innovative and/or costly systems. A major disadvantage of this type of shop is that there is no real reward for getting results. The premium on talent is at a minimum (relative to the rest of the industry). It is very easy to become pigeonholed because there are many individual skills scattered throughout the company. The primary disadvantage is the frustration of never coming to grips with problems, with having problems hidden and glossed over, waiting to reemerge later in an exaggerated and larger form. A by-product of the attitude toward employees is a high turnover rate.

21.4 BUDGET CONSTRAINED APPROACH TO MANAGEMENT

The budget constrained approach contrasts with the infinite budget approach to management. In the budget constrained case, management simply cannot move because of the lack of financial resources. Lack of resources creates a paralysis that affects both the ability to solve immediate problems and the ability to move an organization toward long-range goals. The budget constrained management approach to data processing is typically found in installations where companies operate on a very nominal profit margin. In other cases, such as some government-regulated agencies, the budget is so small that data processing management is unduly constrained.

One characteristic of the budget constrained installation is that it is seldom the leading edge technically because it simply cannot afford to be. Costs of hardware come down over time and budget-constrained environments wait for the decrease. Also, the budget makes management conservative because costly mistakes cannot be tolerated. For these reasons, these installations usually are a step or two behind the industry.

On the other hand, budget constrained shops sometimes are not averse to "exotic" solutions, that is, using technology in ways other installations have not used it. On occasion a manager is tempted to delve into technical areas that *can* be handled, but probably *should not* be. These managers meet with various levels of success—in some cases failing miserably, in other cases achieving a fair degree of success.

Outstripping hardware is a normal way of life. By the time an upgrade arrives, it is already used up. Because these organizations need to get the absolute maximum out of their hardware, they keep the hardware overloaded. These managers try to stretch their resources through hardware, software, or any other available tool that is not expensive.

Because there are never enough resources to go around, these environments often appear to be behind the times. The installations have few frills and use to the hilt what little software they have. Expenses other installations take for granted have to be justified.

Because of the emphasis on resources, managers must come to grips with problems and address problems at the most basic level. Talented people tend to advance because management recognizes and encourages competency. Less-than-able personnel are soon identified and weeded out. Management cannot afford the luxury of unproductive personnel. Because of the lack of resources, there is a definite tendency for this organization to go into a reaction mode even in the face of a fairly high degree of discipline.

One trademark of this approach is an abbreviated development cycle. Systems are put up with little fanfare, usually with a minimum of documentation. Development efforts are usually very efficient because there is a constant awareness of wasted effort. Since there are minimal human resources, the person doing the maintenance is usually the original developer, so documentation can be considered almost a luxury.

People working in this environment tend to become proficient at many tasks because the company cannot hire all the expertise it would like. Thus the job demands that people function in a broad spectrum of capacities. There is always constant pressure on personnel to produce because there are never enough personnel. On occasion, jobs simply do not get done properly because there is not enough staff to do the job.

The approach to solving crises is to review the problem, determine the immediate solution, allocate the minimum amount of resources, and reprioritize the work that is being done. Since current work is understaffed, some work suffers whenever a crisis occurs.

Some of the advantages of the budget constrained approach are that problems are met and handled in a straightforward manner, there is very little wasted work, on occasion innovative solutions to problems are found, and personnel function in a wide capacity of jobs. The disadvantages stem from the fact that there are not enough resources to go around. This means that the organization will most likely not be state-of-the-art, that the actual operation of systems is hamstrung by lack of resources, and that there is unceasing pressure on the entire staff.

21.5 TECHNOLOGICAL APPROACH TO MANAGEMENT

The technological approach to management is somewhat of a hybrid of the other approaches. A shop operating on a lean budget usually has only a few resources and so cannot afford the luxury of solving problems with technology. For this reason, the technological approach aligns closely with the infinite budget approach. The difference in these two approaches, however, stems from the fact that the technologist always looks to technology first for a solution, whereas the infinite budget manager looks for the fastest solution, whatever its nature.

In the technological approach, technology is often used for technology's sake. Many facets of systems are done experimentally, and it is common to see nearly all of the available options (of hardware or software) used whether or not it makes sense to use them. Another trademark is an optimization of one or two aspects of the technology, usually with disregard for more major considerations. For example, in some environments it is considered very smart to make nonstandard modifications to standard software. In this environment a technician is deemed to really know what he or she is doing by making those modifications. However, the technician does not appear smart at all when the release of the software changes and the local modifications either have to be redone or will not work at all.

In the technologist environment (as in the infinite budget environment) it is common to find *many* kinds of hardware and software. Over and over the development that occurs in this environment depends on highly technical approaches and usually runs into technical barriers. Not only does this cause day-to-day production problems, but this approach may mean there are technical barriers to the extension of the system, and in the long run, this may prove to be very inhibiting.

By taking the approach that the technical approach is the best one, quite often these organizations miss easier, more straightforward, pragmatic solutions to problems.

From a personnel standpoint, there are two negative aspects to this environment. The first is that advancement is based almost entirely on technical acumen, and this ultimately produces managers who may not be equipped to manage at all but who are, no doubt, technical wizards. The second problem is that the high amount of technological activity makes the organization more people-dependent than it would normally be. From a different perspective, this type of environment can be appealing to work in because of the exposure to the different tools and equipment.

Crises are *always* handled by reliance on technology, because of the nature of the ways systems are built. This environment is found in several types of shops—academic, research, nonprofit, large-budget shops, and a few high-profit-margin industries.

The advantages of this environment are that the installation is on the leading edge technically, that employees have the opportunity to be exposed to new software and hardware (and thus can stay current with the industry), and that occasionally a company will have a significant competitive advantage because of a technological breakthrough. Disadvantages include the high cost of technology, the dependence on people who are not easily replaced, the options available (and not available) at a time of crisis, and the limitation sometimes imposed on the growth of systems.

21.6 SUMMARY

Few, if any, organizations are at the extremes pictured in the sketches given in this chapter. Most shops, however, have some or most of the tendencies of one approach or the other. In some cases, an installation may exhibit tendencies to go in more than a single direction. Any approach has its advantages and corresponding disadvantages. Usually, the more extreme the approach is the greater the disadvantages.

CASE STUDY

The tuning consultant and expert at Interface Systems has been asked to do a tuning job for three organizations: Consolidated Power, Electro-Engineering, and Dalton County Junior College. He goes first to Consolidated Power, where he inquires into the general background of the company. Power is a large, profitable business. It is primarily a public utility, but its strength lies in the fact that many years ago, the founding fathers of Power bought numerous leases for natural gas in the Midwest and built several large dams that supply a large electrical network.

Since then, Power administers its resources. In essence, it has been living off correct decisions made a long time ago. Public outcry has been made about the large profits Power makes, and as a consequence, Power's profit margins are regulated. From a long-term corporate standpoint, it makes sense for Power to raise its operating expenses so that profits can be raised.

The data processing philosophy at Power is to please the user. Whatever the user wants is correct by definition. The systems produced for the user are large, redundant, not particularly well built, and specialized for each user. Because Power's systems are built in a very undisciplined environment, there is little done to control the design process and the result is poor utilization of resources. This fact, coupled with the never-ending development effort, means that there is always a strain on existing resources.

Management believes the solution to be one of adequate tuning. The problem is that tuning is a chronic problem. In nearly every case, the result of the tuning effort is the purchase of more resources, such as memory or even another computer.

The second company the consultant visits is Electro-Engineering. The environment here is typified by the president, who was a brilliant engineer. The emphasis is on "can it be done?" In many ways, Electro-Engineering systems are state-of-the-art. New features of existing technology are used, and in some cases, whole new technologies are used. In some instances, this has provided an advantage for the company competitively in that customers were able to be offered services not found elsewhere. In other cases, the pioneering attitude has caused the company embarrassment in not living up to customer's expectations.

Electro-Engineering has determined that its systems need to be tuned by several elaborate measuring devices. New software is being considered for one of the focal points of tuning. The software is aimed at organizing data in a nonstandard way that (1) will provide optimal access and (2) will maintain a "clean" state as long as possible. The study has been going on for a while and the strategies for tuning have even been investigated at the vice-presidential level.

Dalton County Junior College presents a different challenge. It is an educational environment where the emphasis is always on finding the least expensive way to get things done. Instead of worrying about making the customer happy or the best way to get things done, the management here has to worry about getting something done first, then hope it is adequate to meet the needs of the user. The junior college has a limited budget and must make do within that budget. Because of this awareness of costs, systems are constructed very carefully. This means that the junior college gets the maximum out of the equipment it has, even if the equipment is a bit dated. Management feels that a tuning effort is in order. Their approach is to consider the full range of options available to them and to select the options that are most feasible in the junior college environment.

The options being considered are:

1. More hardware acquisition—is the purchase of hardware justified? Is it within budgeting constraints?
2. New software-new techniques.
3. More optimal ways of running existing software and using hardware more efficiently.
4. Limiting user expectations.   ■

Comment on the Following

1. Tuning is the major area in which differences in organizational attitudes show up.
2. In the technologist environment, the first criterion for promotion is technical expertise.
3. Aside from the fact that there are never enough resources to go around, the cost-conscious environment is very rational and can be very stimulating.
4. The infinite budget approach becomes so layered with inefficiency and unproductivity that, over time, the environment may not appear to be as bad as it really is. This may stem from the fact that work often expands to fill a vacuum.
5. Most shops usually have some elements of each approach at the same time.
6. The long-term effects of management approaches and philosophies have a profound and widespread effect on the organization. This effect is seen in the budget, the personnel, the types of systems being built, and the way systems are built.

MULTIPLE-CHOICE QUESTIONS

1. In the cost-conscious environment, a data-entry clerk works her way up to programmer. After a while, she becomes a project leader and a designer. After several years of this experience, she becomes an assistant data base administrator.

   A. The cost-conscious environment normally exposes employees to a broad set of experiences in data processing.
   B. Working in a cost-conscious environment can be tedious because there are never enough personnel to go around.
   C. Management tends to weed out unproductive employees in this environment because a "rotten apple" is obvious and an unwelcome luxury.
   D. The cost-conscious environment is much more conducive to feedback to the employee—rewards for good work, penalties for mistakes.
   E. Success as an application designer is not necessarily a stepping stone to data base administration.

2. John works for a large, profitable oil company. He has worked there for two years. In his previous job, he had much latitude and was considered one of the people who "made things run." At his present job, he feels stifled because of the very narrow confines of his job and because his duties seem to be important to the running of the company only on rare occasions.

   A. The seeds for dissension were sown before he took his present job.
   B. This environment is typical of *most* large shops.
   C. This is a good environment to "get lost in" and to consider as a relaxing atmosphere prior to retirement.
   D. Trying to move a project or an innovation through this environment can be *very* trying.
   E. It is a good bet that there is little positive feedback for a good job here and little negative feedback for a poor job.

ESSAYS AND EXERCISES

1. Assume that it is your job to go into a shop you have never been in before and in a two-hour interview classify the shop in many ways—how happy the employees are, what approaches management has, what the degree of system quality is, and so on. Make a list of questions you would ask to discover what is true about the organization. How can

you tell if someone is "painting a picture" for you rather than describing the reality of the matter? At what levels of management would you wish to interview? People with what job skills would you be interested in talking to?

2. Is there a predictable "day of doom" for those organizations that blatantly waste resources?

3. Is a cost-conscious manager better equipped to make judgments or to judge character than the counterpart in a non-cost-conscious company?

4. What impact will a manager of a different philosophy have if the manager is suddenly elevated to a position of responsibility? Where are the roots of resistance?

5. Is technical expertise a valid criterion for promotions into management? Is promotion into management the best path for rising in the corporation? What problems arise when the *only* criterion for management is technical expertise?

XXII

Data Base Administration/ Data Administration

□□

22.1 SYSTEM GROWTH CYCLE

The evolution of the functions of data base administration (DBA) and data administration (DA) and the differences between the functions can be explained in terms of the rather standard system growth cycle found in most installations. This growth cycle is depicted by Figure 22.1.

Computerization	Sequential systems	Data base	On-line systems
(C)	(S)	(D)	(O)

Figure 22.1 System growth cycle.

In this figure, it is seen that the growth of automated systems begins with the initial efforts to computerize—to go from manual to automated systems. The next phase of the growth cycle is the construction of sequential systems—systems characterized by tapes, reports, sorts, merges, and so on. The next phase of computerization is that of data base, where data is stored and used in a direct fashion and can be accessed by a number of users concurrently. Following the trend toward data base is the evolution toward on-line systems, where data can be accessed and updated concurrently and users can access data in an interactive fashion.

The total amount of computer processing usually grows as an installation proceeds along the system growth cycle. This can be measured by the number of systems that are developed, the size of those systems, and the total amount of processing done. This growth of computing activity is shown by Figure 22.2. In this figure, the total amount of processing done grows almost linearly during the days of initial computerization and in the early days of sequential systems. After a certain point, the growth becomes exponential as sequential systems give way to data base and data base gives

286

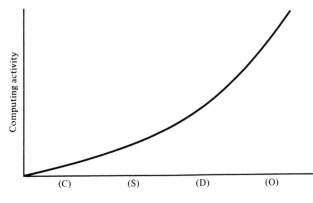

Figure 22.2 Growth of computing activity as the mode of processing matures.

way to on-line systems. This explosive growth is triggered by growing demand for services, new and more effective ways to satisfy that demand, and equipment with new orders of magnitude of processing capabilities.

A rather interesting (and subjective) phenomenon observable at most installations is the degree of organizational complexity arising as computer processing grows. This somewhat subjective measure is shown by Figure 22.3. The complexity here refers not to the individual complexity of a given application, but to the organizational complexity that arises in managing many systems, resources, people, users, and long-term and short-term growth. The focus is on the organizational impact in the face of growth.

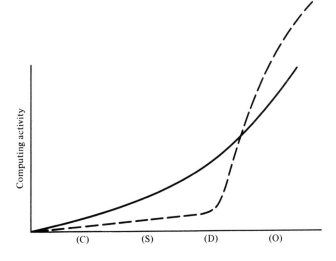

Figure 22.3 Degree of organizational complexity (dashed line) as computer processing grows (solid line).

It is seen that organizational complexity is fairly low (and linear) until data base begins to be implemented and used, at which point the complexity factor rises dramatically. The main reasons for this "knee" in the curve of complexity are:

287

- *Number of systems involved.* Organizational control of a few systems (data base or otherwise) is relatively straightforward. The sheer increase in the number of systems causes organizational complexity.

- *Age of systems.* As systems age, their code and data structures have a tendency to degenerate. This adds greatly to organizational headaches.

- *Interrelationship of systems.* When an installation has only a few systems, the interrelationship of systems during modification or new development is not too bothersome. As time goes on, systems age and increase in number, and the interrelationship of systems becomes a major problem. Furthermore, data base fosters an environment in which systems can be interrelated in ways not possible previously.

- *Amount of data to be handled.* The sheer volume of data in an environment that is exponentially increasing in size carries with it its own considerations for such mundane needs as restructuring, recovery, access, and update.

- *Number of environmental variables that need to be controlled.* The variables of success that need to be mastered in the on-line environment, for example, are more numerous, less obvious, and vastly more critical than the variables of success of the sequential environment.

- *Number of programs and transactions.* The sheer volume of computing activity has its own considerations as the volume increases exponentially.

From an organizational perspective, the problems listed above tend to accelerate somewhere between the waning of sequential systems and the advent of on-line systems. This point in time varies considerably from installation to installation.

22.2 COPING WITH THE PROBLEMS OF COMPUTING GROWTH

From an organizational perspective, there are several ways to attempt to cope with the problems posed by the growth of computing. One approach is to attempt to retrofit solutions on systems after they are built. The effectiveness of this approach is *very* limited. The *single most important* time that the organization can effectively address many of the problems of growth is at the moment of application design, because it is *at that moment* that the system takes its general shape, and any further efforts to modify that shape significantly will be painful. Figure 22.4 illustrates the shaping effect of the design process.

This means that the issues of growth and consequently how the organization reacts to that growth are *primarily* addressed at the point of design. In order to institute organizational control, the functions of the DBA and the DA make their appearance. Previously, the perspective of applications was

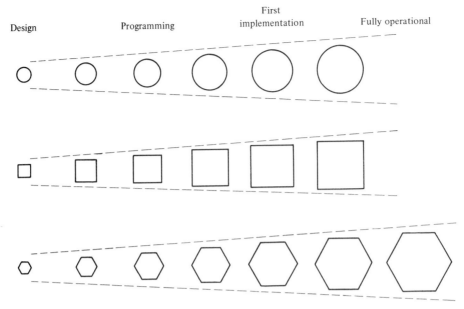

Figure 22.4 Shaping effect of the design process.

limited to the needs of the user being served. As systems, grow, there is a necessary change from the traditional perspective of applications, in that applications can no longer design systems as if they were the only user of computer resources. This means that management must recognize the need for a higher degree of organizational control and applications must relinquish some control, which is usually traumatic but is healthy and mature for the organization. The perspective of the DBA is to protect the DBMS from any misuse by any system that will abuse commonly shared resources. The function of protecting the DBMS is necessary and represents the higher level of control not found in the traditional application perspective. It is the basis of the need for sharing of control of design with applications.

On the other hand, the perspective of the DA is different from that of the DBA. While the DBA worries about the proper usage of the DBMS, the DA ensures the integration of data and systems across *all* systems in an organization. The role of the DA, insofar as influence on design is concerned, starts at the very early moments of design. The DA's influence on design is to ensure that systems are integrated, that work on old systems is being done in the right place, and that work on new systems fits within the framework of system integration. All perspectives need to be effectively represented and balanced at the moment of design. Not having them represented and balanced will cause problems later.

Figure 22.5 shows that it is in the domain of applications to include design exclusively as its responsibility. The mature, necessary sharing of control is shown by Figure 22.6, where DBA, DA, and the applications share

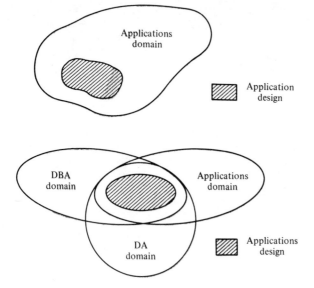

Figure 22.5 Applications domain. Applications design is within the domain of the applications function, where there is no need for organizational control of the complexities of the data processing environment.

Figure 22.6 Sharing control in applications design. Where there is a need for organizational control, applications design falls into the domain of the applications function, the DBA, and the DA.

responsibility and control of the application design from the different perspective of each of the organizations. The recognition for this sharing of design responsibility is illustrated by Figure 22.7, where it is seen that applications' existence and presence is felt throughout the system growth

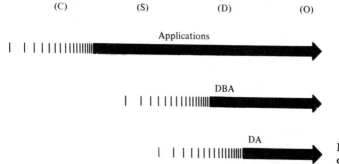

Figure 22.7 Recognition for sharing of design responsibility.

cycle, whereas the DBA makes its appearance somewhere between the midpoint of sequential systems and the advent of data base. The DA function slowly makes its presence felt from the advent of data base systems up to on-line systems.

22.3 INFLUENCE OF DBA AND DA ON THE PROJECT LIFE CYCLE

Once the functions of DBA and DA are established, the project life cycle is affected differently at different times. This project involvement is shown in Figure 22.8.

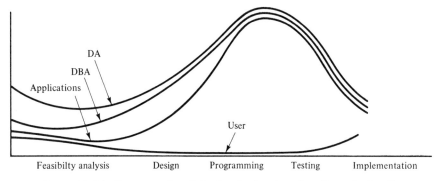

DA

DBA

Applications

User

Feasibilty analysis   Design   Programming   Testing   Implementation

Figure 22.8 Influence and activity level of various functions during the product life cycle.

Here the user is seen playing a very important role in the formative stages of development, a somewhat more passive role during the middle of the development cycle, and an increasingly important role as the implementation phase draws near. The DBA plays an advisory technical role (somewhat passive) in the initial phases of feasibility, an important (perhaps dominant) role during analysis and early design, and an almost clerical role during programming, testing, and implementation. The DA plays a very influential role (dominant) during the feasibility study and early analysis, and a decreasingly important role (passive) during the remainder of the life cycle. Applications plays a role of participation in the early feasibility and analysis, and a clearly dominant role in design (after the foundations have been laid) and programming, testing, and implementation. This blending of the influence of each group at different points in the life of project development ensures that each organization represents its perspective properly. Not allowing a group the proper influence at the right time precludes one or more aspects of the project being designed properly.

22.4 ROLE OF THE DBA

The role of the DBA can be viewed from two essentially different perspectives depending on the problem being addressed. The perspectives are global and local—*global* over *all* the applications in a shop, or *local* to a given application. Some of the global concerns of the DBA are:

- Standard work unit—enforcement, definition, exceptions, and so on
- Installation-wide strategy for data base recovery and reorganization
- Design considerations for recovery and reorganization
- Monitoring of on-line system activity
- On-line system generation and control
- Design review

The global perspective of the DBA can be characterized as that of watchdog over all activity that occurs in the use of the DBMS. In this perspective the DBA considers *all* systems that are or will be on the DBMS. The concerns are resource sharing, system-wide performance, system-wide availability, stability of the system, and operational impact of the running of any one system on the entire system. In this capacity the DBA must have the authority and capability to alter any application for the good of the others. If management chooses *not* to support the DBA in this case, the DBA should clearly document the projected results and openly and formally address the management that is not supportive. The local concerns of the DBA focus on the project as if it were the only system to be run. This perspective is as necessary as the global and should be balanced.

Some of the local concerns of the DBA are:

- Data base definitions of a project
- Recovery procedures for each data base of a project
- Reorganization procedures for each data base of a project
- Data base monitoring
- Implementation of physical data base changes and transaction changes
- Application control block generation
- How business function can be met within the standard work unit

In the "local" capacity, the DBA is concerned with the very immediate aspects of a given application. This includes day-to-day needs such as space allocation, execution of reorganization or recovery procedures, definition of the data (and redefinition when changes need to be made), and technical advice. In this role, the DBA views the immediate needs of the application as his or her primary task.

All of these concerns—both local and global—properly belong to the DBA. Exactly *where* they belong depends on the organization and the corporation.

22.5 ROLE OF THE DA

The role of the DA in the data processing organization is very similar to the role of the DBA. Whereas the DBA is concerned primarily with the performance and availability characteristics of systems going on the DBMS, the DA is concerned with the integration of systems within the corporation. One long-term benefit of a high degree of integration is reduced system maintenance. The DA is thus concerned more with long-term activities than with day-to-day problems. Some of the concerns of the DA are:

- Data as a corporate resource
- System integration for existing and new systems
- Data dictionary (formal and informal)
- Long-range planning
- System flexibility
- Design review

The primary role of the DA is to ensure system integration. To be effective this must be done early in the development cycle. Attempting to integrate systems once the design has been fairly well completed is useless. The DA is more of a "traffic director" than a day-to-day influence on the system development cycle.

It is seen, then, that the roles of the DBA, the DA, and applications together assure that the *total* data needs of a corporation can be met. Not defining each of these functions separately and formally does not mean that the function will not be done; it means that *some part* of the total function will be done haphazardly or by default, thus not achieving the total benefits that could be derived.

One of the major long-term benefits of system integration is reduced system maintenance. When systems are integrated, changes that need to be made are made in only a few places, thus reducing the work of the maintenance programmer. Furthermore, the DA ensures that systems that are being built provide a framework for future additions, rather than causing similar systems to be built in the future. An effective DA, by greatly reducing maintenance, can significantly enhance programmer productivity. The investment return is long-term and is at a macro level (thus making it difficult to see), but the return can be considerable.

22.6 DEFINITION OF RESPONSIBILITIES

For both the DA and the DBA, there are two essential ways that domains and responsibilities can be defined: formally or informally. There are advantages and disadvantages to both. Some of the considerations of a former definition of responsibilities are:

- Minimization of long-term conflicts that would arise from an ambiguity of domain
- Clear definition of organizational domain
- Formalization of communications where necessary
- Boundaries of responsibility clearly defined to management

When responsibilities are defined formally, there are *many* benefits. The interface and responsibilities between departments is clear and the expectations and deliverables are well defined. This goes a long way toward harmonious relations between departments. Another benefit is that management is able to resolve conflicts objectively based on predefined roles and commitments, rather than roles ambiguously defined. There will be conflict enough between applications and DBA and DA without adding an element of ambiguity between the DBA and DA.

Some of the considerations of letting responsibilities evolve informally are:

- Delay of the confrontation with resistance
- Initial ease of evolution of responsibility
- Dependence on management resolution for conflict

Informally letting responsibilities evolve is politically expedient and causes a minimum amount of friction initially. However, that initial lack of friction can lead to a false sense of security because the friction that results later, when conflicts occur, will most likely be very heated and intense.

Clearly, formally, and openly declaring the boundaries of responsibilities creates an environment of order in which roles are well-defined and the people fulfilling those roles can interact with other people with a minimum of stress.

22.7 TOOLS OF THE DA/DBA

Some of the tools (concepts, methodologies, functions, etc.) that can be used by either or both the DA and DBA are:

- Standard work unit
- Design review with explicit and real rights of project approval
- Standards/guidelines/procedures (separately defined)
- Documentation
- Data dictionary (formal and informal)
- Information dissemination (technical, design, etc.)
- System generation
- Formalized communications
- Test/production system control
- System monitoring software

Use of these tools provides the DBA and/or DA with (at a minimum) the opportunity to influence applications to the long-term benefit of the corporation. Each of these tools has an appropriate place. Not all organizations use all of these tools, but most organizations use some combination.

REFERENCE

IMS/VSI Version 1 Data Base Administration Guide, IBM Manual SH20-9025-7, S370-50.

CASE STUDY

The Indiana Insurance Company has had a data base administrator (DBA) for six years, a little longer than they have had their DBMS. The first five years of use of the DBMS have been in the batch environment. In this capacity, the DBA has played the role of guardian of the DBMS and the data that support the application systems. This has been primarily a technical advisory role. When systems need to be debugged, the DBA function is one of the primary contacts.

In the last 15 months, the first on-line development effort has been made and the system has been operational for about four months now. Once the system was cut over, it was a short amount of time from a small utilization to a longer and longer utilization. Each day the system is being used more.

During the initial design phase, the DBA met with applications and suggested strongly that several features be changed. The applications people felt that the DBA had no business telling them what should or should not be done. The applications designers had a long history of successfully building systems and the attention of the DBA was quickly disregarded. Applications management fully supported the people that had performed well for them over the years.

To make matters worse, the DBA was organizationally at a lower level than his applications counterpart. The applications leader regularly had the ear of a higher level of management than the DBA ever had access to; thus it was an easy thing to ignore the influence of the DBA.

One day the on-line system experiences an application-induced failure. The data bases are rendered inoperable and the system becomes unavailable for two working days. The user is livid at the DBA, who the user feels is responsible for the long system outage. The DBA attempts to make the point that design practices initially could have greatly lessened the downtime.

Furthermore, response time grows worse and worse. The DBA has undergone no less than six tuning exercises. The first few were marginally successful.

The last ones did nothing for performance. The user and applications blame the DBA for poor response time. It is rumored that the DBA may not be "technically competent."

The DBA attempts to point out that the seeds of poor performance were laid in the initial stages of design. Attempting to retrofit performance into the system once the system is actually built is difficult if not impossible. Management views the DBA cautiously because they believe in the personnel who have always come through for them in the past—the application designers and developers.   ■

Comment on the Following

1. At this juncture, there is little management can do to rectify past short-comings.

2. The DBA should be allowed to approve or disapprove future designs of on-line systems.

3. The problems of performance, availability, and so on, can be attacked at a technical level. There is no great need to address these problems at the time of design.

4. The DBA, in the current environment, is at the point of having to live with other people's bad decisions. In essence, the whip is cracking and the DBA is at the wrong end.

5. The DBA should be elevated in the organization to a level approximately equal to the head of applications. At the very least, the DBA should have an equal opportunity to explain to management the issues as perceived by the DBA.

MULTIPLE-CHOICE QUESTIONS

1. A data base administration (DBA) function is to be established. Management is aware of the pitfalls of not giving the DBA enough power. The DBA is entrusted with the care of the DBMS, all data base design, transaction design, data dictionary, system monitoring, system tuning, long-term planning, test system generation, productivity aids relating to data base, backup and recovery, security, reorganization, and system review.

    A. The DBA function is probably too powerful. It will be difficult for the DBA to fulfill all of the functions effectively.

    B. The DBA function will probably grow very large and be difficult to administer.

    C. The user is accustomed to interfacing with applications. Now the user must interface with the DBA and this change has upset the user.

    D. If the DBA has fewer functions, it will be difficult to coordinate all activities that relate to data base administration.

    E. Applications view the rise of the DBA as a usurper of the functions that rightfully belong to them and as a roadblock to getting work done.

2. Management has decided that a data administration (DA) function is necessary in addition to the DBA function. A meeting is called to determine the different functions and responsibilities of the DA and DBA.

    A. The DA should be in charge of the data dictionary.

    B. The DBA's primary responsibility is the care and tending of the DBMS, the data bases that run under the DBMS, and the application programs that support those data bases.

    C. The DA has as much interest as the DBA in early system design, in some cases, more interest.

    D. The long-term benefit of building systems that support the DA's perspective is that data can be used beyond the scope of the immediate set of requirements for which the system is justified. The viewpoint of the DA is a global one.

    E. Effective data administration results in a reduction of maintenance costs. The result is long-term, however.

3. The data base administrator has decreed that a system design is not fit to go into production. She feels secure in her belief that any system that goes into production must meet her approval. Accordingly, she pays little or no attention to the test system. The application designer whose design has been rejected by the DBA bypasses the DBA and builds his system as he pleases on the test system. Once constructed, he loads a representative amount of data and demonstrates the system to his user. He then tells the user that he cannot have the system because of the DBA. The user immediately goes to upper management and strongly criticizes the DBA for "holding up progress."

    A. The data base administrator still has control because she controls the production system.

    B. The DBA function is one with a low political profile in the company.

    C. The application designer has done a service to the company because it is his job to please the user at whatever cost.

    D. The reason the original design was rejected is not particularly important to the user.

    E. If the data base administrator gains control over both the production and test systems, her problems will be over.

EXERCISES AND ESSAYS

1. Given a brand-new DBA organization, what areas are the most important for the DBA to stress for the greatest and most immediate payback? For the DA? What are the long-term considerations of the DBA?

2. How can the DBA make the most of its technical expertise and control?

3. In the following phases of design, where should the DBA and the DA exert the most control?

    a. Feasibility study
    b. User requirement and definition
    c. System analysis
    d. System design
        (1) Data base design
        (2) Transaction design
    e. Programming
    f. Testing
    g. Implementation
    h. Production
    i. Maintenance

4. The perspectives of the DA and DBA are both global. How do they differ? How are they similar? Which is more important? How should a difference of opinion be resolved?

5. Describe the shortcomings of the DBA when the DBA is *not*:

    a. Adequately technical
    b. Adequately political
    c. Adequately cognizant of application problems and concerns

6. It has been said that the role of the DBA is in great flux throughout the industry. Project what the role will look like in five years. What impact will changing technology have on the role of the DBA?

7. Why is the balance between applications and DBA so delicate? What impact does the SWU have on that balance? What factors *other* than performance are relevant to the balance of the DBA and applications?

8. What is the proper relation between DBA personnel and application personnel?

XXIII

Organization
of Data Base Administration

□□

For the most part, little distinction is made in this chapter between data administration (DA) and data base administration (DBA), even though those distinctions exist (see previous chapter for a discussion of the differences). The function of DBA will be traced from its origins to the present, and at least initially there is little distinction organizationally between the DA and DBA. Of course, as an installation grows and more systems are built, the data processing environment becomes more complex and the distinctions between the two functions become more clear. The role of the DBA is emphasized in this chapter because, from the DBA the DA is borne.

23.1 ORIGINS OF THE DBA

The need for the function of DBA is usually recognized at the point of the acquisition of a DBMS, or shortly thereafter. The more complex the DBMS, the greater the need for the function of DBA. This initial recognition of the need for a DBA is due to the complex nature of DBMS, especially a fully functioned DBMS. Consider Figure 23.1, where it is clear that the DBMS must interface with and manage many diverse environments. Some of those environments are data communications, physical storage and structure of data, application programs, and the host SCP. Each of these environments has its own considerations and is quite different technically from other environments, and *all* of these diverse environments must be tied together successfully by the DBMS. In addition, *none* of these environments is static, so the DBMS must not only bring together complex and diverse environments, it must also dynamically change with them. Thus it is no wonder that a DBMS is a complex piece of software. One of the primary motivations for the function of the DBA is as a controller of the complexities of the DBMS.

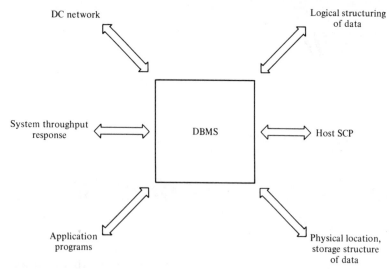

Figure 23.1 Variety and complexity of environments interfacing with the DBMS. Furthermore, the diverse environments are constantly changing.

Although it is the initial justification, complexity of the DBMS is by no means the *only* justification for the function of the DBA. The data base environment is usually singled out for the critical and voluminous applications of a company. Even if the DBMS were simple to use and control, the criticality of the applications running under the DBMS warrants the function of DBA. Another reason for the DBA function is the growth of the processing needs of the corporation. Another function of the DBA is to provide a vehicle for the control of growth as well as control of the DBMS.

23.2 RESPONSIBILITY OF THE DBA

It is unlikely that the function of the DBA is the same in any two installations. This is true because (as will be seen later in the chapter) the role of the DBA is in an evolving and unstable state. However, a consensus of some of the responsibilities of the DBA might be:

1. To oversee the DBMS as a precious resource of the company (this includes the DBMS itself and all applications run under the DBMS). Some of the concerns of the DBA are:

    a. Integrity of data. What are the exposures? What are the costs?
    b. Recovery of data. What are the exposures? What levels of recovery exist? At what cost?
    c. Coordinating needs and usage of data—for year-end processing, audits, special processing, and so on.

300

    d. On-line system availability. Is the DBMS up? Are the applications that run under the control of the DBMS up?

    e. On-line system capacity. What is the transaction balance today? In the future? What resources are needed?

    f. System security. Is data secure at all levels? What security features are used under the DBMS? External to the DBMS?

    g. System response time. What is the average response time? Is it reasonable? If not, what can be done? Immediately? In the short term? In the long term?

2. To take part in data base and transaction design. The DBA has an interest in data base and transaction design as far as performance and system availability are concerned. If an application is to be put on-line that will negatively affect existing on-line applications, it is the job of the DBA to see to it that the offending application is *not* allowed to go into production. The same considerations hold for the issues of availability. It is in this area that an organization experiences the most difficulty, because traditionally it is the domain of the applications to do what it wants without regard for the effect this will have on others.

3. To provide technical leadership. Provide the organization with leadership in the following area:

    a. Tools/mechanics of DBMS. What are they? How can they be used? When should they be used? Not used?

    b. Standards. What practices should always be followed?

    c. Guidelines. In the absence of standards, what practices should be followed by default?

    d. Review and design methodologies. What are they? How should they be used?

    e. Information source. When technical problems (especially data base) arise that the organization is not equipped to handle, the DBA should be the focal point for the solution of these problems. Often, the DBA provides a link in the chain between systems programming and applications for problem resolution and diagnosis.

4. To monitor existing data bases and on-line systems. The primary interests are average activity, maximum activity, transaction arrival rate, response time, data base size, and internal data base organization. Based on the state of affairs, the DBA will tune the data bases and/or on-line system.

23.3 INTERFACES TO THE DBA FUNCTION

The software interfaces to the DBMS are shown in Figure 23.2, together with the organizational interfaces to the DBA function. The DBMS must interface with software from data communications, the host SCP (operating

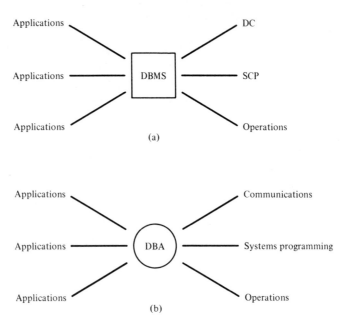

Figure 23.2 (a) Software interfaces to the DBMS, and (b) organizational interfaces to the DBA function.

system), computer operations, and applications. The DBA must interface with representatives of communications, systems programming, operations, and applications. It is interesting to note the very parallel relationship between the software and organizational interfaces. It is also interesting to note that the most difficult interface (in both cases) is with applications— whether on the software or organizational level. This does not mean that the other interfaces are not important; it means that again and again the difficult interface is with applications.

How does the critical interface normally get defined? In most installations the application/DBA interface informally evolves as the function of DBA evolves. Very few shops formally lay down the responsibilities, obligations, and rights that define the relationship from the beginning. This works fine until a conflict develops and one or the other side is unable to perform necessary functions; and conflicts are almost *sure* to develop. Organizations that have gone to the trouble of formally defining the interface between DBA and applications preempt future misunderstandings.

23.4 IMBALANCE OF THE DBA/APPLICATIONS INTERFACE

Why does the interface between the DBA and applications *normally* tend to become imbalanced? First, the DBA function is new and that itself is cause for imbalance. But the main reasons stem from the fact that the DBA is exerting a new and necessary level of control and that control is resisted by applications. It becomes politically expedient to bypass the control of the DBA until such time as the needs for that control become obvious (at which point it is too late to retrofit necessary control). The fact of the matter is that *both* applications and DBA have an equal and valid stake in the same thing—the design and running of applications—and because the DBA is the newcomer, the organization is not prepared (psychologically, organizationally, or otherwise) for the role of the DBA. Organizations that define very carefully the rights and responsibilities of the DBA and applications in the area of design remove some of the causes for future conflict.

How does the DBA/application interface become imbalanced? Figure 23.3 shows the two ways. In one case, the application organization "overpowers" the DBA function. In the other case, the DBA function "overpowers" the application. Both cases of imbalance lead to undesirable results and one or the other is the *normal* result of evolution. What, then, are some characteristics of these imbalances and problems caused by them?

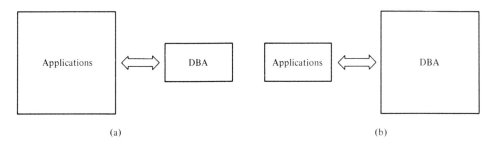

(a)   (b)

Figure 23.3 Two ways the DBA/application interface can become imbalanced: (a) applications is stronger and more influential than DBA and can ignore the influence of the DBA function; (b) DBA is stronger than applications and can do as it wishes in spite of applications.

23.5 APPLICATIONS OVERPOWERING DBA

When the applications function overpowers the DBA (which occurs more often than the reverse), the initial result is "status quo" and organizational harmony (with the exception of the DBA). Applications designs systems as if their user were the only user in the system. It is normal for little or no consideration to be given to the resources consumed or to other systems that will be sharing common resources. This attitude is a holdover from the application attitudes of batch development. One of the major problems with this interface is that the ill fruits are not obvious until the design process runs its course (i.e., until the system designed is run under a full transaction load with a full volume of data competing for resources with other systems).

It may take *years* for the full set of problems to surface, at which point redesign and redevelopment are not feasible. The role of the DBA is (among other things) to ensure wise usage of precious resources. Ignoring the advice of the DBA ultimately can be very costly, although heeding the advice requires organizational discipline from the beginning. Management must be prepared to deal with the trauma of removing some application responsibilities. The fact is that the DBMS will not allow any application to abuse resources without paying an overall price even though designers have the tools to build such applications. Ignoring the DBA only postpones the eventual and expensive pain of poor performance that can only be addressed by redesign.

23.6 DBA OVERPOWERING APPLICATIONS

On a few occasions the DBA function ends up in a more powerful position than the applications organization. When this happens the DBA function tends to create unnecessary "red tape" for applications. In the worst case, applications does not have all the tools it needs to satisfy the user and the DBA becomes a real roadblock to progress. Too many design decisions are taken out of the hands of applications. Typically, the DBA tends to become very large, bureaucratic, and in some cases secretive. The DBA tends to view itself as an end in itself, not a means to an end. The DBA loses sight of the fact that it is only a part of the developmental, design, and operational part of data processing. The application group becomes a coding organization and development time takes much longer than is necessary.

23.7 BALANCING THE DBA/APPLICATION INTERFACE

Despite the *normal* tendency toward imbalance of the DBA/application interface, it is possible for applications and the DBA to exist in harmony. Some of the characteristics of shops where the functions exist in stability are:

1. *Formalized responsibilities.* The rights, responsibilities, and domains of the DBA and applications are well thought out, written, and are understood and supported by management.
2. *Adoption of the standard work unit.* This specific issue is discussed in Chapter 12 of *Design Review Methodology for a Data Base Environment*, by Inmon and Friedman. The standard work unit provides a set of objective parameters under which the DBA and applications can interact.
3. *Effective and consistent usage of design review methodology.* Design review creates an open forum for discussion that can only be healthy (in addition to offering many other advantages).

4. *Management support and understanding.* Since it is inevitable that conflict will develop, management support is mandatory. Without support, the organization being overpowered will not have backing at the most critical times when backing is needed.

5. *Placing the DBA function in the correct place organizationally.* This means that the DBA should be neither too high nor too low in relation to applications.

23.8 PLACING THE DBA IN THE ORGANIZATION

The next section discusses several organization charts in which the DBA and applications are positioned in several configurations. All of these configurations are taken from real company organizations. Each configuration has its strengths and weaknesses. Because the function of DBA is in a somewhat unstable and undefined state, there is a tendency for the application/DBA interface to become unbalanced—the DBA becoming much stronger than applications, or vice versa. This is further evidence of the evolutionary nature of the function of the DBA within the organization.

What can be termed the "standard" placement of the DBA is shown in Figure 23.4. Here it is seen that the DBA is at the same level, organizationally, as the applications with which it interfaces. This arrangement is typical of organizations initially establishing the DBA function. The number of people in each organization depends on the total number of people in the

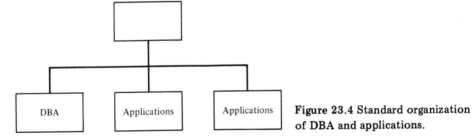

Figure 23.4 Standard organization of DBA and applications.

company—in a small company there may be one or two people in the DBA, in a large company, many more people. This organization is characterized by informal communications between the DBA and applications. Often, the DBA is staffed with personnel from applications and they carry with them ties from their former job.

As time passes and the differences between applications and DBA begin to manifest themselves, the interface goes into a state of imbalance. Unless management is fully aware of the need to control the data base environment, there is a tendency to follow the most expedient path, which is to allow applications to overrule the DBA. The result of this expediency is a short-term organizational truce and the creation of a long-term problem in the design and operation of systems. Figures 23.5 and 23.6 show two ways in which the function of the DBA is organizationally neutralized to the advantage of the application.

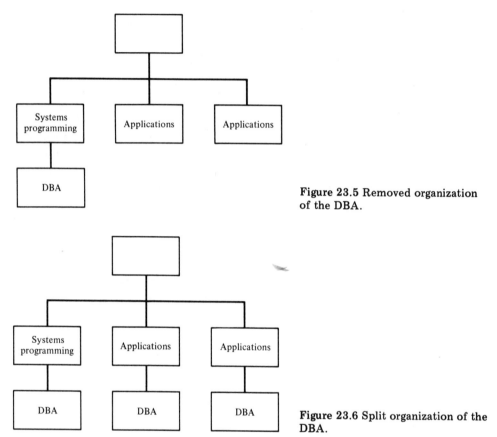

Figure 23.5 Removed organization of the DBA.

Figure 23.6 Split organization of the DBA.

In Figure 23.5 (the "removed" organization of the DBA function) the DBA is organizationally moved to a level below applications, usually under systems programming. This makes it difficult for the DBA to assert necessary influence since the application management has access to a higher level of management within the organization. This organization is politically expedient and the need for the control of the DBA is not perceived because of the "delayed feedback syndrome."* The application organization quite naturally overpowers the DBA function. The reason the DBA function is placed under systems programming is that a certain part of the job of the DBA is technical in nature. Given the reality of this environment, the DBA

*Described in Chapter 3 of *Design Review Methodology for a Data Base Environment.*

function becomes technical and clerical, without any real influence on the important design decisions (hence, the control) of applications that will run under the DBMS.

A variation of the "removed" organization of the DBA is what can be termed the "split" DBA organization, as shown by Figure 23.6. In the split organization, it is recognized that there is some validity to having the application influenced by the DBA. Each application creates its own subordinate DBA function (primarily to solve technical problems) and the organization deludes itself into thinking that the problems of the DBMS have been mastered. What is missing is that the DBA has no real control. Each application can still design systems as it likes, but ultimately there is a heavy price to be paid, because once the systems are operational, the DBMS will not allow *each* application to consider itself the most important. The split organization provides some of the services of the DBA without any necessary control. It is obvious that the applications function completely overpowers the DBA function.

23.9 THE EXALTED DBA

Up to this point, organizational approaches have been discussed which lead to the DBA not being allowed to exercise the necessary level of control. It is only a matter of time before application overrules the DBA. In an attempt to correct this instability by means of an organizational structure, the "exalted" DBA approach has been tried. This is shown by Figure 23.7. In the figure, the applications function reports to the DBA. In this case, it is *not possible* for the DBA to be overruled by applications. The problem with this approach is that the DBA function overwhelms the application function and that ultimately the user is dissatisfied. The results of this organization are the lengthening of the development cycle and the evolving of the role of the DBA as an end in itself rather than a means to an end.

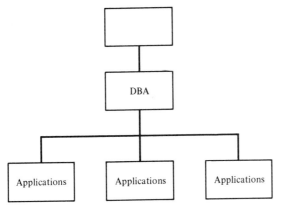

Figure 23. 7 Exalted DBA organization.

A variation of the "exalted" DBA organization is the "exalted, removed" organization, shown in Figure 23.8. Here it is seen that the DBA is higher (organizationally) than the applications areas. This means that the DBA is not likely to be overruled by applications. This organization (unlike the previous one) has quite a few merits. One drawback is that the DBA function has a tendency to become distant from the applications. Applications may not have access to the DBA when needed, and in this manner the DBA becomes a roadblock to progress. In the worst cases, the DBA function may begin to overpower applications and upset the stability of the DBA/application interface. In some cases, the DBA grows to the point that it is larger than any application, and administrative and management problems grow within the DBA function itself.

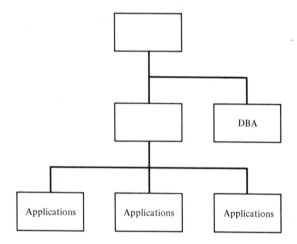

Figure 23.8 Exalted, removed DBA organization.

23.10 THE EVOLUTIONARY DBA

The preceding examples have shown the DBA function to be in a state of flux, and that is a fair statement of the world as it exists today. The reason for this instability is the need of both applications and the DBA to influence the design of applications and each with a different perspective. This represents a major change in the data processing organization and is difficult to achieve because the design of applications traditionally is the domain of the applications. To develop what can be termed the "evolutionary" DBA, consideration must be given to the actual needs of applications and the DBA in their influence on the design of applications.

The needs of applications (as it related to the DBA) are:

1. Access to the technical expertise of the DBA
2. Tools to satisfy the needs of the user

3. Ability to build systems quickly
4. Ability to build useful systems

The needs of the DBA (as it relates to applications) are:

1. Control of systems that will go on DBMS because of performance
2. Control of systems that will go on DBMS because of availability
3. Ability to prevent an application from negatively affecting other systems on the DBMS

Are the needs of applications and the DBA mutually exclusive? Not at all, but they certainly are where one organization does not *allow* the appropriate organizational influence to occur. What organization, then, can be constructed to meet the needs of the two perspectives? As an organization first builds the function of DBA, the "standard" organization is usually the form adopted. Because of the organizational instability and the need for the DBA function, the application and DBA functions go into a state of imbalance.

Over time, a few organizations have evolved into a state of balance with what can be termed an "evolutionary" organization of the DBA. One of the forms of this evolutionary organization is shown in Figure 23.9, where the DBA function appears in two places: higher in the organization at the DA/DBA level and lower in the organization at the APPL/DBA level. It is here that the function of data administration (DA) begins to make its appearance.

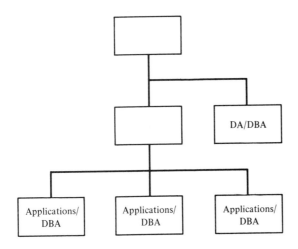

Figure 23.9 Evolutionary approach to DBA organization.

The role of the DA/DBA is (1) to ensure the quality of system design for applications going onto the DBMS, and (2) to provide direction for the integration of systems. The APPL/DBA function is concerned with such issues as (1) recovery of data, (2) reorganization of data, (3) technical support, and (4) applications of sound design principles at the application level.

The DA/DBA takes a broad perspective of systems, whereas the APPL/DBA takes a more immediate, localized view of the world. Two tools the DA/DBA uses for communication and control are the standard work unit and the design review. This "evolutionary" organization becomes more formalized as the systems to be controlled grow. In a small installation there may be a need for only a small amount of formalized communication, whereas in a larger environment the needs for formalized communication may greatly exceed the needs of the former. The difference in the DA/DBA and the APPL/DBA can be described in terms of perspective. Figure 23.10 shows that difference.

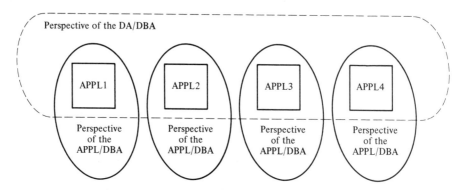

Figure 23.10 Differences between the perspectives of the APPL/DBA and the DA/DBA.

The APPL/DBA is the person responsible for the recovery of a given data base. The DA/DBA is the person responsible for the overall strategy of recovery in the shop. These two perspectives are joined by the standard work unit and design review. Both perspectives are represented in the design process.

REFERENCES

Inmon, W. H., and L. J. Friedman, *Design Review Methodology for a Data Base Environment*, Prentice-Hall, Inc., Englewood Cliffs, N.J., 1981, Chap. 12.

Ross, Ronald, *Data Base Systems—Design, Implementation and Management*, AMCOM, New York, 1978.

CASE STUDY

The Mendocino Mint and Chocolate Company has been in data processing for about 15 years. For the past six years, they have been operating in a data base environment. Years ago they acquired a DBMS. They set up a data base administration (DBA) group to handle the complex piece of software. The DBA was put in the technical support area together with systems programming, data communications, and operations control.

Initially, the DBA installed the DBMS and helped applications get their programs up and running in the batch environment. Very soon applications became independent of the DBMS as application personnel became familiar with the tools the DBMS had to offer. From this point on, the DBA function became something of a clerical job. The DBA's role was that of tending to the DBMS, but the DBA really had little to say in the major decisions that were being made.

About four years after the DBMS was brought in (in the batch mode), management saw a need to use the DBMS as the foundation of an on-line system. A data communications monitor was purchased that was compatible with the DBMS and applications were planned for the on-line environment. At this point, the DBA made an attempt to become more involved in the design of the application. These attempts were quickly rejected by applications and management, which solidly supported them. Management based its support on the fact that applications had been doing a good job for many years.

Time passed and the first few on-line applications were failures. The expense of the failures was significant, not to mention the political embarrassment. At last management came to the realization that the DBA needed to have a greater influence at a moment in time that would do the most good— the moment of design. One of the major roots of the early failures was in not allowing the DBA to influence applications design with a broader perspective.

Management realized that organizationally it was easy to ignore the DBA because (1) the DBA was buried deep in a technical organization, and (2) the DBA was not consistently afforded the opportunity of management's ear. This meant that the DBA was too far from where decisions were being made and that the corporate level of the DBA was such that the DBA was easy to ignore. Management wished to correct those deficiencies in the hopes of averting any more on-line failures.

Finally, management brings in a consultant to help them consider the following alternatives in placing the DBA:

1. The DBA should report to the applications director.
2. The applications director should report to the DBA.
3. The DBA should be at the same level as the applications director but not in the same organization. ■

Comment on the Following

1. If the DBA reports to the applications director, the imbalance of influence at the point of design probably will not be solved.

2. If the applications director reports to the DBA, there probably will be other kinds of problems.

3. If the applications director and the DBA are at the same level, there will still be conflicts to be resolved. How can those conflicts be resolved? What will they be over? Are they avoidable?

4. The progression of change of the role of the DBA is predictable. Was it necessary to have costly failures to demonstrate the problem? Where could the problem have been addressed initially? Why wasn't it?

MULTIPLE-CHOICE QUESTIONS

1. The position of DBA has just been created to deal with the DBMS that has been purchased recently. Management has read about problems other companies have had and wants to avoid those problems. To make sure that the DBA has the necessary political clout, all applications personnel are to report to the DBA.

   A. The development process will probably slow down substantially.

   B. The applications groups will probably have many tools they use to satisfy user removal from their control.

   C. A unified DBA effort is now possible.

   D. Just because the DBA has all the political clout it needs does not mean that systems will necessarily be integrated or better designed.

   E. Applications personnel will probably be justified in claiming that the DBA is creating unnecessary roadblocks even though they report to the DBA.

2. The DBA mandates that all programmers use the data dictionary. In this fashion the DBA will "control" data.

   A. Programmers can find *many* ways to circumvent the DBA's "control."

   B. The DBA may be placing an unnecessary obstacle before the applications designer.

   C. Data redundancy and unintegrated systems can be built on a data dictionary as easily as they can without a data dictionary.

   D. If the DBA wishes to succeed, he will "sell" the data dictionary, not legislate it.

   E. Control of data is a much greater issue than merely installing and using a data dictionary.

EXERCISES AND ESSAYS

1. Why does the DBA function become clerical and technical in a batch environment? Why does that function change greatly in the on-line environment?

2. What checks and balances are appropriate, even when the DBA is properly placed in the organization?

3. How does the role of the DBA differ as the organization grows in size?

4. How can applications resistance to the influence of the DBA be minimized?

IN SUMMARY
□□

XXIV

Controlling the

Data Processing Organization

□□□

Managers of data processing face as difficult a task as there is in management because of the complexity of the data processing environment, the changing role of data processing in the corporation, the continuous demands on the environment, and its ever-changing nature. This book attempts to alert the manager to the bare minimum that will be needed for survival.

There is another aspect of management that is crucial to success that is not stressed here. No amount of discussion on the forces that shape the data processing organization can replace good judgment, common sense, and judgment of character. These traits are essential to successful data processing management (indeed, any management!), but they are beyond the scope or intention of this book. The fact that they are not stressed should *not imply* that they are not important or are not recognized.

24.1 MANAGEMENT CONTROL — AVOIDING CRISIS

The key to management control is to avoid crisis. At the time of crisis, there is *no choice* as to what must be or can be done, thus removing the options and controls available to management. Since control implies the ability to make choices, a crisis is the *last* thing a manager wants. The key to avoiding crisis is to plan ahead—to anticipate problems before they reach crisis proportions. Like the ship a few seconds before crashing into the reef, the time to avoid the reef was long before the collision. Too many managers do not open their eyes until the force of the ship is about to carry them into the reef. Operating in an anticipatory mode implies that the manager knows what should be anticipated. The forces leading to crises that a manager should be able to anticipate form the subject of this book.

The ultimate in lack of management control is the manager who allows an installation to operate on a "crisis treadmill." One crisis leads to another, which leads to another, and so forth, so that life in that organization is merely running in a reaction mode from one crisis to the next. Management in that environment can be labeled "management by crisis." This is a very difficult environment because there is never the time or resources to "do things right"—to address the roots of the problem. Instead, resources are spent addressing symptoms of problems, not causes, and the real cause of the problems is never cured. Management by crisis is the worst possible environment for all concerned—managers, users, designers, programmers . . . everyone.

To anticipate problems in data processing, the manager can look at three different categories of considerations: problems related to the user of data processing services, technical problems, and organizational problems.

24.2 USER-RELATED CONSIDERATIONS

Because of user demands, the growth of systems and computer utilization is a fact of life. Users want more systems, bigger systems, and more functions in existing systems. Users often find ways to use a system that were never anticipated. All of this leads to a backlog of requests for data processing services that is insatiable, even if adequate resources exist on which to run the systems. Adding to the backlog of data processing requests is the fact that the user's environment is not static. As the user's environment changes, so must the systems that support the environment, because a computer system is really a static snapshot of a dynamic environment. The only real difference between users is the rate of change of their environment. However changing computer systems is no trivial task.

Another consideration the manager must be aware of is that users traditionally operate in a very undisciplined manner. They often consider data processing services to be free and give little or no consideration to the human and machine resources they use in building or operating their systems. The user often has an attitude of not caring about technical or practical limitations. This attitude is usually based on the assumption that all problems have an available technological solution—an attitude that the data processing department, with its early marketing approaches, may have been responsible for. Users feel that they are not accountable for the data processing resources they consume. This attitude is a by-product of the way systems originally were built in a corporation. The fact that initially data processing had to sell the users on automation produces this attitude as a side effect.

This "selling" of data processing is aimed at overcoming the resistance users have to making changes. The problem is, once users have decided to make changes and use computers, they forever expect the same attitude and attention from data processing, which is not realistic or organizationally mature. The manager who wants to control the data processing environment must be aware of the forces that drive the user, the attitudes of the user, how those attitudes came about, and the difference between user wants and needs.

24.3 TECHNICALLY RELATED CONSIDERATIONS

Just as the user's environment is undergoing constant change, so the technical environment of data processing is undergoing change. New capabilities, new modes of operation, and new capacities are a day-to-day fact of life in data processing. These changes occur in hardware, in design methodologies, and in software techniques. The mastery of these tools is overwhelming if the manager addresses them only at a detailed level; the manager who controls the data processing environment understands the technical world at a high, conceptual level, and then delves into detail when appropriate.

If there is a key to success in managing the large, complex, multifunction technical environment, it lies in the realization that desirable system attributes are put into a system at the point of design. Retrofitting desirable attributes into a system once the design of the system has been architected is either impossible or impractical in nearly every case. In an on-line environment, some of the major attributes which are usually desirable are performance, availability, and flexibility. Managing a project that is optimized for speed of development often greatly reduces the quality of the system design.

The manager should also understand that technology has its proper and improper uses. Using technology for something that *can* be done but *should not* be done normally entails a long-term cost, usually quite large. The manager should also understand the limits of technology and how to determine when a problem is caused by constraints of technology or by surmountable obstacles.

The manager's job is one of constantly evaluating trade-offs. These trade-offs are constantly being made either consciously or by default. In the planned environment (or action mode) the trade-offs are made actively; in the unplanned environment (or reaction mode) the trade-offs are made by default.

There are always costs related to trade-offs. Sometimes the costs are between the short term and the long term. Other times the costs are between human resources and machine resources. On other occasions the trade-off is between the degree of user satisfaction and development resources. Whatever the trade-off and set of considerations, the manager who controls the environment is *always* better off making those decisions with as much enlightenment as possible and doing so consciously.

There is a temptation in data processing to approach all problems as if they can be solved technically. Certainly, some problems can be addressed this way, but an organization is in trouble when the attitude is that *all* problems have a technical solution. The manager should be aware of an overemphasis of the technical aspects. In addition, the manager should be cautious of the consultant or employee who operates under the veil of a technical guru.

24.4 ORGANIZATIONALLY RELATED CONSIDERATIONS

The third set of considerations of which the manager should be aware are those that relate to the organization. An organization should mature over time. The vehicle by which it matures is pain, the pain of experience. These pains can be and should be a very useful tool for maturation. It is up to management to see to it that the pain of experience is utilized in a beneficial manner.

The manager who attempts to control the environment must understand that technical change has an impact on the organization. The traditional organizational roles and functions need to be changed as the environment that is shaped by technology changes. Maintaining traditional organizational roles in the face of massive technological change results in a very uncontrolled environment and is one of the largest reasons for an organization getting on the crisis "treadmill."

In a large, complex, on-line environment it is necessary to have both the local and global perspective of problems. The local perspective—that of looking at a single user's needs—has been recognized for quite a while. The global perspective—that of all the users who share a common resource, such as an on-line controller—is also necessary, but is largely unrecognized in an environment where there are ample resources. However, once those shared resources become precious, it is mandatory that the global perspective be recognized. It is that *sharing of responsibility*—both local and global—that troubles many organizations because it is nontraditional, and transfers organizational control from one unit to another. The organizational unit that is giving up control *always* resists, to the long-term detriment of the organization.

The manager who would control the data processing environment must be aware of the issues of productivity. Productivity must be approached at both a micro and a macro level. The micro approach is typified by new software capabilities, coding practices, and such. The macro approach is typified by such things as design review methodology, quality control of system design, and strategies for user satisfaction, such as subsystem manipulation of extracted data (i.e., prototyping and/or high level query facilities). The manager should be very careful in the measurement and comparison of productivity.

Another very major pitfall the manager should be aware of is the temptation to try to use technology to implement or effect a solution that should be attacked organizationally. For example, bringing data dictionary software in-house *does not mean* that an organization's data is under control. The control of data is an organizational issue, not a technical issue. There are many other examples of the misuse (and ultimate failure) of software solutions for organizational problems. If experience has shown anything, it has indicated that organizational problems *must* be addressed at the organizational level to be effective. The manager is often tempted to use technology because the technological approach does not require the manager to make the appropriate organization change, which most managers find to be very difficult. The technological approach may superficially effect the desired change, but eventually the organizational problem will manifest itself in a different, usually more obstinate form.

Communications within the organization and a clear-cut definition of responsibilities are essential for the reduction of organizational friction. When responsibilities are not defined, there is a large and unnecessary strain among different organizational units because the job of developing, running, and maintaining complex computer systems is difficult enough.

A last temptation that managers should be wary of is the temptation to buy their way out of a crisis, instead of understanding the causes for the crisis and addressing the real problem. Managers often attempt to buy more hardware to address problems when design practices are at the root of the problem. Managers create more positions to do more maintenance when design and debugging practices are the problem. Managers often allocate more staff time to a user rather than to try to understand the user's problems and educate the user as to what should and should not be done. And so forth. Above all else, this attitude of buying one's way out of a problem rather than addressing the problem is most expensive and most wasteful.

Index

□□

A

Abstraction of data, 55, 198
Accountability, 97, 98, 254, 318
ACP, 144
Action/reaction mode, 6, 61, 63, 77, 95, 154, 178, 188, 247, 248, 249, 318
ADF, 116
Ad hoc requests, 22
Airline industry, 18, 82, 144, 155, 251
Analysis, 27, 30, 31, 291
Analytical approach, 95, 96, 97
Applications (organization), 83, 84, 174, 178, 180, 188, 196, 289, 290, 291, 301, 302, 303, 304, 305, 306, 307, 308, 309, 310
Archival of data, 40, 41, 70
Arrival rate limitations, 204, 205
Auditing, 124, 125
Automatic code generation, 110, 112, 113, 114, 115, 194
Automatic teller (ATM), 155
Availability, 19, 20, 43, 44, 61, 62, 63, 65, 69, 70, 111, 138, 165, 167, 169, 214, 228, 237, 248, 253, 292, 301

B

Backlog of requests, 22, 105, 106, 107, 108, 147, 213, 252, 261, 262, 318
Banking industry, 18, 144, 155, 205, 251
Batch, 14, 17, 19, 39, 44, 65, 80, 81, 99, 108, 109, 111, 155, 156, 157, 159, 161, 162, 163, 165, 168, 169, 170, 213
Batch to online transition, 7, 154, 160, 161, 165, 166, 173
Batch window, 156
Benchmark, 135, 136

B (continued)

Bits and bytes approach, 95, 96, 97
BMP, 156
Budgets, 224
Business function, 79, 80, 81, 82, 83, 84, 90

C

Calculation intensive process, 79
Canonical data structures, 30, 230
Capacity planning, 6, 7, 77, 95, 96, 98, 99, 100, 101, 179, 301
Charge back scheme, 99, 254
CICS, 75, 182
CMS, 110, 115, 214
COBOL, 111, 115
Coding styles, 110
Compatibility, 184
Concatenation (of key), 51
Constraints (software), 204, 206, 207
Copylib, 110, 112, 113
Cost analysis, 226
Cost conscious approach (management style), 275, 279, 280
CPY, 100
Crisis, 3, 4, 5, 6, 61, 196, 277, 278, 280, 281, 317
Crisis treadmill, 6, 317, 318, 321
CRT, 18

D

Data administration (DA), 54, 55, 56, 101, 149, 150, 156, 174, 187, 193, 196, 197, 198, 237, 253, 268, 286, 288, 289, 290, 291, 292, 293, 294, 295, 299, 310
Data base (environment), 53, 66, 68, 69, 70, 142, 143, 144, 145, 146, 148, 149, 150, 156, 159, 168, 170, 286, 288

Data base systems, 11, 15, 16, 17, 19, 29
Data communications (DC), 70, 122, 138,
    294
Data dependence, 42, 106
Data dictionary, 53, 56, 110, 113, 192,
    193, 194, 195, 196, 197, 198, 199,
    200, 277, 293, 294, 321
Data driven process, 79, 80
Data integration, 38, 45, 47, 49, 50, 51, 52,
    53, 54, 55, 69, 151, 157, 171
Data model, 31, 45, 46, 218, 230, 231
Data modeling, 30, 55, 56
Data sharing, 144, 150, 156
DBA (data base administrator), 83, 84,
    237, 253, 267, 286, 288, 289, 290,
    291, 292, 293, 294, 295, 299, 300,
    301, 302, 303, 304, 305, 306, 307,
    308, 309, 310
DBMS, 17, 62, 70, 75, 76, 77, 78, 79, 83,
    87, 88, 112, 122, 124, 133, 134, 135,
    137, 138, 142, 144, 150, 169, 170,
    289, 292, 299, 300, 301, 307, 309
Deadlock (deadly embrace), 143, 144
Design, 27, 31, 291
Design review, 7, 56, 227, 235, 236, 237,
    238, 239, 240, 241, 291, 293, 294,
    304, 320
Development costs, 213, 215, 217, 219,
    220, 226
Development time, 28
Disaster planning, 125, 126
Discipline, 7, 53, 54, 87, 195, 196, 199,
    215, 216, 247, 250, 251, 252, 278,
    318
Disjunction, 65, 66, 69, 78, 188
Disk, 16, 143, 146
Distribution of processing, 172
Domain, 252, 289, 293, 304
Down time, 70
Driver program, 166, 168

E

Elasticity, 29, 48, 52, 106, 225, 231
Encoding/decoding, 123, 143
Encryption (of data), 123
Error isolation, 62, 63
Errorless approach (to design), 211, 219
Evolution of systems, 6, 11, 22, 23
Exclusive control (of data), 43, 44, 63, 65

F

Fail soft, 44, 65, 69
Feasibility, 27, 29, 30, 55, 123, 126, 291
Feedback loop, 4, 97, 98, 100, 250, 254,
    306
Flexibility, 44, 51, 61, 108, 111, 138,

145, 150, 167, 169, 170, 214, 237,
    248
FOCUS, 22, 146
FORTRAN, 112

G

Global data bases, 171, 172
Global view of data, 54
Growth, 3, 4, 15, 16, 20, 22, 77, 95, 105,
    178, 179, 260, 286, 318

H

Hardware, 3, 6, 44, 61, 62, 78, 88, 96,
    100, 125, 145, 159, 162, 165, 169,
    178, 179, 180, 181, 184, 204, 205,
    207, 212, 216, 247, 252, 261, 278,
    279, 280
Hierarchical model of data, 47, 48, 144
High level language, 115, 116
Hyperproductive approach (to design),
    211, 213, 214, 215

I

IDMS, 112
Implementation, 27, 28, 29, 30, 32, 33,
    44, 49, 51, 53, 291
IMS, 75, 76, 112, 181, 182
Infinite budget approach (management
    style), 275, 277, 279, 280, 281
Information cycle, 13, 17, 18, 20, 21, 22,
    23
Integrated environment, 32, 51, 108, 263
Integration, 7, 46, 48, 51, 159, 170, 194,
    199, 231, 240, 253, 264, 289, 293
Inventory of data, 192, 193
I/O (input/output), 75, 76, 77, 79, 86, 89,
    97, 169

J

Job specialization, 263, 267, 268

L

Lists and tables, 167

M

Main storage, 38
Maintenance, 5, 7, 27, 32, 33, 52, 108,
    145, 194, 205, 293
Management styles, 275

MARK IV, 116
Measuring productivity, 109, 110, 111
Message size, 76, 89
Micro level of productivity, 105, 106, 320
Mode of operation, 81
Modularity, 84
Mongolian Horde approach, 278
Monitoring, 98, 125, 291, 292, 294, 301
MP-AP, 180
Multifunction process, 79

N

Naming conventions, 198
NCSS, 99
NOMAD, 146
Normalization, 30, 145, 230
Number of data base calls, 75, 76, 78

O

Online performance, 89, 90, 165, 170, 228
Online systems, 11, 17, 18, 19, 20, 28, 29,
    32, 40, 43, 61, 70, 80, 81, 82, 83, 87,
    88, 90, 107, 108, 109, 111, 112, 142,
    143, 144, 146, 147, 150, 154, 155,
    156, 157, 159, 160, 161, 162, 163,
    164, 165, 167, 168, 169, 170, 204,
    206, 210, 236, 269, 286, 301, 319
Operations cost, 213, 215, 217, 219, 220
Overspecified process, 79, 80
Ownership of data, 15

P

Password/authorization, 123, 124
Performance, 44, 51, 61, 88, 108, 111,
    123, 150, 162, 167, 169, 180, 206,
    214, 218, 230, 231, 237, 248, 253,
    292, 301
Physical model of data, 31
PL-1, 112, 115
Postdevelopment costs, 213, 215, 217, 219,
    220
Postimplementation design, 28, 29, 34,
    107, 214, 262
Process iteration, 80, 81
Processor upgrade, 179, 180
Production costs, 226
Production environment, 32, 33, 147, 149
Productivity, 52, 105, 106, 107, 108,
    109, 110, 112, 114, 116, 145, 224,
    293
Productivity (at the macro level), 52, 105,
    106, 108, 109, 320
Profit, 251, 276, 277, 278, 279
Program error, 5

Programming, 27, 31, 291
Prototyping, 69, 116, 173, 225, 320
Private code, 124

Q

QBE, 22, 146
Query language, 115, 116
Queuing model, 97

R

RAMIS, 22, 146
Recovery, 43, 63, 65, 69, 70, 126, 144,
    147, 150, 156, 169, 170, 172, 228,
    291, 292, 300, 309, 310
Redefinition (of data), 63
Relational, 47, 48, 144
Reorganization, 43, 63, 64, 65, 69, 70,
    150, 170, 291, 292, 309
Resistance, 54, 55, 160, 195, 199, 238,
    248, 294, 318
Response oriented system, 96, 99
Rewrites, 165, 204, 206

S

SCP, 61, 62, 88, 99, 134, 294
Security, 7, 121, 122, 123, 124, 125, 143,
    145, 237, 301
Semantic, 22, 41, 42, 43, 45, 49, 70, 133,
    170, 183, 187
Sequential systems, 11, 15, 16, 17, 19, 29,
    53
Shifting of data, 169
Simulation model, 97
Skeleton programs, 110, 115
Software, 3, 44, 96, 100, 122, 123, 125,
    133, 134, 136, 147, 150, 159, 169,
    174, 178, 180, 181, 182, 184, 192,
    193, 194, 195, 204, 205, 207, 216,
    247, 252, 261, 278, 279, 280, 281
Spinoff systems, 147, 148, 149, 150
Splintered systems, 108, 109
SQL, 116
Staff turnover, 5
Standard approach (to design), 211, 212
Status, 45, 47
Stress test, 32
Surveys, 136
SWU (standard work unit), 7, 75, 77, 78,
    79, 80, 81, 82, 84, 85, 86, 88, 89, 90,
    99, 172, 173, 206, 291, 294, 304
System life cycle, 6, 27
System priorities, 28
System quality, 19, 31, 106, 107, 108,
    109, 235, 237, 238, 320
System test, 32

T

Technological approach (to design), 211, 215, 216, 217
Technological environment, 3, 4, 22, 54
Technologist approach (management style), 275, 280, 281
Technology, 53
Testing, 27, 32
Theoretical approach (to design), 211, 216, 217
Threshold of pain, 7, 95, 96, 97, 101
Throughput oriented systems, 96, 99
TOTAL, 112
Traditional approach (management style), 275, 276
Transaction throughput, 205
Transportability (data base), 138
TSO, 99, 110, 115, 181, 214

U

Unit test, 32
Upgraded reconfiguration, 180
Usable systems, 11, 20, 22
User environment, 38, 49, 52, 225, 240
User requests, 106
User requirements, 28, 29, 30, 33, 69, 161, 162, 211, 224, 225, 226, 227, 228, 229, 230, 231, 237
User satisfaction, 34, 224

V

Vendor, 62, 99, 100, 134, 135, 136, 139, 160

W

Work or hold data bases, 167, 168
Workload distribution, 184, 185
Workload split, 69, 181, 182, 184, 186